Journal of Roman Pottery Studies

The Study Group for Roman Pottery

The Study Group for Roman Pottery was founded in 1971 to provide a forum for the discussion of all aspects relating to Roman pottery found in Britain. The Group holds an annual conference in different locations each year and there are a number of regional sub-groups which meet occasionally. Since 1986 it has published the *Journal of Roman Pottery Studies*. The Group also aims to provide both a lead in Roman pottery studies and guidance towards best practice. It has produced *Research Frameworks for the Study of Roman Pottery* and *Guidelines for the Archiving of Roman Pottery*. Other projects in hand are a revision to the Council for British Archaeology Research Report 6 – *Romano-British Pottery: A Student's Guide* and updates to sections of the 1980 Directorate of Ancient Monuments and Historic Buildings (now English Heritage) document *Guidelines for the Processing and Publication of Roman Pottery from Excavations*. The Group also collaborates with other specialist groups on aspects such as Minimum Standards for Project Designs and Assessments and the United Kingdom Ceramic Thin-Section Database. The Study Group for Roman Pottery now has its own website – www.sgrp.org

Membership of the Group is open to all those with an interest in Roman pottery.

Journal of Roman Pottery Studies

Volume 9

The Roman Pottery Kilns at Rossington Bridge Excavations 1956–1961

A report on excavations carried out by
J. R. Lidster on behalf of
Doncaster Museum

P. C. Buckland, K. F. Hartley and V. Rigby

with contributions by
M. Aitken, S. Esmonde Cleary, G. Crawley, M. J. Dolby, M. Henig,
G. Lloyd Morgan, J. Samuels, T. O'Connor, G. H. Weaver and J. P. Wild

Published by
Oxbow Books
for
The Study Group for Roman Pottery

Originally Published in the United Kingdom in 2001. Reprinted in 2017 by
OXBOW BOOKS
The Old Music Hall, 106–108 Cowley Road, Oxford OX4 1JE

and in the United States by
OXBOW BOOKS
1950 Lawrence Road, Havertown, PA 19083

Paperback Edition: ISBN 978-1-84217-049-6
Digital Edition: ISBN 978-1-78570-780-3

A CIP record for this book is available from the British Library

For a complete list of Oxbow titles, please contact:

UNITED KINGDOM
Oxbow Books
Telephone (01865) 241249, Fax (01865) 794449
Email: oxbow@oxbowbooks.com
www.oxbowbooks.com

UNITED STATES OF AMERICA
Oxbow Books
Telephone (800) 791-9354, Fax (610) 853-9146
Email: queries@casemateacademic.com
www.casemateacademic.com/oxbow

Oxbow Books is part of the Casemate Group

Contents

Abstract

The eight excavated kilns at Rossington Bridge and material from the waster heaps provide a sample of production and wastage on a site with at least 15 other unexcavated kilns and ancillary structures lying either side of the Roman road. The bulk of the finds clearly belong to the main period of activity on the site during the mid-2nd century when the mortarium potter Sarrius and his associates were involved in the production of mortaria, 'parisian' fine wares, black-burnished and grey wares intended at least partly for the military markets on the Northern frontier. Earlier material is largely associated with roadside settlement, initially around the Torne river crossing north of the Claudio-Neronian vexillation fortress, although the scatter of human bone in the water- main trench may reflect a disturbed pre-Roman burial, to which a number of other finds may also belong. Occupation continued along the roadside through the 3rd century and probably into the 4th. Pottery production, however, appears to be largely restricted to the Antonine period, although a number of types imply production at least into the early years of the 3rd century.

Note

The first draft of this report was completed in 1976, after the processing of all finds from the 1956–61 excavations, and was archived with Doncaster Museum, with the intention of completion for publication as soon as the relevant specialist reports were available. The departure of the senior author (PCB) from the Museum in 1978 led to further delays in completion. The material was incorporated in the Nottingham doctoral dissertation of John Samuels (1984), and he carried out additional counts of the material as part of his research. His data are incorporated in the body of this paper, although there has been considerable inevitable re-interpretation, particularly of the kilns. The authors are aware that the report, like them, is beginning to show its age, particularly in terms of quantification, although it should be added that the recording and subsequent history of the finds would make any attempt at this a somewhat dubious pursuit. Often referred to but rarely seen, Rossington Bridge is here presented, warts and all, hopefully to provide a basis for further research.

P. C. Buckland,
Department of Archaeology and Prehistory,
University of Sheffield.

Excavations at Rossington Bridge 1956–1961

Introduction

The Roman road from Lincoln to Doncaster, the site of the Roman fort of Danum, and the North diverges from the modern A638, 1.5km south of Rossington Bridge, continuing in a straight line to cross the River Torne, 600m E of the modern bridge (Figs 1–5). The valley is sharply incised into Quaternary deposits, here the Older River Gravel of Gaunt (1981; 1994), and is partly infilled with peat (Whitehouse 1999). North of the river, the course of the road is evident as a broad depression giving way to a raised *agger* on the crest of the ridge, where the line is preserved beneath a field boundary (Fig 5). The field, bounded by the river, railway and Warning Tongue Lane, is unploughed, largely occupied by a rough grazing, and is currently being overgrown by birch and oak, with a dense growth of bracken giving way to hawthorn scrub towards the A638.

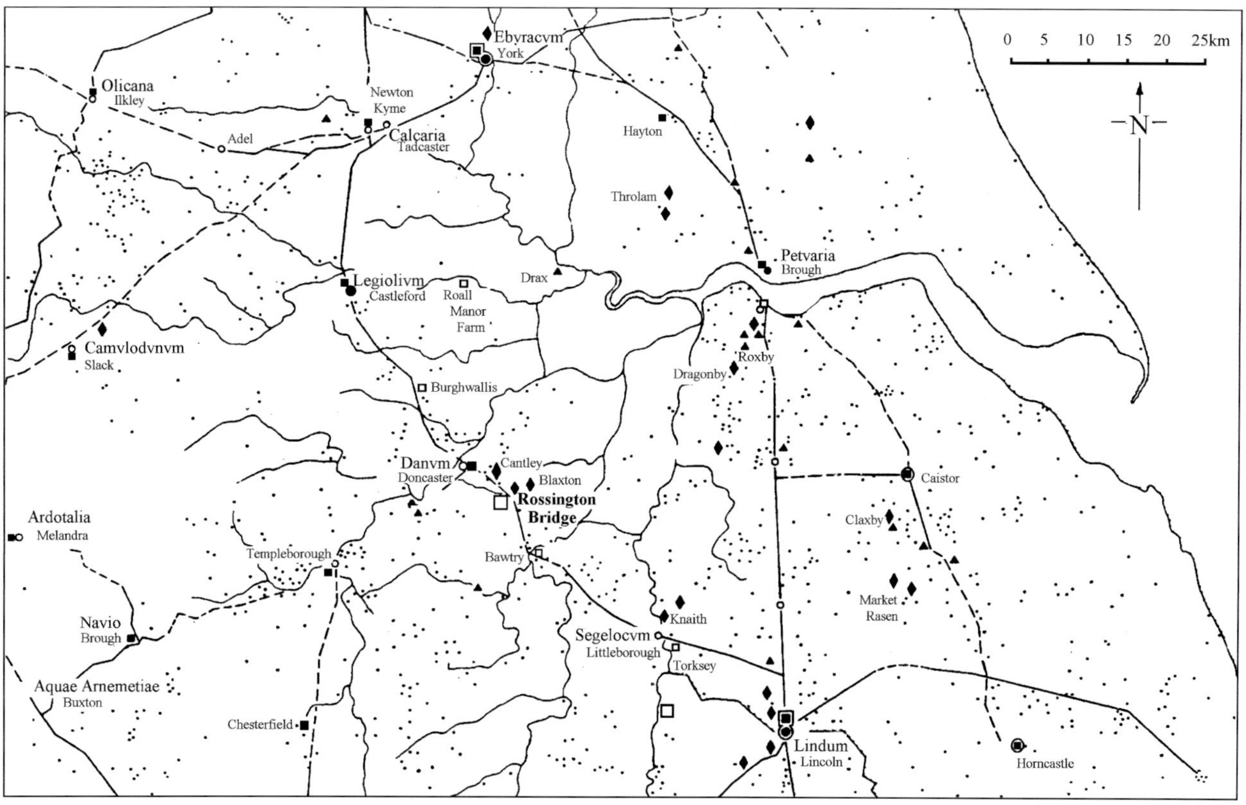

Figure 1. Location Map. The Rossington Bridge kiln sites in relation to other Roman sites in the East Midlands. (redrawn from Buckland and Magilton 1986, fig 1). Key: ▬ Roman Road – course known; ▬▬▬ Roman Road – course unknown; ▣ Fortress and (open square) Julio-Claudian vexillation fortress; ◉ Colonia; ■ Fort (long term occupation), open square temporary site; ○ Principal civilian settlements including vici; ⊙ Walled settlement; ▲ Villa; ⧫ Pottery kilns; ✦ Other Roman finds.

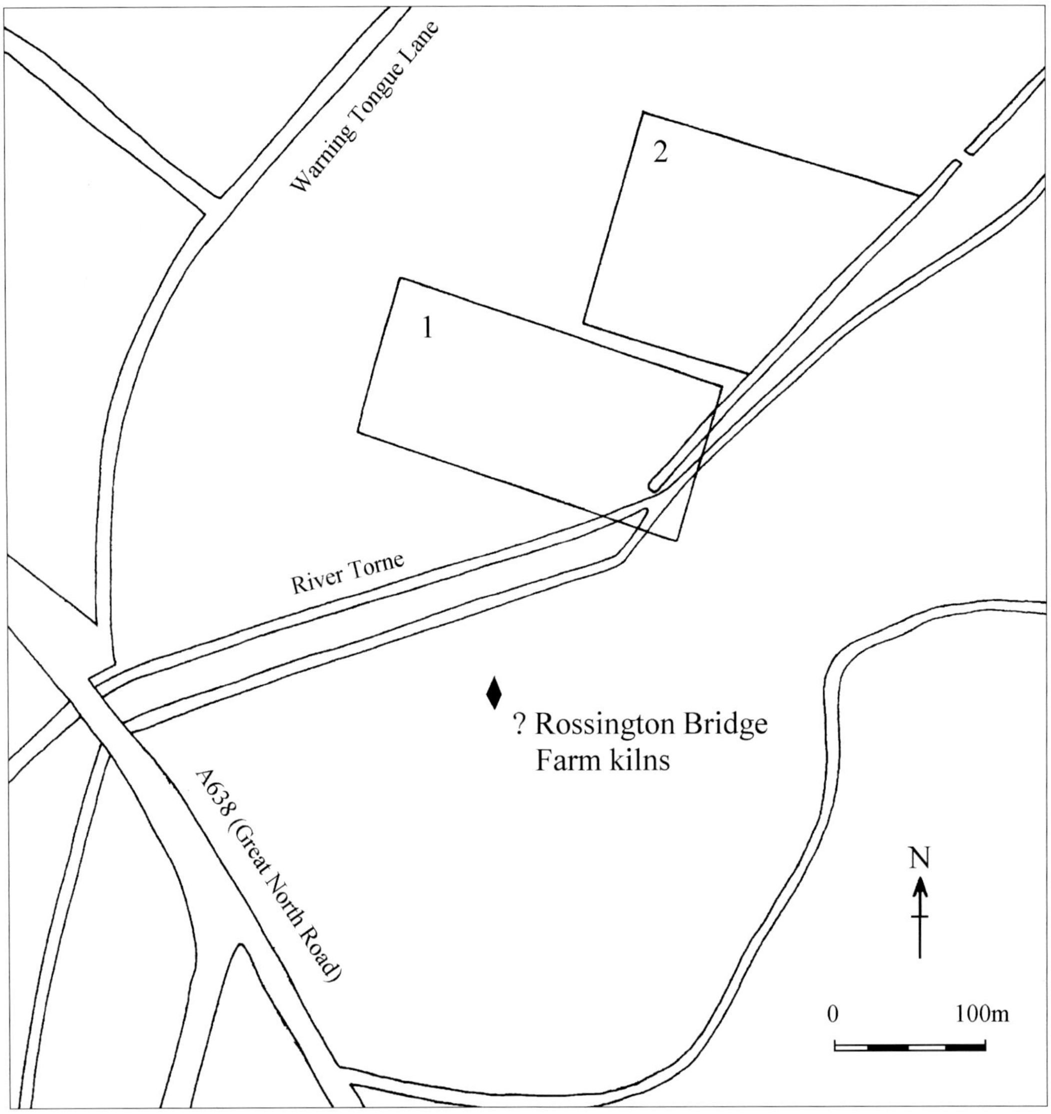

Figure 2. Rossington Bridge: location of known kilns (Areas 1 and 2) and the probable position of the Rossington Bridge Farm kilns. Plan: M.J. Dolby.

In the latter part of 1956, a large trench, 5.7m (18' 9") wide, was cut for a water-main leading westwards to a pumping station at the top of the slope from across the River Torne. This produced large quantities of Roman pottery and domestic debris (centre of site at NGR SK 631998). The material included not only evident kiln waste but also two hippo sandals and an Iron Age fire iron or blacksmith's paddle. Doncaster Museum was notified and, between 1957 and 1961, J.R. Lidster, the Museum's Keeper of Antiquities, carried out a series of excavations, which revealed five Roman pottery kilns, a "domestic" oven and other evidence of extensive occupation (Fig 3). The finds included much leather and woodwork, and it is apparent that archaeological deposits in the former meander of the river have considerable potential for palaeoenvironmental research (van de Noort and Ellis 1997; Whitehouse 1999), as well as excellent preservation of artefacts. The quality of recording was unfortunately poor, and many finds, including any peat and sediment samples, have since either been disposed of or lost their documentation. Plans, profiles and sections were partly drawn for most of the features, to a variety of often undisclosed scales, and it is evident that some of the recorded information, on unlabelled scraps of graph paper, has been subsequently lost. The data are sufficient, however, to understand much of what was found, if not sufficiently detailed to enable some of the stratigraphy to be interpreted.

In 1960, a local amateur archaeologist, W. Ingram, excavated two further kilns at Rossington Bridge Farm

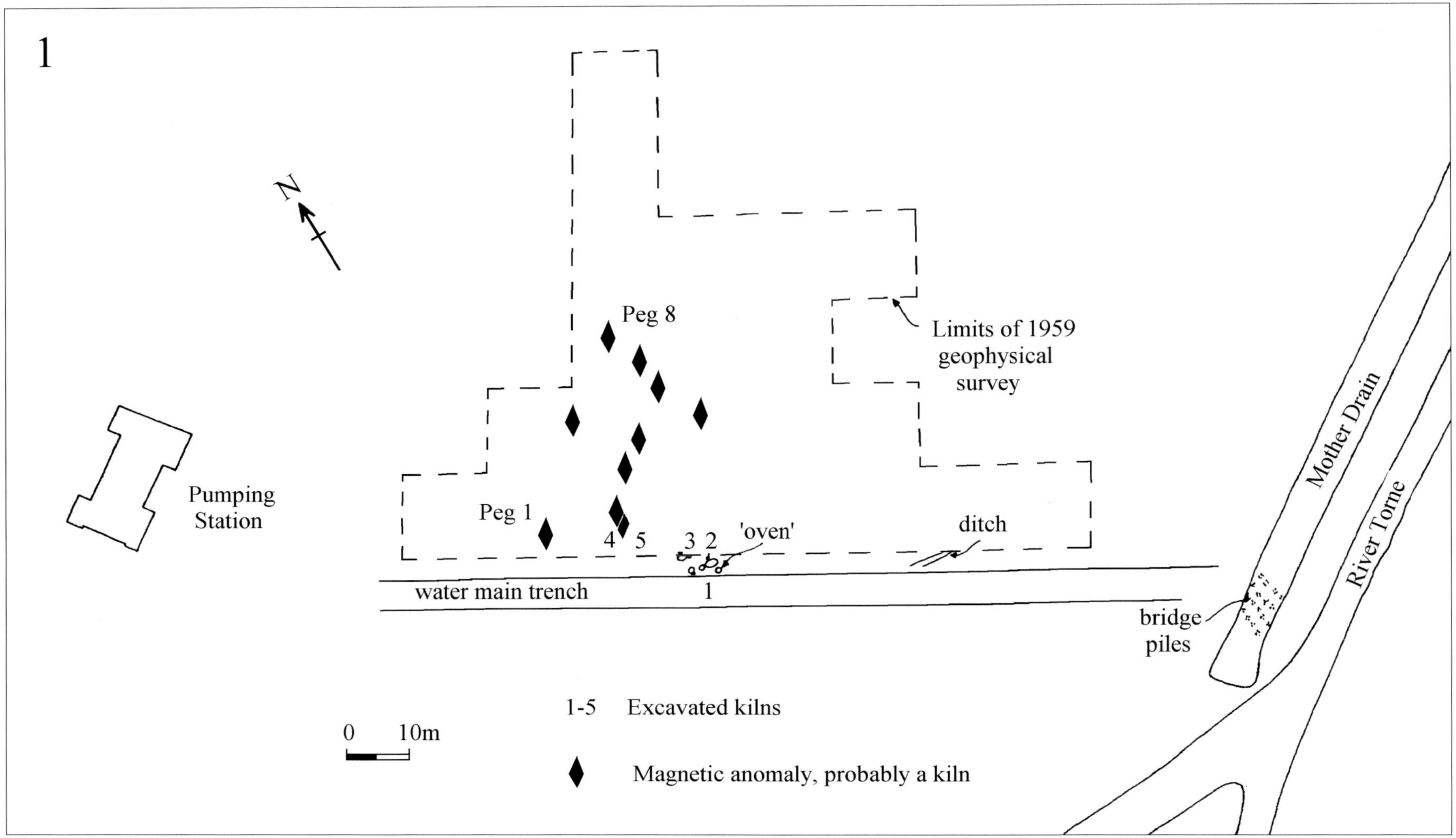

Figure 3. Rossington Bridge Pumping Station (Area 1 on Fig 2): water main trench of 1956, excavated kilns and other features (1957–61), Roman bridge piles, and magnetic anomalies located during the 1959 geomagnetic survey. Kilns 4 and 5 and features at Pegs 1 and 8 were subsequently excavated. Plan: M.J. Dolby.

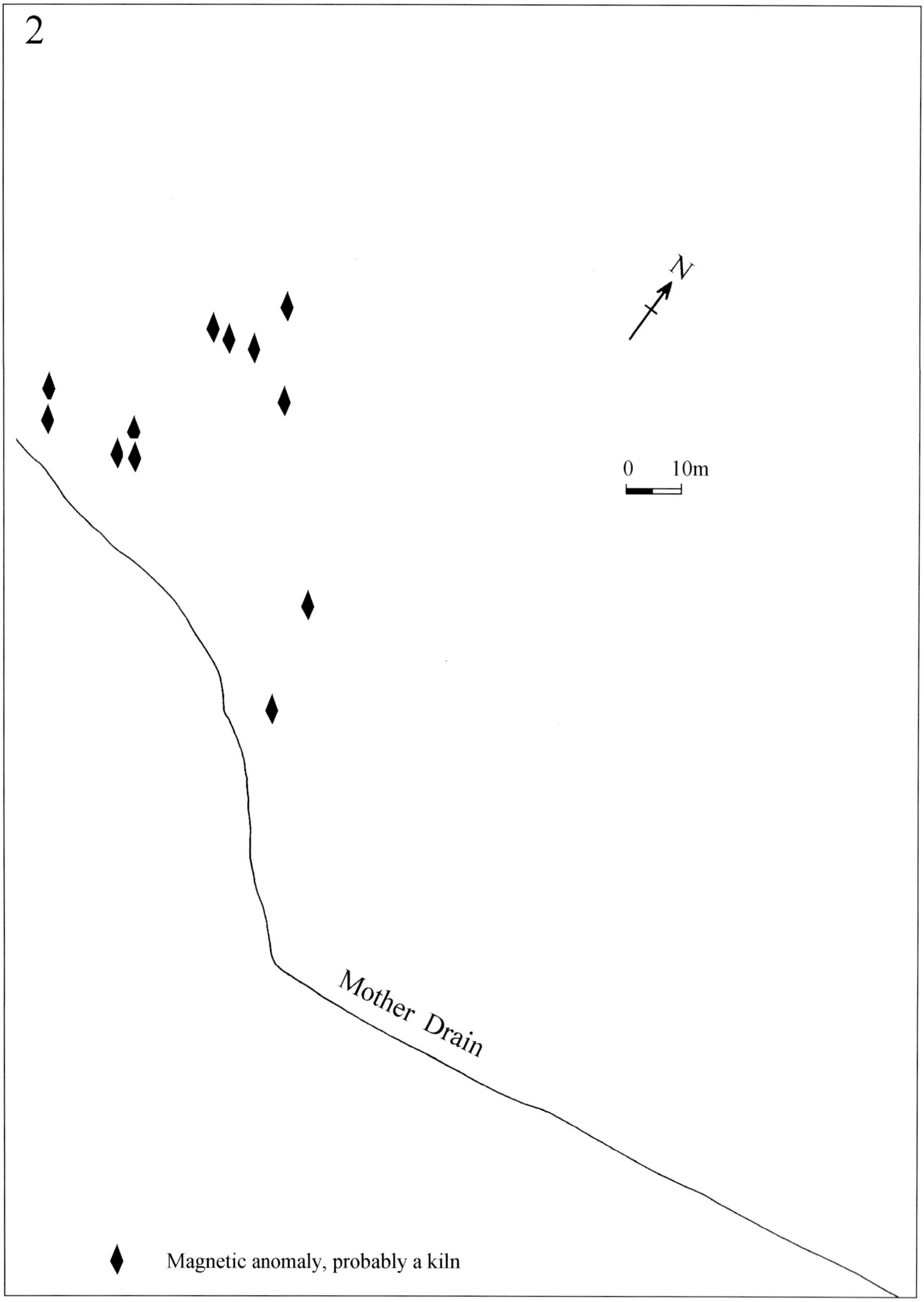

Figure 4. Rossington Bridge Pumping Station (Area 2 on Fig 2): unexcavated kilns located by geomagnetic survey 1963–64. Plan: M.J. Dolby.

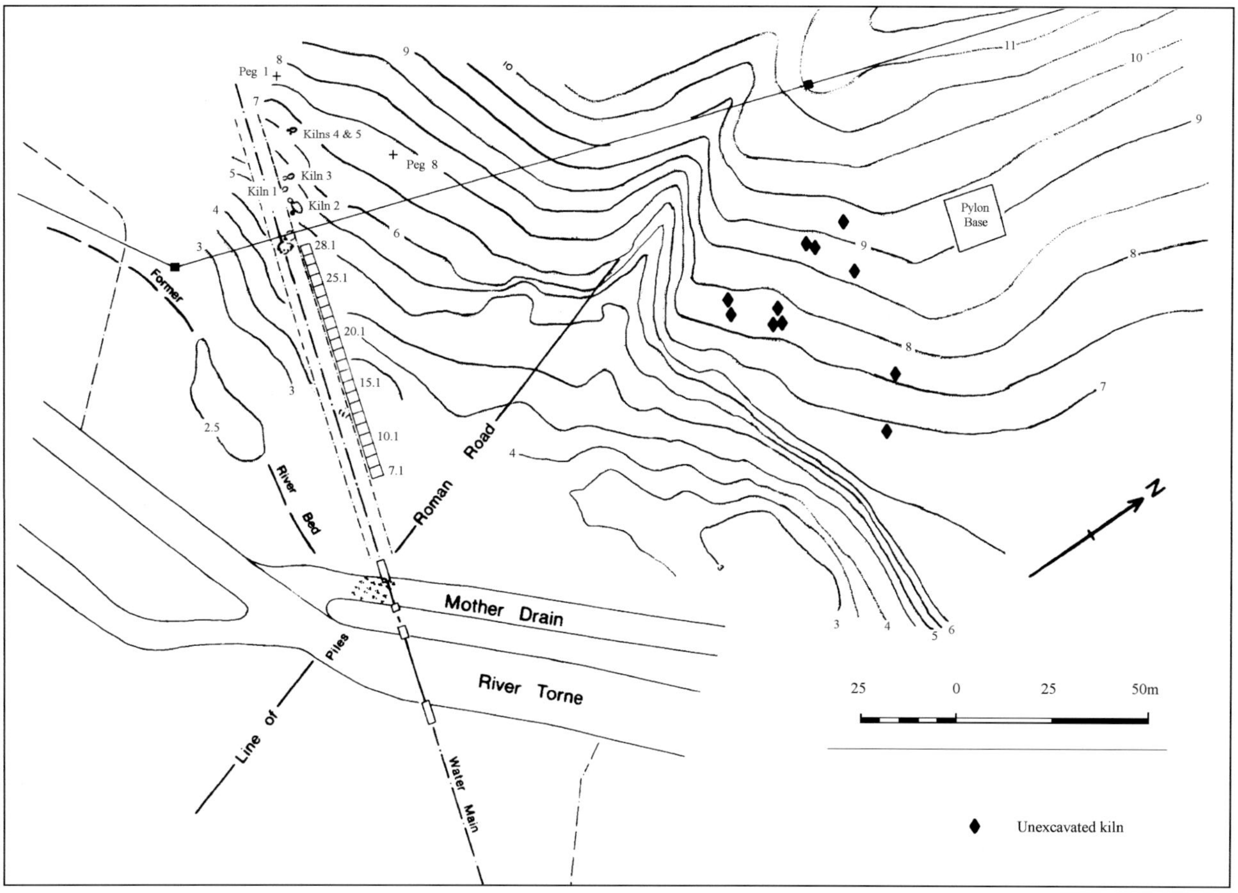

Figure 5. Rossington Bridge: site plan, contour interval 0.5m. The line of trenches (28.1–7.1), north of the water main trench of 1956–7, is indicated, as well as the kilns and the piles in the former bed of the river Torne. The contours are based on an arbitrary level adjacent to the River Torne and indicate the cutting of the Roman road, with kilns distributed to either side. Survey: P.C. Buckland and D.R. Ingram (1984).

across the River Torne from the main site (Fig 2) (NGR SK 637982); these were also partly recorded by Lidster.

Rossington Bridge Pumping Station

Excavation was at first concentrated on the material cut through by the water-main trench (finds labelled 1–28 WM), including three kilns (kilns 1–3), and the excavation was later extended as a series of 22 box sections, each 2.75m (3 yds) square (1.1–22.1) parallel to the water main trench and separated from it by an unexcavated baulk, 0.38m (18") wide, parts of which were later demolished (finds – 1–22 WMB) (Fig 5). Although the sections laid out close to the river (1.1–6.1) were not excavated, an area was cleared in the bed of the Mother Drain, exposing the piles of the Roman bridge (Figs 3 and 10). In 1959, a magnetometer survey located ten anomalies of sufficient intensity to suggest further kilns. Four of these (kilns 4 and 5, Pegs 1 and 8) were subsequently excavated. During 1963–5, before the construction of a new power line across the site, further geomagnetic survey was undertaken by M.J. Dolby, then the Museum's Assistant Keeper of Antiquities. This revealed 10 additional kilns to the north-east of the excavation (Fig 4). This implies a total of at least 21 kilns, and it is probable that further structures lie in the scrub, west of the water-main trench.

The Kilns

In view of the problems with the site records, the best documented structures, the excavated kilns, are dealt with first. All had been shallowly dug into the natural gravel subsoil and were clay-lined.

Kiln 1 (Fig 6 and Pls 3–5)

This was discovered in 1956, when the water-main trench cut obliquely through the flue destroying the stokehole but leaving the oven intact in the baulk. Clearance to the base of the topsoil exposed the wall of the kiln, orientated north-south, standing level with the Roman ground surface, shown by the overspill of soot, ash and pottery and the finished tops to the oven walls. The kiln wall was continuous and unbreached from one side of the flue to the other. The flue lacked a solid fired arch, and was

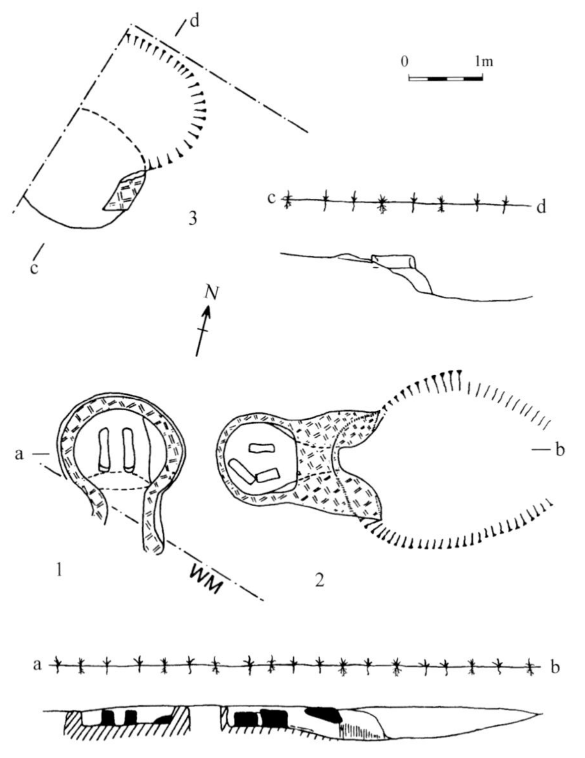

Figure 6. Rossington Bridge Pumping Station: Kilns 1 to 3, plan and profiles, 1957. WM = edge of water main trench. The plinths and kiln walls have been projected onto the line of section. Redrawn from original by J.R. Lidster (1957).

plugged with a mass of 'tough, flaky fire-reddened clay', with pottery sherds interspersed through the mass. Its extremity, and the whole of the stokehole had been cut away by the mechanical excavator digging the water-main trench. Excavation of the interior of the kiln disclosed quantities of pottery sherds lying in the mixed sooty sand filling. Almost level with the walls, the tops of two parallel rectangular pedestals were encountered and, on the east side a little lower, a shelf or side plinth was found. Pottery in quantity occupied the spaces between plinths and walls, and the northern end of the western pedestal, damaged in antiquity, had been repaired by placing over it one half of a large wide-mouthed bowl. From the space between the eastern pedestal and the side plinth, came sherds which make up a complete small cooking pot. One sherd of rustic ware within the kiln chamber at floor level suggested contemporaneity of this ware with the kiln. A sherd of mortarium with the stamp SARRI came from a similar position, and a stamped sherd of parisian ware (*sensu* Corder 1956), examples of which had been found in the trench excavations, implies a similar date for this material.

The oven was roughly circular, with a maximum internal diameter of 1.25m, and the walls were 0.17–0.2m (7–8") thick and 0.25m high, fired grey to a depth of 50–60mm. Internally, the oven contained two pedestals, placed parallel, rectangular in section and smoothly finished on their top surfaces, measuring 0.5m long by 0.10m wide and 0.17m high. The ends of the pedestals towards the flue were rounded off, perhaps to minimise damage in stoking and raking, and had been fired to a hard grey almost to their centres. Both had been damaged at the end away from the flue. The side plinth, about 0.15m high and attached to the east wall of the oven, in effect squaring off one side of the kiln, had been built up in two layers, its top surface approximately level with the other pedestals, and 50mm (2") below the top of the oven wall. No traces of insertion points for fire-bars in the kiln walls were recorded, and it seems probable that the furniture was laid to the contemporary ground surface before the oven was extended upwards, presumably in turf. The walls were continuous with the base, which was smooth and grey fired, joining with a small bevelled curve. The oven floor sloped very slightly towards the flue, which had a softer clay floor, and fell away sharply from the oven. The flue walls and floor were also lined with clay. Unfortunately most of the flue had been destroyed by the water-main trench. A line of small stakeholes, running tangentially eastwards from the back wall of the chamber, evident on the photograph (Pl 3) but unplanned, may have held a wicker fence, acting as a wind-break.

Fragments of kiln furniture were recovered from the chamber filling. Pieces of firebar were at least 70mm by 100mm and 70mm by 50mm in cross-section, in a hard fired, grey, sandy fabric. The debris also includes fragments of what might be described as 'clay-plates' in a similar reduced fabric. The largest, incomplete, is rectangular, 120mm by 100mm and 14mm at its thickest. Uneven, it shows evident finger impressions on one surface and large lumps of fired clay, grog temper. A similar, more irregular piece, 130mm by 90mm with one right-angled corner and smoothed out towards the other edges, is a maximum of 20mm thick. Two smaller irregular pieces also survive. It is probable that these fragments represent *ad hoc* repairs to pedestals and firebars, which have subsequently spalled off, rather than pieces made specifically to assist in stabilising or covering a load. There are similar pieces associated with kilns 4 and 5.

A feature of this kiln was the use of a large number of water-worn pebbles, mixed with the clay of the kiln structure. This mixture was used in the chamber walls, but the flue walls, continuous with these, contained a much higher proportion of clay to pebbles; few pebbles were present in the pedestals and none in the flue floor. Whilst the kiln chamber floor over most of its area had few pebbles intermixed, the proportion of pebbles increased in a patch beneath the plinths, possibly with the object of increasing the strength of this area. The kiln walls and floor were continuous in structure. The side plinth was formed in one with the wall besides it, and the pedestals were integral with the floor. All parts of the structure surviving, with the possible exception of the soft clay floor of the flue, appeared to have been constructed at the same time, and had undergone no modification or repair between construction and abandonment. A waster sherd on the reddened sand surface beneath the floor, and sealed in by the laying down of this, indicated that pottery was being made on the site before the construction of this particular kiln.

Kiln 2 (Fig 6 and Pls 3, 6 and 7)

The back wall of this kiln lay 0.4m east of kiln 1, orientated at about 90° to it, the stokehole being towards the east. Neither site notes nor drawings provide any evidence of stratigraphic links between the two structures, but the finds would suggest that they were virtually contemporary. The oven was less circular than that of kiln 1, with a maximum internal width of 1.0m, flattened towards the flue. The walls of the oven were 0.18m thick, fired hard grey on the inside, and survived to a maximum height of 0.32m, again coinciding with the Roman ground surface. Initially, the floor appears to have sloped gently towards the flue. Although not evident in the drawn section (Fig 6, a-b), the remains of a pedestal positioned along the centre line were located. The shattered remains of the pedestal, 0.41m long, sealed beneath the later floor, imply that the pedestal was of a single build with the floor, and had been broken up when the kiln was rebuilt. The second phase of the structure involved the laying of a more horizontal floor within the oven and a reflooring of the flue, the raised floor being laid over the reduced pedestals and a filling of "sooty sand, clay and pot sherds". The resultant shape of the kiln (Fig 6) presented a shelf between flue and oven, and this must have directed the heat from the fire more directly upwards, since the plan would suggest that the form is not the result of the raking out of the flue. Three rectangular pedestals, all approximately 0.2m high, were disposed irregularly on the oven floor. The more southerly, 0.33m long by 0.11m wide, was positioned immediately south of the centre line of the kiln at about 10° to it. Although no evidence was recorded, it seems probable that this had been initially twinned with a second pedestal, placed symmetrically to the north of the kiln axis, and the addition of two pedestals, 0.34m by 0.12m and 0.43m by 0.14m, in an irregular V-form to supplement it, may reflect an *ad hoc* arrangement to utilise shorter lengths of firebar among the moveable furniture in the kiln. None of the pedestals would appear to have been integral with the floor. Despite the fact that the tops of the pedestals lay 80mm below the finished top of the kiln, there was no evidence for the insertion of fire bars into the walls, and the furniture must have rested directly onto the slightly bevelled edge of the walls.

In contrast with kiln l, the flue of kiln 2 was complete, constructed with massive cheeks of clay, 0.4 m thick. The flue itself was 0.33m wide by 0.2m high at the stokehole end, splaying westwards to the full width of the oven, the roof, at a maximum 0.26m thick, also sloping upwards towards the oven. The stokehole was well preserved. Roughly oval, it was 3.32m long by 2.1m wide and 0.48m deep, shallowing eastwards away from the kiln. The stokehole produced a considerable group of pottery, indistinguishable from those in the adjacent kiln 1, although the presence of a small sherd from a Castor box provides additional dating evidence.

Kiln 3 (Fig 6 and Pls 3, 8 and 9)

The poorly preserved remains of kiln 3 lay about two metres north of kiln 1. The structure had been only shallowly dug into the ground and interpretation is difficult. Part of the oven and stokehole were in the baulk, and the kiln appears not to have been completely excavated. Only a short length of oven wall, approximately 0.22m thick and 0.08m high, remained, and the oven had perhaps been 1.2m in diameter. An irregularly circular layer of fired clay appears on photographs of the oven, and this was perhaps the floor, although it does not seem to have been continuous with the oven walls. A sherd of parisian ware was recovered from this. The nature of the flue is uncertain but, if the feature interpreted as this kiln's stokehole is contemporary, then it can only have been short. The incompletely drawn section, however, (Fig 6) might suggest that the kiln has been cut away by a later pit, 1.60m long by nearly 2.0m wide and 0.60–0.70m deep. Photographs of this feature, perhaps a stokehole, suggest that this might have been of several phases. Swan's (1984, fiche) suggestion that this was an uncompleted, unfired kiln does not appear to be substantiated by the site notes.

Kilns 4 and 5 (Fig 7 and Pls 10–13)

A pair of kilns, situated approximately 15m north-west of kiln 1, were located by a magnetometer survey in 1959 and subsequently excavated. Each had at least two phases of use and their stokeholes overlapped; the section (Fig 7, a-b) shows the smaller kiln 5 to have been the later. No description of these kilns appears to have been made and the details have to be reconstructed from the site day books and comments on the drawings.

Kiln 4

Although there are many problems with the recording of this kiln, the photographs, with the incomplete plans and sections, allow a reasonable interpretation. The kiln was orientated west to east, with the flue in the latter direction. Initially, the circular oven was 1.3m in diameter, with clay walls 0.12–0.18m in thickness. The kiln lay 0.4m below the modern ground surface, and it is probable that it survived to its original full height. The rim of the oven curved outwards at the edge as if for a finished lip; its

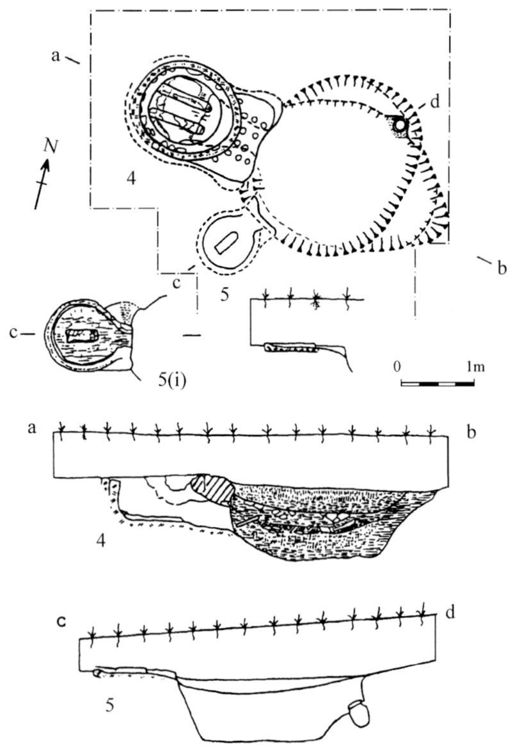

Figure 7. Rossington Bridge Pumping Station: Kilns 4 and 5 (Peg 5), plan and sections, 1959. There is some doubt about the orientation of the structures and both plans and sections have been reconstructed from incomplete fragments to varying scales. Redrawn from originals by J.R. Lidster (1957).

maximum depth was therefore 0.6m, to the floor of the combustion chamber. The nature of the floor and furniture of this phase of the kiln is not evident, as the oven had been extensively relined, whilst still utilising the same flue alignment. In its first phase, the mouth of the flue sloped steeply down into a stokehole, 1.05m deep and 2.56m long by 1.95m wide. On the north-east side of the stokehole, a complete cooking pot, a distorted waster, had been set into a small, irregular clay hearth, 0.33m by 0.24m (Fig 7, c-d). Much charcoal was noted around it and the site notes suggest that the vessel had been set in clay to half its height. North west of the hearth, a shelf 'at sitting height', a maximum of 0.36m wide, continues the line of the stokehole around to the flue. That there was a significant gap, although perhaps only a season, between the two phases is suggested by the survival of the cooking pot (No **171**), upright in the stokehole filling to phase 1, the new stokehole floor lying immediately above it. The extent of the rebuilding of the kiln was considerable, including the complete relining of the oven, and probably the reconstruction of the flue, although the evidence for the latter is only tentative. The oven was reduced in diameter to 0.94m, and the thickness of the clay relining was such that the division between the two phases is clearly apparent on the photographs. Some patching occurred on this lining to the south side near the flue. A number of 'pockets', infilled with sand, survived between the two phases of lining, and the excavator considered that these may have held some form of support for the temporary part of the kiln, rebuilt for each firing. The remains of two parallel tongue pedestals, 0.67m long by 0.06m wide, were found on the floor of the oven. These lay either side of the centre line, attached to the rear wall of the kiln, but survived only to a maximum height of 25mm, apparently having been broken off, perhaps for reuse before the kiln was infilled with a mixture of soft red-yellow clay and fragments of fired clay. The oven floor sloped gently towards the flue, which was 0.43m long in its primary phase and 0.61m in its later. At the stokehole end, the flue mouth was 0.49m wide and 0.3m high, sloping upwards into the oven. The second phase of the kiln was equipped with a much shallower stokehole, partly floored with rubble and including firebar pieces and two fragments of a flat rotary quern, a further fragment of which was found in the oven. The site notes suggest that this shallower stokehole, 0.58m deep, led horizontally into the flue, although the section (Fig 7, c-d) is less clear, the later phase with quern appearing to lie level with the top of the flue. The stokehole contained much kiln debris and fragments of kiln furniture, both oxidised and reduced. The splayed end of one firebar, 65mm by 50mm in cross-section and a fragment of a larger bar, 90mm by 50mm, with both upper and lower surfaces spalled, survive. Fragments of 'clay plate', similar to those from kiln 1, were also recovered; the method of manipulating the clay appears identical in these two kilns. Much decayed, amorphous fragments of a Mayen lava quern were also recovered from the stokehole, and a large, lozenge-shaped object of fired clay is perhaps best regarded as a loom weight (Fig 32).

The top of the flue, constructed partly of a prefired bar set in soft yellow clay, showed a symmetrical arrangement of 12 stake-holes, approximately 75mm in diameter and 130mm deep. These are disposed in two rows of three either side of the flue, with four posts over the flue and one to either side against the outer edge of the oven. No postholes were recorded elsewhere about the kiln and the nature of the structure is uncertain; it is possible that the potter constructed a drying rack for vessels, utilising the heat emanating from the top of the flue and the oven. It is also possible that the stakeholes and the 'pockets' around the oven lining, which had a similar filling of reddish sand, relate to a single superstructure of uncertain form.

Contemporaneity with kilns 1–3 is suggested by sherds of parisian ware in the black, sooty sand at the base and stamps of SARRIVS in the stokehole.

Kiln 5 (Fig 7 and Pls 10–11)

Set at 60° to the flue of kiln 4, some 0.20m away to the east and partly overlying its stokehole was kiln 5. This was less well preserved than kiln 4, being set less deeply into the ground. It had a circular clay-lined oven, 0.76m in interior diameter, with walls 0.12m thick, but remaining to a height of only 0.10m. Part of the west wall of the oven, close to the flue showed evidence of repair, having given way into the poorly consolidated filling of the stokehole of kiln 4. A single, much damaged pedestal, 0.42m long by 0.14m wide, placed on the centre line of the kiln, sat on the fired clay floor. The remains of a short flue, 0.25m long and 0.26m wide, were recorded. The kiln appears to have had an earlier phase (5(i)), with a similar, slightly larger pedestal associated with a narrower flue (Fig 7, 5(i)), although the notes are insufficient to be certain on this point. The almost circular stokehole, 2.60m in diameter and 0.74m deep, cut across the stokehole of kiln 4, against the edge of the flue of the earlier kiln. This effectively sealed wastage from the earlier kiln. The filling of the chamber and flue contained much firebar debris, the largest surviving piece being a wedge-shaped end of a bar, 90mm wide by a maximum of 60mm thick, the upper surface having spalled off in firing. All fragments are in a very hard sandy grey fabric, with scattered quartz pebbles and some burnt out vegetable temper.

Kiln 6 (Fig 8 and Pls 15–16)

Although described by the excavator as a domestic oven in a potter's hut, there is no supporting evidence for this statement, and only the small size and lack of surviving associated pottery cast doubt on its function. The recording of the feature is particularly obscure, and its precise location is uncertain. The feature, noted as Peg 1 in the site records, was found by magnetometer survey in 1960, and lay approximately 26m west-north-west of kilns 1–3 (Fig 3) A rectangular area, approximately 2m square, was excavated. The kiln was either associated with or dug through a clay floor, and a group of six stakeholes, curving away from the kiln may be the 'potter's hut' of the notes. It is difficult to reconcile plan, section and photographs, but the impression is of an oval clay-lined oven (Fig 8), approximately 0.65m diameter internally, with walls 0.16–0.30m thick and surviving to a maximum height of 0.62m. Several blocks of stone were found in the oven, perhaps the remains of a raised floor, and stones were also included in the construction of the short clay-lined flue which spread out apron-like from the oven. The flue, orientated to the south-east, was complete, and its floor sloped upwards to the stokehole giving it an internal height of between 0.22 and 0.30m. The stokehole tapered towards a rounded end, about 0.50m in length, but the section does not give an adequate impression of its depth except at the flue, where it was about 0.48m deep. It appears to lead into a further

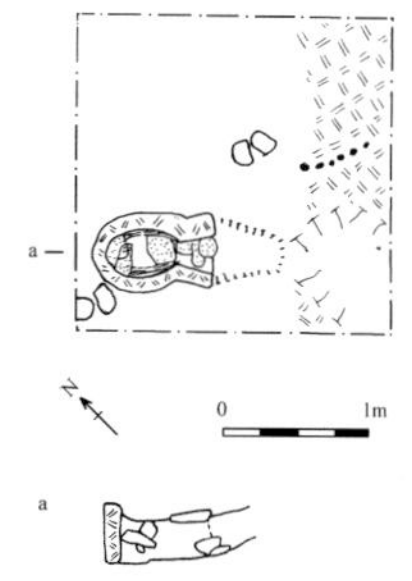

Figure 8. Rossington Bridge Pumping Station: Kiln 6 (Peg 1 "domestic oven in potter's hut"), 1959. The profile through the kiln does not include any relationship with modern ground level or any other features. The clay surface, 'platform', appears to have been burnt and the short arc of stakeholes is later. Redrawn from original by J.R. Lidster (1957).

depression in a burnt clay floor, described in the site notes as a 'platform'.

The small size of the kiln is not unique; Cantley kiln 39 was only 0.9m in internal diameter and kiln 43 was similarly small at 0.7m; both seem to have been associated primarily with the production of oxidised wares and mortaria (Buckland and Magilton, in prep).

Clamp

Until recently (cf Hearne and Smith 1991), there has been a virtual absence of kilns associated with black burnished ware (BB1) production in Dorset, and this has led several researchers (Farrar 1973; 1975; Peacock 1973, 64; Williams 1977, 189) to suggest that the principal method of production was in clamps or bonfires; this has been supported by both ethnographic parallel and experiment (Swan 1984, 53–4). Despite the intimate association of BB1 with the other wares in the kilns at Rossington, it has been suggested (Buckland *et al* 1980) that bonfires or clamps formed part of the process there. The basis of this statement is a note for 8th September 1957, in J.R. Lidster's hopelessly inadequate site books:

> "Worked on 21.01, fragments of broken vessel, in situ between charcoal layers in burnt sand indicating a firing process, followed by clearing of good pottery and leaving of broken – hence dishes etc. At least 2 firings"

A photograph (Pl 14) shows BB1 bead rim dishes apparently set upside-down on a rough pebble surface and this may be the remains of a clamp firing. Unfortunately, the matter cannot be resolved without further excavation.

Other features

Apart from the pottery kilns and their associated spread of pottery, evidence of domestic occupation north-west of the river Torne is extensive, and some sort of roadside settlement alongside the Lincoln to Doncaster road is indicated. The site, however, is not sufficiently well recorded to allow detailed interpretation. Geophysical survey located a clay floor north of kilns 1–3, and a square 2.5m wide, labelled Peg 8 in the site book, was opened over the feature. A sketch plan shows a rustic jar and carinated bowl associated with the floor, but there are no further details. A series of upright wooden stakes, and a 'semicircular wickerwork fence' were found some 50m east of kiln 2 in the excavated section alongside the water main trench (see Pls 17–18). No intelligible plan of these has survived, although in the opinion of the excavator, they were the remains of a 'potter's hut'. In the same area, associated with an iron cauldron chain was a wooden moulding (Pl 19) and a single plank trackway laid across logs (Pl 20); no other information survives. Clay floors elsewhere are also referred to in the site notebooks, but there are no detailed records of these.

Some 40m south east of kiln 2, (Fig 9 and Pl 22) in Areas 19.1–21.1, a ditch was found running east to west. As recorded, it was 0.25m deep and 0.70m wide, and the excavator suggested that it formed part of a boundary ditch around the kilns. The drawn section, however, shows that the feature post-dates a burnt layer, apparently that associated with black burnished ware production, and the ditch may reflect a property boundary, at right angles to the Roman road, subsequent to the main phase of pottery production in this area. Its filling is recorded as peat, contiguous with a layer described as 'upper peat' (layer 3?). The alignment of the ditch is oblique to the extensive field systems to the south of the river (Riley 1980, map 8). Throughout the site notes there are references to 'pebble surfaces', and it seems probable that the area around the kilns was roughly metalled. The relationship with the road, which ascends from the river crossing in a broad cutting (Fig 5), is uncertain.

Further south-east, on the bank and in the bed of the drain, a series of timber piles, between 0.35m and 0.18m in diameter, were found with a mechanical excavator during the dredging of the Mother Drain and River Torne. These were below a layer of peat, and covered an area of 25m × 14m. The site plan is rather inadequate (Fig 10), but from the photographs (Pl 21) the piles appear to be arranged in groups of 2, 3 and 4. More recent evaluation work (van de Noort and Ellis 1997, 444–447) has shown the piles to be of oak. It is probable that these are the uprights for a bridge across the river, carrying the main Roman road northwards to Doncaster. Additional piles were noted further east in the bed of the canalised Torne, but were unplanned. The finds from this area, largely made by the workmen during the construction of the water main in 1956, include much leather, wood, human bones and several of the better preserved items of iron.

Rossington Bridge Pumping Station stratigraphy

The poor quality of recording causes major problems in overall interpretation. The kilns are not accurately tied into the general site stratigraphy, and only their stratigraphic relationship to each other, where they overlap, can be worked out from the notes. Using the distribution of evident wasters amongst the pottery however, it is apparent that they relate to the 'occupation layer', layer 5a. A record was made of some of the layers observed in the watermain trench and the excavated trench beside it. The basic stratigraphy appears simple, thickening southwards towards the river (Fig 11), although the absence of a continuous drawn section and the practice of numbering each sketch of the baulks between pits consecutively from the top, regardless of correlation, adds to the interpretative difficulties. Most of the excavated finds were stratigraphically recorded, although several important pieces have since lost their documentation. The basic stratigraphic division was into five units, with two peat units being separated by a wedge of varying thickness of occupation debris and gravely sand:

Section at 7WMB (as recorded by J.R. Lidster)

1.	Topsoil	0.21m
2.	Upper Peat	0.32m
3.	Rooty sand	0.38m
4.	Light gravely sand	0.32m
5.	Heavy gravely sand	0.38m
5a.	Occupation Layer	0.19m
5b.	Sand, gravely at upper level	0.51m
5c.	Green, clayey peat	0.25m
6.	Peat	

Numerous discontinuous lenses of clay and sand also occurred, but it would seem from the site notebooks that the above layers were the only ones regularly observed and recorded. The thickness of the basal peat was not ascertained but, to the north east the borehole records of the Water Authority record nearly 4.0m of 'black organic silts', and Whitehouse's (1999) work in sections excavated for fishponds 500m to the north east shows a similar succession extending back into the early Holocene.

The bulk of the finds away from the kilns are recorded from the 'occupation layer', 5a, a variegated, black organic sand with much pottery, burnt clay and soot, with, in the sections towards the river, excellent preservation of wood and leather, the latter largely consisting of the remains of shoes and sandals. The waterlogged animal bone from this layer was initially well preserved, but the lack of conservation has left most of it in very degraded state. Still recognisable are bones of cattle, sheep/goat, horse, pig, and hare (below p 81). Mixed with this material are several fragments, including the greater part of the pelvis, of a human, presumably a disturbed burial. The deposit consists essentially of domestic and kiln waste thrown down the slopes, and as

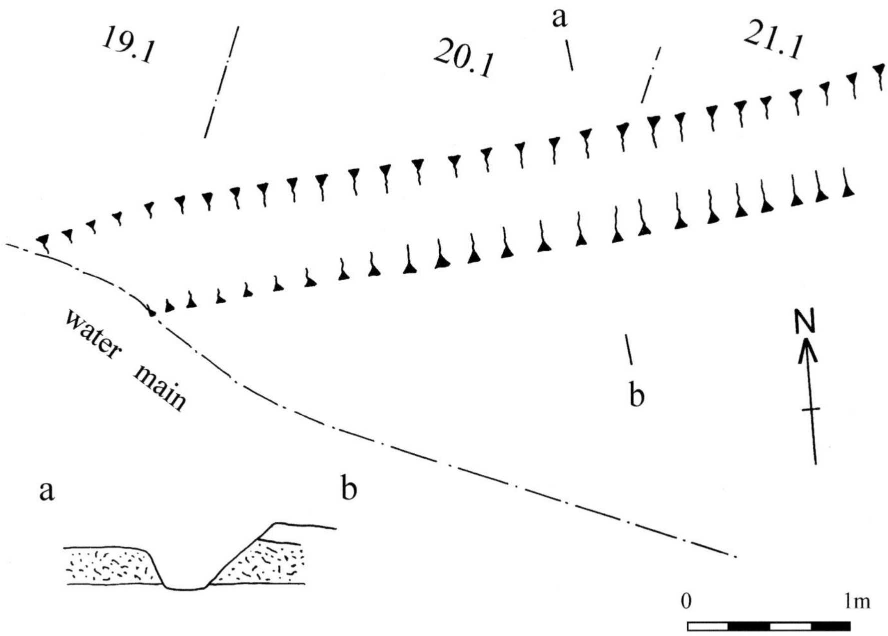

Figure 9. Rossington Bridge Pumping Station : Plan and profiles of ditch, cut at right angles to the line of the Roman road through the area of apparent clamp firing in sections 19.1 to 21.1, 1961. No relationship with the modern ground surface is recorded, but the partial section a-b shows the ditch infilled with peat and cut through the 'burnt layer' into the underlying natural sand. Redrawn from original by J.R. Lidster (1957).

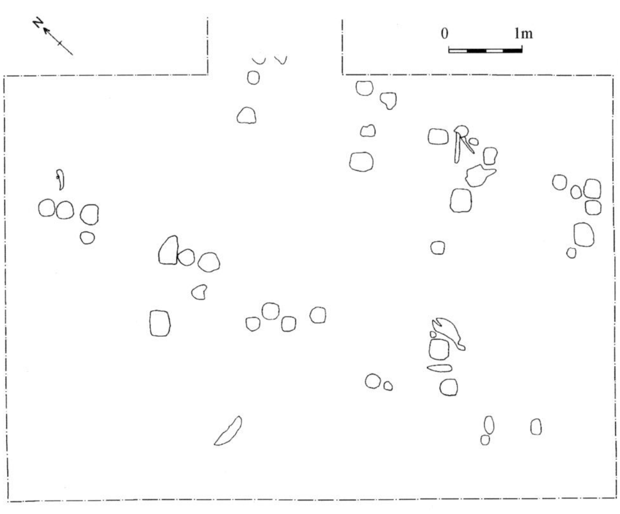

Figure 10. Rossington Bridge Pumping Station : Plan of timber piles for the Roman bridge across the river Torne, exposed in the bed of the Mother Drain, 1958. The position of the trench is only evident because of the survival of the degraded traces of the rectangular extension to the north east in the overgrown bed of the drain. The excavation has been lined up with the orientation of the Roman road. Redrawn from original by J.R. Lidster (1957).

such it appears a remarkably consistent group, well sealed by the over-lying sands and gravels of layers 4 and 5. The pottery includes a considerable amount of samian, colour-coated wares and Mancetter mortaria; the overall impression is of detritus from an occupation site of higher status than a pottery production centre – only a few sherds of plain samian are recorded from all the Cantley kilns. Although the non-local building debris consists merely of several unworked blocks of Lower Magnesian Limestone and fragments of Roman brick and tile, a 'paved surface' was reported to the Museum in 1955 (Doncaster Museum Sites and Monuments Record) during the construction of the pumping station itself (Fig 3), and the possibility of more substantial domestic structures away from the kilns remains. Some confidence in the sealed nature of the assemblage is provided by the close dating of the samian (Table 1), and a *terminus post quem* for cessation of deposition at some time in the first half of the 3rd century is indicated by the denarius of Septimius Severus, minted in AD 196–197, towards the top of the deposit, and the scale-indented beaker in colour-coated ware (**364**), although some bioturbation of such an accumulation must have been inevitable. A date range from the middle of the 2nd to the second quarter of the 3rd century must be allowed for the finds. Later occupation on the site is indicated by some of the pottery and a coin of Magnentius (AD 350–353).

During the analysis of the pottery, a number of joins were noted between sherds in different layers, (particularly evident in the samian), and the layers above the occupation layer 5a contained some rolled pottery, including redeposited sherds of Flavian date.

The accumulation of occupation debris down the slope (Layer 5a) appears to have been abruptly terminated over the lower part of the site by a rapid influx of clean sand and gravel (Layer 5), containing some rolled sherds of pottery, ranging from Flavian to the late 2nd century in date. Some Claudio-Neronian or Flavian material was recovered from both Layer 5a and the peat (Layer 6) beneath this occupation layer, for example, the butt beaker (**370**), but the sherds incorporated in the sands and gravels must derive from upstream, and the 1st century sherds may represent debris associated with the vexillation fortress discovered by St. Joseph (1969), some 750m to the south west. The fragments of human bone recorded by the excavator may also belong to this reworking. Only a right femur, 245mm long, rolled and lacking both epiphyses, has been located in the Museum collections. Although the site books include reference to a humerus, sharpened at one end, as well as cranial and pelvic fragments, the probability is that all pieces belong to a single burial, disturbed from upstream, rolled and redeposited.

In the overlying Layers 3 and 4, the latter containing both eroded peat fragments and minor phases of peat growth, sherds of redeposited early pottery continue to occur, and Layer 3, capped by a soil, represents the gradual re-establishment of a stable regime with renewed peat growth, a condition which apparently continued until the canalisation of the river in the 18th century.

The drawn archaeological sections (Fig 11) suggest that Layers 4 and 5 were deposited by fluviatile action over a relatively short period of time, with some suggestion of cross-bedded units occurring towards the base of Layer 5 and a sharp contact with the underlying occupation debris (5a). Some idea of the range of the date is provided by the pottery, since occupation, and probably pottery manufacture in kilns unexcavated, continued on the site. The flanged bowls provide the most useful evidence. In layer 5a, the type is represented by bowls with grooved lip (**87–89**). The true straight-sided flanged bowl, with flange set well below the lip, (**91**, and **95–96**) only appears in Layers 3 and 4 (*contra* Buckland *et al* 1980); a mid-3rd century date is probably indicated. Whether this phase of sand and gravel deposition, to a maximum depth across the site of 0.5m, reflects a purely local phase of erosion is uncertain, but the borehole sections recorded by the Water Board engineer, Mr. M. Cawley in 1955, show that deposition in the Torne valley was characterised by organic silts and peats for much of the Holocene, and an anthropogenic origin for the event should perhaps be sought. Samuels and Buckland (1978) record a change in fluviatile deposition at the site of Sandtoft close to the confluence of the Don and Idle, to which the Torne is tributary, and

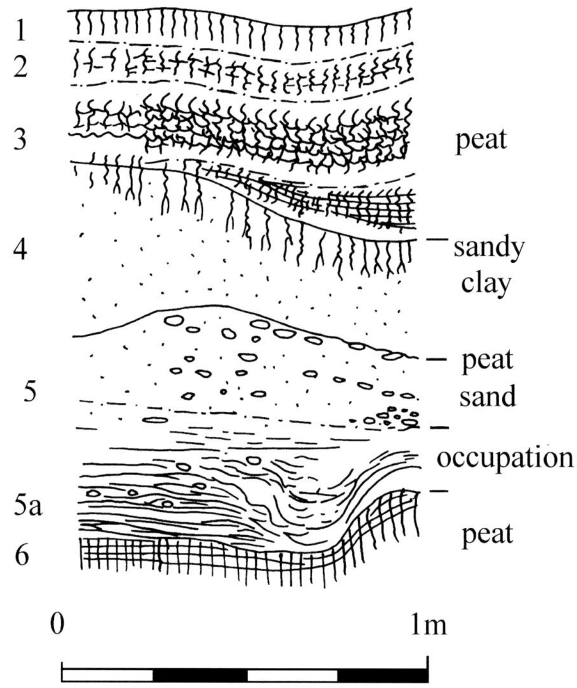

Figure 11. Rossington Bridge Pumping Station: Section of the deposits in the abandoned meander of the river Torne, 1957, providing the basic stratigraphic units. Occupation = "dirty occupation layer (5a)" of the site notes. Layers 7 and 8, from which finds were recorded on the bags are not apparent in any section. Redrawn from original by J.R. Lidster (1957).

Buckland and Sadler (1986) have discussed this in its wider regional context. It is uncertain whether the deposits can be correlated, although recent work on the Trentside settlement at Littleborough has produced similar evidence of later 2nd century flooding (Riley *et al.* 1995)

Proton Magnetometer Survey

During the period of J.R. Lidster's excavations in 1959, a proton magnetometer survey was carried out by staff from the Geophysics departments of both Oxford and Cambridge Universities. This located another ten probable kilns to the north of the water main trench and excavation at one of these sites revealed kilns 4 and 5 with overlapping stokeholes. Kiln 6 was also located during this survey.

In 1963–5, in advance of the construction of a high voltage power line across the site, the area subjected to magnetometer survey was extended eastwards (Fig 4) by M.J. Dolby and colleagues from Doncaster Museum. Each of the 21 anomalies isolated was tested by augering, and it would seem that at least a further 10 kilns exist in this area; the thick scrub south of the water main trench probably conceals more. The present total of 21 probable kilns, of which six have been investigated, is supplemented by two further examples across the River Torne on the Rossington Bridge Farm site (Fig 2).

Rossington Bridge Farm

Introduction

In the ploughed field, about 220m south of the kilns excavated at Rossington Bridge Pumping Station, on the south side of the River Torne (Fig 2), excavations in 1959 by a local amateur, W. Ingram, located two Roman pottery kilns. The exact location and orientation of these kilns is open to some doubt and the plans and notes are often mutually contradictory. The data on the plan (Fig 12) have been preferred in interpretation. The kiln products show considerable overlap with the material from the other Rossington kilns and waster tips. The kilns lay immediately beneath 0.5m of ploughsoil, kiln 1 orientated approximately east-west and the other at 90° to it. The stokeholes overlapped, kiln 1 being the earlier. No details of the primary excavation were recorded, and the following account is based upon notes, plans and photographs by J. Lidster, who took over the excavation on behalf of Doncaster Museum.

Kiln 1 (Fig 12 and Pls 23–25)

Kiln 1, orientated north west to south east, with flue to the north west, was the larger of the two kilns, and was infilled with a 'fire reddened and flaky mass of clay', overlying a layer of sooty sand. The circular oven was 1.30m in diameter, with clay walls 0.15–20m thick, and it survived to a height of about 0.45m, having been dug into the pebbly clay-sand subsoil to this depth. Nothing survived of the upper edge of the chamber, a result of plough damage. The plan (Fig 12) was initially interpreted as showing the remains of a pierced clay floor (Samuels 1984), but this appears uncommon in association with the tongue pedestal, 0.83m long and 0.50m wide, also recorded. The notes, however, are more explicit and fragments of the ends of fire bars were recovered from the oven, suggesting a radial pattern, and the small ledges represented on the plan and sections would have been to take the ends of the bars; at least nine firebars were arranged radially in the kiln. The arched part of the flue was 0.50m long, and had an average height of 0.45m. It is difficult to work out the detailed history of the flue, as plan, section and notes do not usefully coincide. Into the south wall of the flue a large pre-fired slab of clay had been incorporated, probably the re-use of a pedestal, 0.58m long by 0.28m high and of undetermined width, from an earlier kiln. The flue arch had also collapsed and been repaired at least twice, the later repair incorporating several large sherds of pottery. At one stage, the width of the flue was substantially narrowed from 0.55m to 0.30m, and this appears to be associated with a relining of the body of the kiln.

During sectioning of the kiln for archaeomagnetic

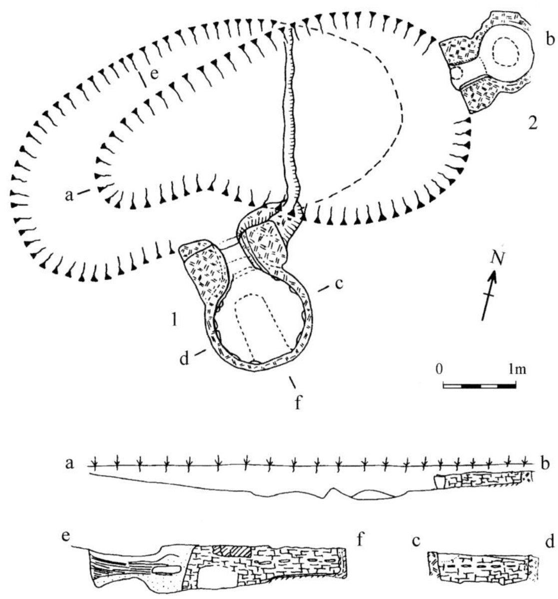

Figure 12. Plan and profiles of the Rossington Bridge Farm kilns, 1959. The exact location of the site remains in doubt, north is magnetic north as of 1959, recorded on one of the incomplete drawings. The profiles are difficult to interpret; a-b provides a cut across kiln 2 and its stokehole, but does not include the stokehole to kiln 1 below, and the sandy clay ridge, forming a shelf in kiln 1's stokehole, appears in a different place in plan and profile. The section through kiln 1 and its stokehole (e-f) does not include the overlying stokehole to kiln 2, although its position is evident. Redrawn from original by J.R. Lidster (1957).

samples, it became apparent that an earlier kiln, represented by a 'hard burnt layer' under the floor, had existed on the same site. Although it does not appear on any of the surviving drawings, part of the flue of this earlier kiln was noted in the side of the stokehole, indicating a similar alignment to the later structure.

The stokehole was directly overlain by that of kiln 2 and was roughly oval, 3.9m by 1.75m, and at least 0.5m deep. It contained much soot and pottery, but recording was insufficiently precise to indicate to which phase individual finds might belong. It is apparent, however, that the stokehole to kiln 1 lay open when kiln 2 was built, as a layer of clean sand separates the two phases, suggesting that material excavated during the construction of the later kiln was distributed across the older feature; there can be little difference in date between the features.

Kiln 2 (Fig 12 and Pls 23 and 26)

The second kiln lay at 90° to the long axis of kiln 1, 1.5m away to the north-east. It was of a similar shape, but smaller, the sub-circular clay-lined oven being approximately 0.84m in diameter and its walls, hand-smoothed and fired to a hard grey fabric, 0.15m thick. The excavator's notes contain the comment 'little trace of plinth on kiln floor', although the plan (Fig 12) shows the ghost of a roughly circular pedestal, 0.4m in diameter. Only one scar for firebar insertion remained on the wall near the flue opening, although, since the walls survived only to a height of 0.20m below the ploughsoil, it is unlikely that any trace would have been evident. The flue, 0.40m long, had no surviving roof, and the whole had been badly damaged by the plough. What remained, suggested an arch, pointed in the stokehole, and flat in the oven. The kiln was infilled with a variegated mixture of 'black sand, clay lumps, fired and unfired' and 'much pottery'. Standing upright just inside the mouth of the flue was the greater part of a grey ware jar. The stokehole was irregularly oval in plan, 2.60m long, and had cut away much of the stokehole of kiln 1, impinging on its flue wall. The stokehole was shallow, about 0.4m deep, and a mass of clay was noted in front of the flue.

Both kilns and stokeholes contained a wide range of pottery types and the presence of parisian, 'roller stamped' and rusticated sherds confirm the connection with the main site over the river, although it is unfortunate that the entire group can no longer be reconstructed. A trademark stamp on a mortarium from kiln 2 (Fig 33) is matched by a further example, unstratified, on the Rossington Bridge Pumping Station site across the river. The stokehole to kiln 1 produced one find of interest other than pottery, a split quartzite pebble, heavily polished on one face. The excavator considered that this was more probably a burnishing tool than a dreikanter out of the local Drift deposits. Several other scatters of potsherds were noted over the field, and it is possible that other kilns exist in the field.

Discussion

All the excavated Rossington Bridge kilns fall into the category defined by Swan (1984) as 'semi-sunken', with all or part of the combustion chamber or furnace below ground level and the oven, containing the load, raised in turf as a temporary structure above the finished lip of the kiln. Kilns 1, 2, 4 and 6 at the Pumping Station site retained at least in part evidence for the careful finishing of the top of the chamber wall, and it is evident that the site had not suffered plough damage (*contra* Swan 1984, 106). The top of the flue to kiln 1 must have been constructed above contemporary ground level. Across the river, at the Rossington Bridge Farm site, the upper surface of the two excavated kilns showed similar evidence of finishing to the top of the kiln walls. Although kiln 2 on this site was very shallow, about 200mm (Fig 12), the depth to the floor of the furnace differs little from the earlier kiln 1, where slight ledges in the kiln wall show that the firebars had been set at a similar height; the furniture could have been reused in kiln 2, laid across onto the contemporary ground surface.

It is unfortunate that little kiln furniture was either retained or accurately recorded during the excavation of the kilns. The notes make frequent reference to firebars, and it appears that none remained *in situ*. Reuse of plinths and pedestals, as well as firebars, is particularly evident in kiln 2 at Rossington Bridge Pumping Station, but the removal of cylindrical pedestal and even a tongue plinth at the Farm site also suggests that these were taken for reuse, an earlier, rectangular pedestal having already been incorporated in the flue wall to kiln 1. Removable kiln fittings and temporary ovens have a number of advantages over more permanent structures, especially where potting activities were seasonal and subject to major fluctuations in demand. In two cases, smaller kilns superseded larger ones on the same site, Pumping Station kiln 5 succeeding 4 and Farm kiln 2 replacing 1. In both examples, the later kilns are less deeply set into the ground, and firebars could have been reused, their excess length being accommodated within the turf walling. In addition, the turf oven could be built up during loading, and its height varied as to the available load of vessels. The majority of the Rossington kilns fall within the range of variation evident in the larger group excavated in Cantley parish (Annable 1960; Gilmour 1954, 1955, 1956; Buckland and Magilton, in prep), largely semi-sunken, with rectilinear or cylindrical plinths and pedestals. Although the small kiln 6 is unusual, it is not the only example amongst the Cantley kilns (Buckland and Magilton, in prep). The tongue pedestals of Rossington Bridge Pumping Station kiln 4 and Farm kiln 1, however, are so far unique in south Yorkshire, probably a reflection of the relatively early date of the site. Swan, (1984, fiche), however, perhaps influenced by the other evidence from south Yorkshire kilns, chose to interpret the evidence differently, suggesting that the former had become joined to the back wall of the kiln as a result of relining, and the latter was a detached pedestal; neither explanation is supported by the site notes, drawings or photographs, although, without re-excavation, if anything survives, they remain remote possibilities.

Although the distribution of various late 1st to early 2nd century vessels, in particular the dishes of Gillam (1970) types 330 and 337 stamped by CEN, REDITAS and SACE (Rigby 1998; Buckland *et al* 1980), suggests that activity began in the area earlier, it is the establishment of SARRIVS and other mortarium potters at Rossington *c* AD 140 (below pp 45–6), which provides the earliest excavated kilns. In the Mancetter-Hartshill potteries, from which the Rossington industry partly derived, single tongue pedestals occur in some of the smaller kilns of the first half of the 2nd century (Hartley 1973), but later structures tend to have free-standing pedestals, a pattern more general at Cantley. The combination of a tongue pedestal and corbels or pilaster strips to support the ends of the firebars was widespread in the 4th century in the Oxfordshire potteries (Young

1977), and appears in a contemporary kiln at Hartshill (Hartley 1973); Rossington Bridge Farm provides a much earlier example of this technique, although the slight corbels recorded here may be merely the results of pushing pre-fired firebars into the soft clay lining of the kiln before firing. The single tongue pedestal form is particularly widespread (Corder 1959), but the paired tongues of Rossington Bridge Pumping Station kiln 4 appear atypical. The basic construction of the two kilns with tongued pedestals is similar, utilising massive cheeks of clay either side of the flue, and there are clear ceramic connections across the river between the two sites, but the twin tongue of kiln 4 is sufficiently unusual to seek other parallels. Although a continental origin is possible, in view of the Gallic antecedents proposed for parisian ware (below p 56), Duhamel (1973, quoted in Peacock 1982), in a study of kilns in Roman Gaul, noted only two examples out of a total of 134 kilns with circular chambers. The problem cannot be resolved without further excavation.

North-west of the excavated areas, in the gardens of properties fronting onto Warning Tongue Lane, west of the line of the Roman road, Atkinson and Merrony (1994) excavated a circular enclosure in advance of housing development. Whilst the authors were tempted to relate the structure to the pottery industry, the few sherds (31) of 2nd to 3rd century pottery found, suggests that the site was not directly involved in production.

Archaeomagnetic Measurements
M. J. Aitken and G. H. Weaver

Kilns 1, 2 and 4 were studied and eight, eight and 17 samples respectively were obtained from each. The samples were obtained by enclosing a stump of clay in potters' plastic with a horizontal surface on which a direction with respect to geographic North was marked by means of a sun-orientated theodolite positioned outside the kiln. The direction of the remanent magnetisation was measured, in the Laboratory, by means of a spinner magnetometer after removal of any viscous component. Details of measurement procedure have been given elsewhere (Harold 1960; Aitken and Weaver 1962).

The results are given in Table 1. In this, the quoted Inclination (**I**) has been corrected to the latitude of London by subtraction of 1.5°; this is on the assumption of an axial dipole field. No correction has been made to the Declination (**D**). The circle of confidence, O_{80}, is the Fisher Index at the 80% level of confidence; the error limits for **I** and **D** corresponding to this level of confidence are a little under ± 0° and ± 20° respectively.

The indication of magnetic reliability is as follows: **A** – complete confidence, **B** – reasonable confidence, **C** – doubtful but worth considering, **D** – very doubtful. Despite kilns 1 and 2 being in category **C**, it will be seen that, within error limits, they are in agreement with the **A** kiln, 4, which is to be expected since all three are attributed to the third quarter of the 2nd century. However, because of the much higher reliability of number 4, the value is utilised rather than an average.

There was not much variation of **D** during the first three centuries AD, but a marked shallowing of **I** to 57° during the 3rd century has been evidenced by kiln 18 at Hartshill. In the first half of the 2nd century, the value was around 65° (kilns 11, 19 and 22 at Hartshill), and so the value of 60° obtained for the present kiln 4 is consistent with the presumed date (for further details about these related kilns, see Aitken and Weaver 1962; Hartley 1962).

We are grateful to John Lidster for his help in the sampling of these kilns and to the Leverhulme Trust for supporting one of us (GHW).

The Coins
S. Esmonde Cleary

The three stratified coins are from the layer designated 5a in the site books, and described as 'dirty occupation layer'. It is probable that this deposit reflects a progressive accumulation of debris downslope from the main activity areas, and the coin of Severus high in the deposit effectively closes the sequence before renewed alluviation, represented by sand and gravel accumulation from the river Torne, covered the lower part of the site.

Table 1. Archaeomagnetic results for kilns at Rossington Bridge (Lat. 53.5°N, Long. 1.05°W).

Kiln No.	Direction of remanent magnetisation		Circle of confidence	Magnetic reliability
	Inclination (I)	Declination (D)		
1	58.5°	2.8°W	2.6°	C
2	58.2°	2.4°E	1.4°	C+
4	60.0°	2.2°E	1.0°	A-

Table 2. Roman Coins from Rossington Bridge Pumping Station site.

Emperor	Date	Denomination	Site data
Domitian	81–96	*Dupondius* illeg.	Unstratified 'river bed' (10)
Trajan	103–117	*denarius* RIC 271	RB/16WMB/L.5–5A Depth 1.52m (9)
Hadrian	119–121	*Sestertius* illeg.	Unstratified 1956 (in private possession)
Antoninus Pius	154–155	*Dupondius* RIC 937	RB/12WMB/L.5a Depth 1.6m. (8)
Septimius Severus	195–196	*denarius* RIC 64	RB/12WMB/L.5a Depth 1.27m (11)
Magnentius	351–353	LRBC as 19	Unstratified (12)

(-) = small find number.

An Intaglio from Rossington Bridge
Martin Henig

Carnelian intaglio, ovoid in shape, 12mm × 8mm × 3.5mm. (Fig 13)

This gem has been published as Henig (1978), p 212, no 213. The surface seems to be somewhat worn, but the subject is clearly *Bonus Eventus* standing with his body towards the front, and facing left. He holds ears of corn in his left hand and a patera in his right hand. The subject is extremely common on gems, cf Henig (1978), pp 210–212 nos 203–215; pp 288–289 no App 21, pp 22; p 301 no App 115, and the type may be derived from a statue by Praxiteles (*ibid*, 77).

The rather slapdash manner of cutting approximates to Maaskant-Kleibrink's 'incoherent grooves style', which she ascribes to the later 2nd and to the 3rd century AD.

RB/10.1/L.5. (39).

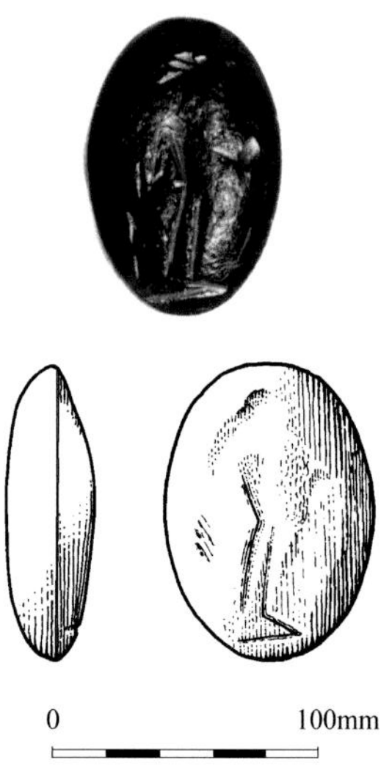

Figure 13. Intaglio from Rossington Bridge Pumping Station.

Small Finds from Rossington Bridge
Glenys Lloyd Morgan, F.S.A.

1. Trumpet brooch, Collingwood Group Riv (Collingwood and Richmond 1968) type with lobed scroll shaped decoration on the head, and remains of ? yellow enamel still *in situ*, and also in the two narrow panels on the bow beneath the stylised acanthus moulding. Virtually complete. Length 57.2mm.
RB/WMB/L.5a. (Fig 14, 1).
Compare a similar piece from Finsbury Circus, London, which is set with blue enamelling (Wheeler 1930, 96; fig 28, 30), and another from Verulamium enamelled in blue, yellow and red, on the head, lower bow and the underside of the foot and also the loop holder (Frere 1984, 25; fig 7, 31). Compare also the unenamelled but related piece also from Verulamium, from a context dated AD 145–150. (Frere 1984, 25, fig 7, 30).

2. Trumpet brooch, Collingwood Group R sub group (i) or (ii)? (Collingwood and Richmond 1968), perhaps originally enamelled, head loop broken and most of spring and pin now lost. Length *c* 55mm.
RB/- unstratified. (Fig 14, 2).

3. Trumpet brooch, Collingwood Group R (iii) (*op cit*), head loop damaged, pin and catch plate broken. Traces of slight decoration on lower part of bow. Surviving length 52mm.
RB/17/L.5a/6. (Fig 14, 3).

4. ?Dolphin brooch, ?hinged pin lost and catch plate damaged. Length 39mm.
RB/- unstratified. (Fig 14, 4).
Compare the Dolphin brooch with hinged pin dated by Hattatt to AD 55–80 (1985, 76, fig 32, 359 and the examples from Winterton, Lincolnshire (Stead 1976b, fig 99, 14 and fig 100, 17), dated to the 3rd century. Collingwood and Richmond (1968, 295) suggest that the type was current from Neronian times to the mid-2nd century.

5. Headstud brooch, with setting for enamel, Collingwood Group Q (Collingwood and Richmond 1969, 296), with sprung pin and lacking the head loop. Traces of red and ? yellow enamel in rectangular settings on bow. Length 45mm.
RB/- unstratified. (Fig 14, 5).
Compare the very similar piece from Doncaster (Lloyd Morgan 1986, 88, fig 19,16 and parallels quoted therein), Late 1st to 2nd century AD.

6. Dolphin brooch, Collingwood Group H (Collingwood and Richmond 1969, 295), with pierced catchplate and sprung pin, now lost. The fore edge of the catchplate is decorated with incised lines as the example from Icklingham (*op cit* fig 102, 15). Length 67mm.

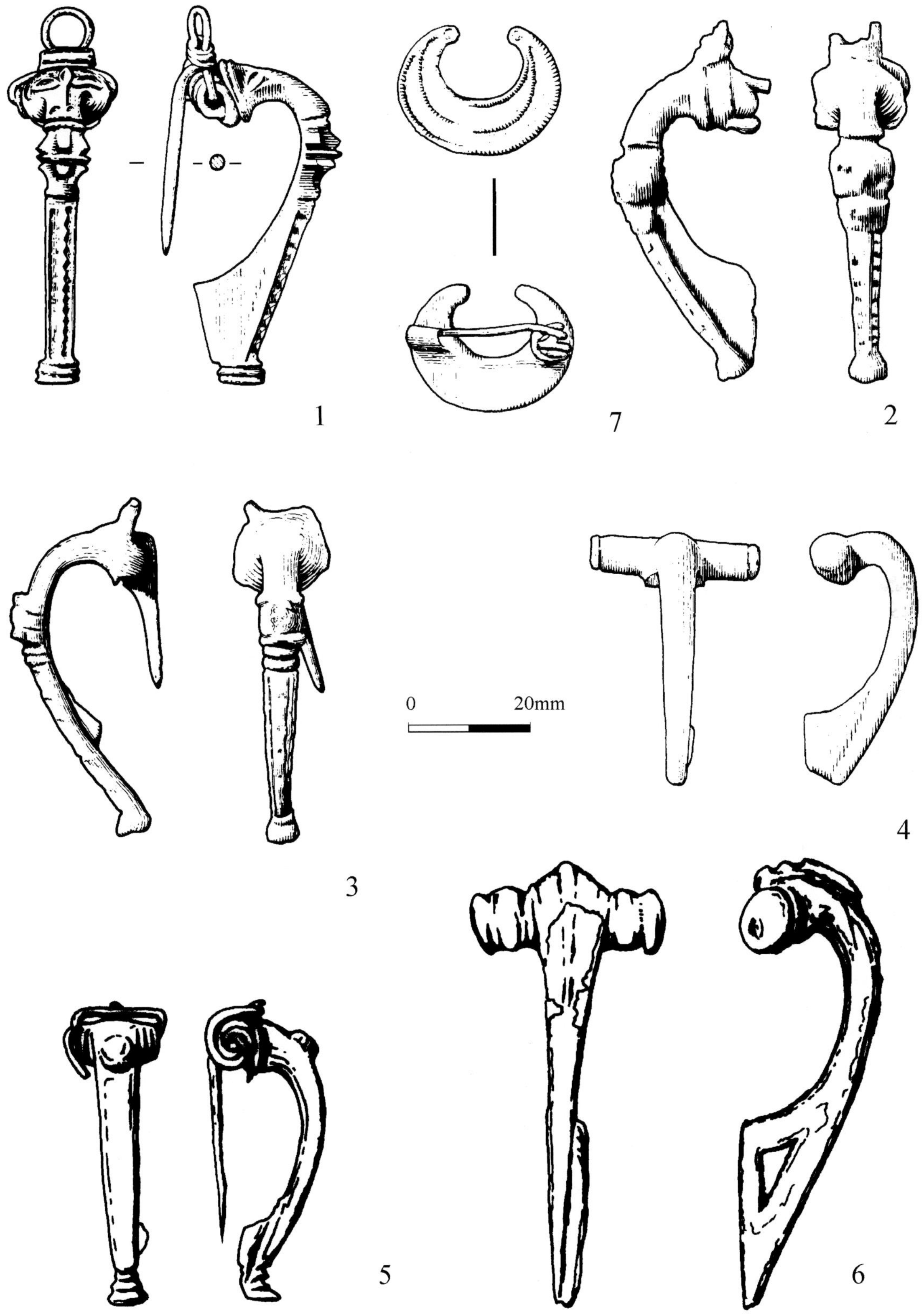

Figure 14. Brooches from the excavations at Rossington Bridge, 1956–1961, Nos 1–7. Drawings: M. Durrant.

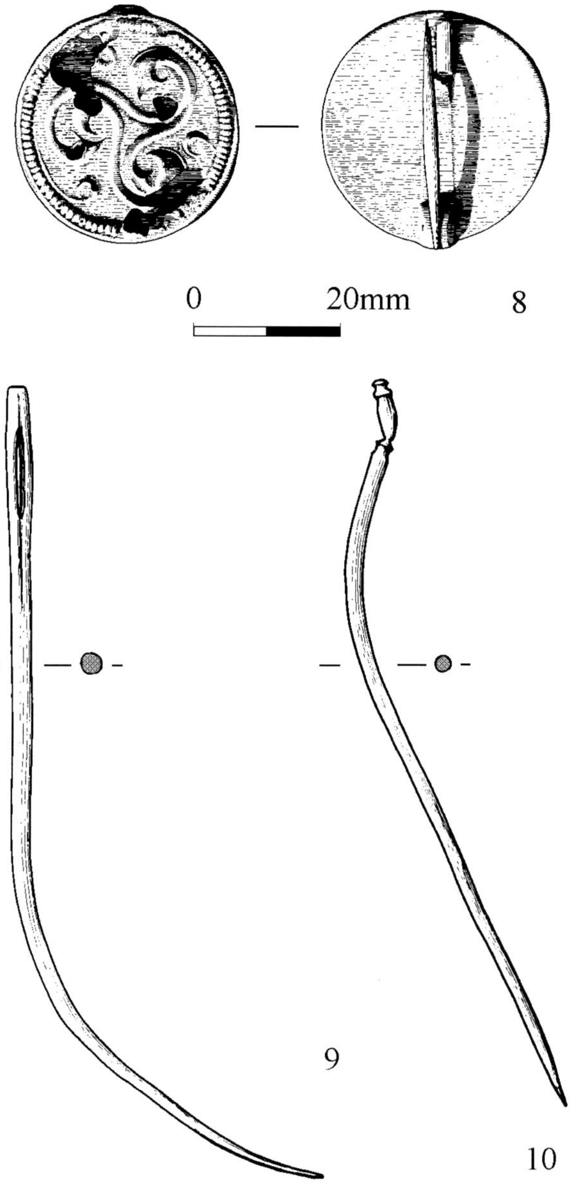

Figure 15. Plate and triskele brooches, needle and stylus from Rossington Bridge Pumping Station, 1956-61. Drawings: M. Durrant.

RB/- unstratified. (Fig 14, 6).
Again Doncaster (Lloyd Morgan 1986, 88, fig 19, 16) provides a very close parallel, unfortunately also unstratified. Mid-1st to mid-2nd century.

7. Crescent-shaped plate brooch inlaid with red enamel in the inner crescent shaped field, and a blue green enamel in the outer field; complete with spring pin. *c* 25.5 × 19.5mm.
RB/9.1/L.5a (51). (Fig 14, 7).
Hattatt illustrates a much narrower enamelled crescent-shaped example, and notes a further piece from Canterbury (1985 fig 68, 597 p 166). As lunular pendants are commonly found as amulets, both in simple and elaborate style and materials, it is perhaps curious that more brooches have not been found with the same design (Zadoks-Josephus, Jitta and Witteveen 1977).

8. Disc brooch with hinged pin, and applied plaque decorated with a repoussé triskele pattern set within a border of ovolo beading. Inside the border are three small scrolls set at intervals, turning in towards the gaps between each curving arm of the central motif.
Diameter *c* 31mm. RB/12WMB/L.5. (Fig 15, 8).
Megaw and Merrifield illustrate a similar brooch from Silchester, and the plaque from another found at Brough-under-Stainmore, and suggest a mid 1st century AD date for the type (1969 pl XVIIc, fig 1g, p 157–158); two examples are reported from the fort at South Shields, where the decorated plaque is described in both cases as gilded silver (Miket 1983, 111 fig 70, 50 from topsoil; Allason-Jones and Miket 1984, no 3. 148, p 118 with fig opp). The latter is virtually identical to the Rossington piece both in decoration and manufacture. A further example is illustrated by Hattatt (1982, p 145, fig 62, 136).

9. Needle, a little bent but otherwise complete. When found, the needle had 'a strip of metal ribbon threaded through its eye. Length *c* 120mm.
RB/10.1/L.5. (Fig 15, 9).
1. A similar example from Castleford (Cool 1998, fig 34, 443) also comes from an Antonine context.

10. Pin with baluster shaped head, consisting of a low cone-shaped terminal separated by a collar from a longer moulded section, then below this a collar with an incision beneath to separate it from the shaft of the pin. Length *c* 101mm.
RB/10WMB/L.5. (Fig 15, 10).
An example from Camerton was said to have come from a context dated AD 250–380 (Wedlake 1958, 64, fig 60, 44), another from Gestingthorpe, Essex was dated by associated pottery to the later 4th century (Draper 1985, 36, fig 13, 91 with dating on p 94, also a second example p 36, fig 13, 92). A further pin is reported from the baths at Newstead (Curle 1911, 337, pl XCII, 20).

11. Two small studs with slightly domed heads, now damaged. Present lengths *c* 8mm.; 8.2mm.
RB/- unstratified 1956 (21). (Fig 16, 11).

12. Domed head of stud, a little chipped and damaged. Diameter of the head *c* 17mm.
RB/- unstratified 1956 (17). (Fig 16, 12).

13. Similar to **12** above. Diameter of the head 17.5mm.
RB/- unstratified (15). (Fig 16, 13).

14. Stud, originally with a flat or slightly concave head, and the edge turned back, now damaged and incomplete. The piece shows traces of gilding. Diameter of the head was *c* 33mm.
RB/8.1/L.6. (16). (Fig 16, 14).

15. Flat strip used as edging or binding with nail hole and marks of edge of stud used for attachment, probably one similar to **14** above. Width 34.5mm.; length 34mm.
RB/- unstratified (19). (Fig 16, 15).

16. Binding strip with C-shaped cross-section and serrated edge. Examples from military sites are usually interpreted as shield or scabbard edging and the piece may be associated with the pre-Flavian vexillation fortress. Length *c* 76mm.
RB/- unstratified (23). (Fig 16, 16).
Compare Templeborough (May 1922) pl XIV, 20, Watercrook (Potter 1979) fig 85, 38 and 39, and Old Winteringham (Stead 1976b) fig 114, 132 and 133.

17. Strip rolled into a crude, narrow tube, now in two pieces. Length 48mm.; 29mm.
RB/8.1/L.5a (49) (20). (Fig 16, 17).

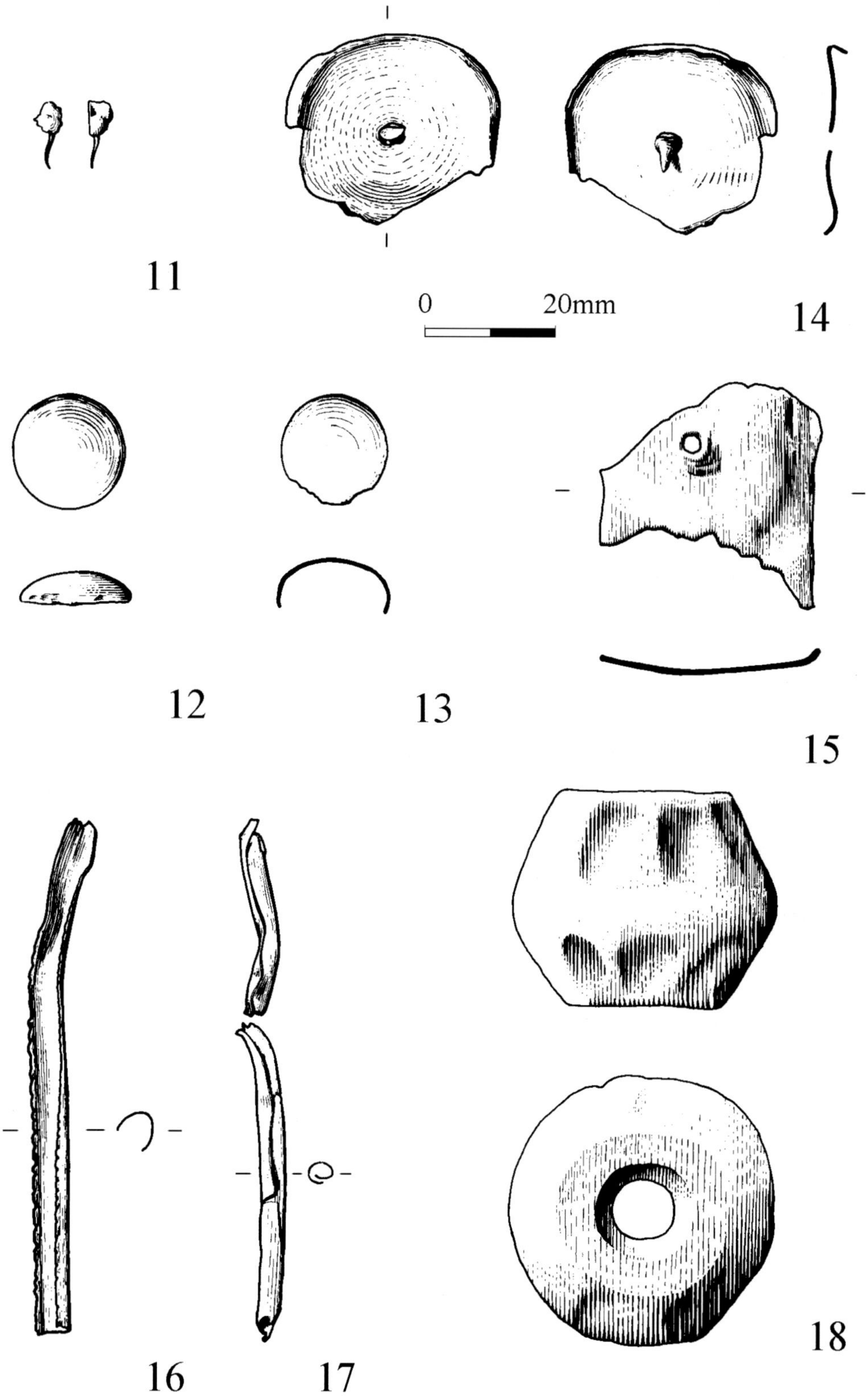

Figure 16. Objects of bronze, Nos 11–17, and lead, No 18, from the Rossington Bridge excavations, 1956–1961. Drawings: M. Durrant.

Object of Lead

18. Faceted spindle whorl or ?bead, with central counter sunk hole. Diameter *c* 21mm. height 17mm.
RB/17.1/L.3. (Fig 16, 18).
Compare the larger example from Camulodunum, described as a spindle whorl (Hawkes and Hull 1947, 344, fig 64, 4). A number of amorphous, melted pieces of lead occur in L.3.

Objects of Iron

19. Fragment of a figure of eight shaped chain link, probably part of **20** below. Length *c* 116mm.
RB/-/L.5a. (Fig 17, 19).
Compare a similar complete loop from Hod Hill, Dorset now in the British Museum, 1893.6–1.69 (Manning 1985, 139, pl 64, S14).

20. Part of a cauldron chain comprising an iron ring, with remains of three figure of eight shaped links similar to **19** above. Diameter of the ring *c* 134mm. length of complete link *c* 126mm.
RB/-/L.5a. (Fig 17, 20 and Pl 19).
Manning (1983) provides a discussion of cauldron chains in Iron Age and Roman contexts in Britain.

21. Iron poker, with flat, paddle-shaped terminal at one end, and at the other a lobed decorative finial with the remains of a loop for suspension or some attachment, now lost. Stead (pers comm) has suggested that this item is a 'blacksmith's paddle' or 'slice', rather than a simple poker. Length *c* 896mm, maximum width 84mm.
RB/- from the bed of the Torne, 1956. (Fig 17, 21).
A similar piece from Southcote, near Reading, Berks., is described as a 'poker' (Piggott and Seaby 1937) and belongs to the early Iron Age. Rodwell (1976) brings together several examples in La Tene II–III contexts. For the Roman period, however, compare the incomplete portions of similar items with paddle-shaped sections now in the British Museum, 1964.7–2.65 from Great Chesterford, Essex; 1915.12–8.345 from Sandy, Bedfordshire, and 1811.6–7.6 from Rodmaston, Gloucestershire (Manning 1985 S128, pl 69, p 143; S129 pl 69, p143; S134, pl 70, p 144). The type is widespread in Late Iron Age contexts on the Continent, and Collis (1984) figures an example, similar to the Rossington piece, from the oppidum at Manching in Bavaria. It is unfortunate, in view of these early contexts, that the Rossington find has no associated stratigraphic evidence.

22. Incomplete iron stand or gridiron, now consisting of two legs which appear to be joined at the upper ends by an outwardly curving bar. Fragments of two other curved bars which do not join also survive, as do one incomplete, and a shorter fragment of another straight bar which would also have been part of the grid section of the stand. Legs height *c* 145mm cross-section *c* 15 × 15mm; curved bar complete length 150mm, cross-section 16 × 12mm curved bar incomplete length 97mm curved bar complete length 113mm straight bar complete length 134mm cross-section 17 × 13mm; straight bar 57mm, cross-section 22 × 12mm.
RB/4/F – apparently pushed into the flue at the abandonment of the kiln, providing thereby a firm mid to late 2nd century date for the artefact. (Fig 18, 22; for X-ray plate, see Pl 31).
See the better preserved example from the 4th century hoard from Sibson, Huntingdonshire (Manning 1998). A near complete example of a gridiron with the upper section consisting of six straight parallel bars, comes from Lion Walk, Colchester, and was found in a context dated *c* AD 44–49/50. (Crummy 1983, 73, fig 77, 2052). Manning illustrates a more complex piece from Icklingham, Suffolk, now in the British Museum (1844.2–23.21: 1937.12.17.2), which has two omega-shaped bars joined together at the centre and surrounded by straight bars. This seems to be the most decorative example known, but see also the discussion (Manning 1985, 100, no P8, pl 45).

23. Corroded head of a pilum or possibly the proximal end of a gouge bit. No trace of a socket exists and the former seems the most likely identification.
RB/- unstratified. Fig 18, 23.
cf the group of *pilum* heads from Bar Hill (Keppie 1975a, fig 33, 18). Antonine.

24. L-shaped lift key, in two pieces, undecorated. Length 140mm.
RB/10.1/L.5 (46). (Fig 19, 24; drawing × 0.5).
Compare a similar piece from Colchester now in the British Museum 1870.4–2.455 (Manning 1985, 92, pl 40, O34).

25. L-shaped lift key with simple moulded decoration on the shaft just below the loop, now broken. Present length 133mm.
RB/10.1/L.5 (47). (Fig 19, 25; drawing × 0.5)
Compare the examples from Gestingthorpe, Essex (Draper 1985, 54, fig 24, 21b), and from Scole, Norfolk, from a context dated to the late 3rd and 4th century (Rogerson 1977, 144, fig 61, 11, for dating see pp 120–1).

26. Consolidated mass with about five figure-of-eight shaped loops. Length of links 22mm.
RB/- unstratified. (Fig 19, 26; drawing × 1)
Compare the chain with similar links from Camulodunum (Hawkes and Hull 1947, 343, pl CV, 14) and from Hod Hill, Dorset, now in the British Museum (1893.6–1.116) (Manning 1985, 139, pl 64,S8).

27. Nail, its virtually unrusted condition suggests that it has been burnt. Length *c* 35mm.
RB/12.1/L.5. (Fig 19, 27; drawing × 1)

28. Nail. Length *c* 26mm.
RB/12.1/L.5. (Fig 19, 28; drawing × 1)

29. Fragment of bent iron rod of unknown function. Length 56mm, 3mm square in section.
RB/12.1/L.5. (Fig 19, 29; drawing × 1).

30. Hipposandal of Type 2, with the wings running together and meeting in a loop above the toe. The back, which is now flattened, would have risen slightly; it ends in a hook. Overall length 190mm, width 118mm.
RB/1–2WMB/- unstratified, 1956. (Fig 19,30; drawing × 0.5).
For a discussion of the type, see Manning (1985), where it is suggested that this form was in use before the 3rd century with two examples now in the British Museum (1856.7–1.1272 and 1871.7–14.22), both from London (Manning 1985, 65, pl 27, H5, H6). Some examples have been found in later contexts and are noted by Manning, to which can be added another piece from Silchester, found with two other hipposandals and a coin of AD 335–345, at the south gate (Corney 1984, 112, fig 37, 2).

31. Hipposandal of Type 5, a half shoe type with the sole only half the usual width, and only one wing on the left side. There is a loop at the front and a hook rising at the back in line with the straight edge of the sole. Overall length 150mm, width 88mm.

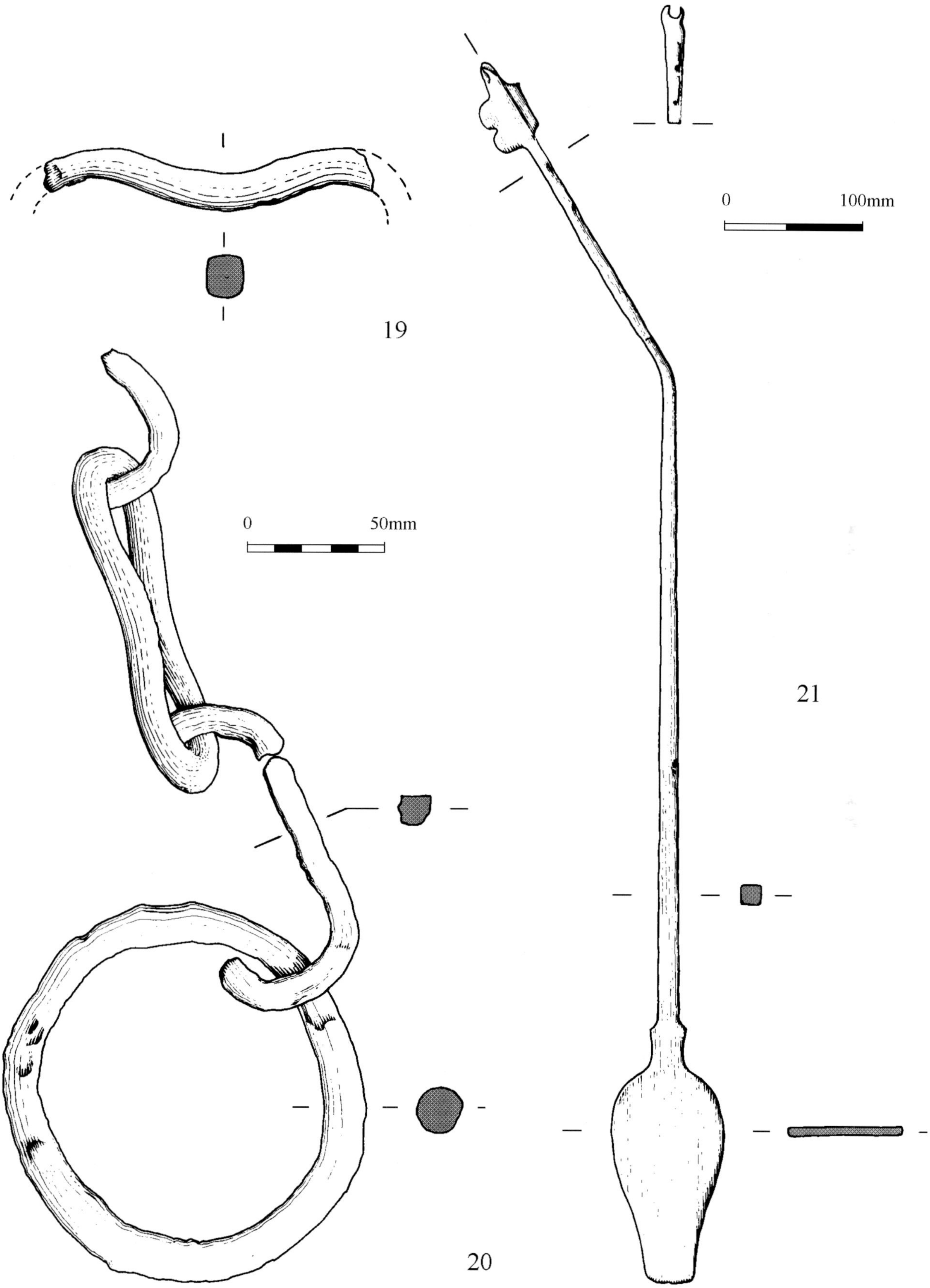

Figure 17. Iron 'poker' and cauldron chain from the bed of the river Torne at Rossington Bridge, 1956 and 1957. Drawings: M. Durrant.

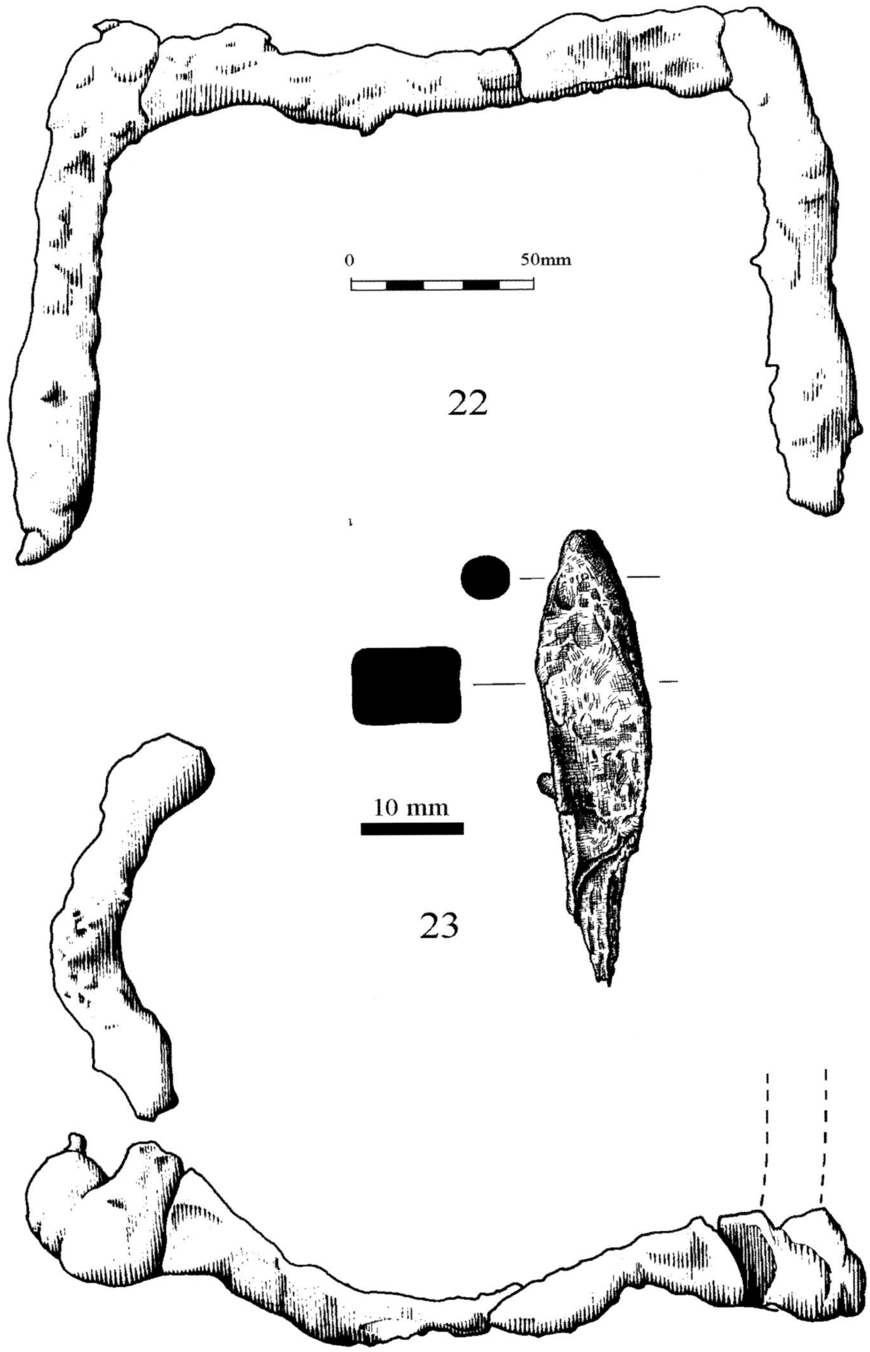

Figure 18. Iron pilum *head or gouge, No 23, and stand or gridiron (found in the flue to kiln 4 at Rossington Bridge Pumping Station, 1959; see also Pl 31). Drawings: M. Durrant.*

RB/1–2WMB/- unstratified 1956. (Fig 19, 31; drawing × 0.5).
The type is discussed by Manning (1985) with parallels, and it is suggested that it may have been used for a damaged hoof. The example in the British Museum (1856.7–1.1274) from London, has the wing on the right hand side (Manning 1985, 66, pl 28, H8).

Object of Amber

32. Orange, annular amber bead, a little irregular. Diameter *c*13mm, height *c* 5mm.
RB/- unstratified, 1956. (Fig 20, 32).
Although known from late Iron Age burials (eg Welwyn Garden City (Stead 1967) fig 10A), amber beads are not common on Roman sites in Britain, and when found tend to come from late contexts. Wheeler and Wheeler (1932, 84, fig 18, 81). noted that the one from Lydney was 'found in

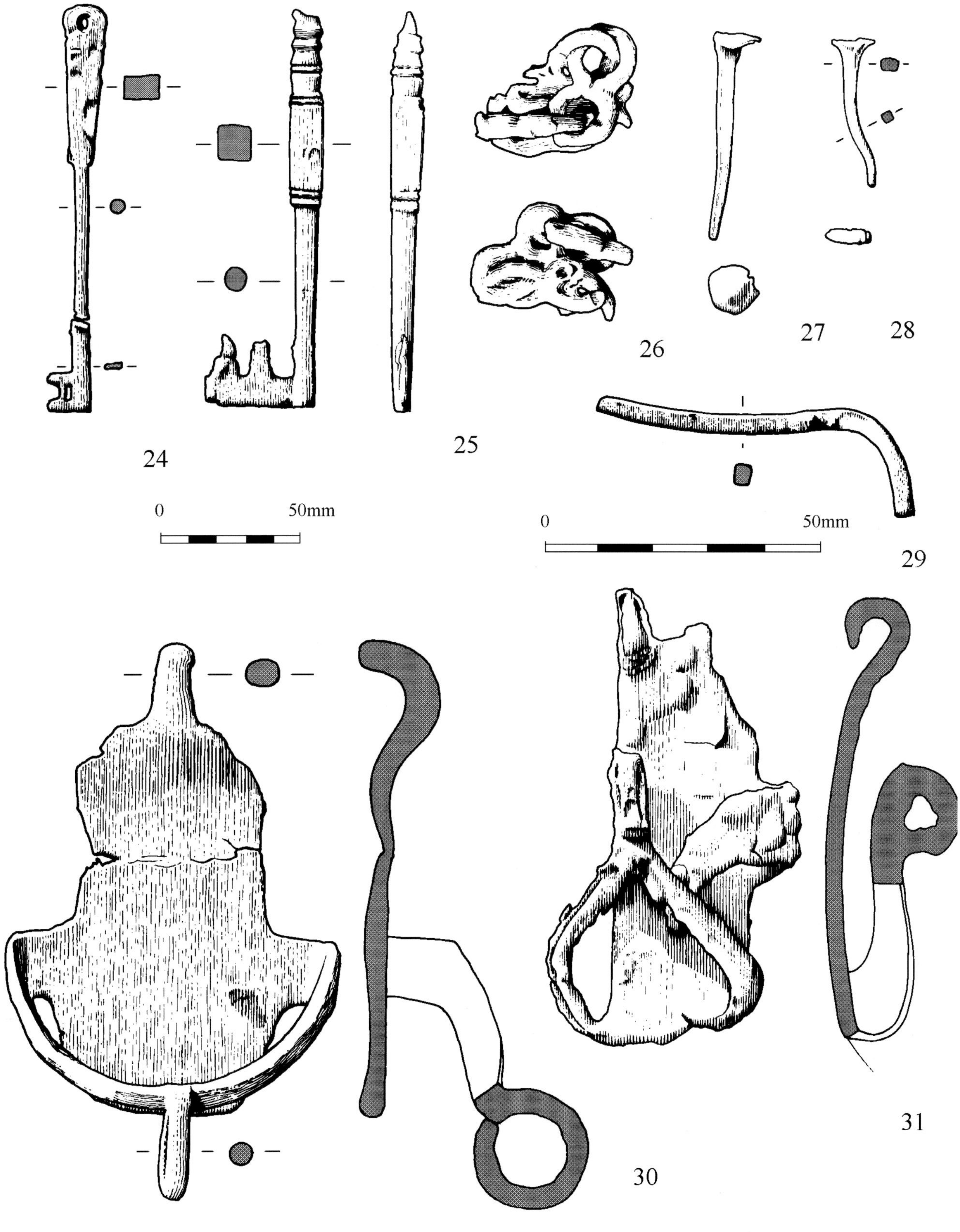

Figure 19. Iron keys, nails, hipposandals and other objects from Rossington Bridge, 1956–1961. Drawings: M. Durrant.

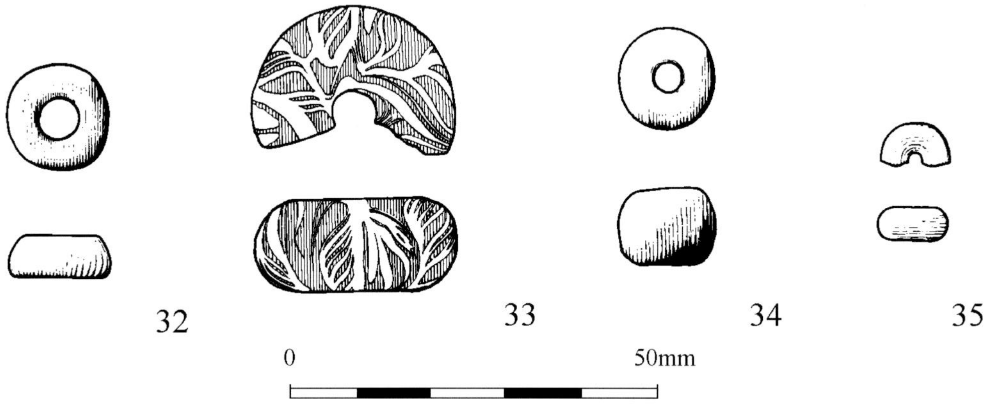

Figure 20. Beads of amber (32) and glass (33–35) from Rossington Bridge. Drawings: M. Durrant.

the core of one of the original walls of the Temple. Several coins of late 3rd and 4th century date were found in a similar position in the structure' (*op cit,* 84, fig 18, 81). Similarly, a bead from a necklace found in the Lankhills cemetery, Winchester, came from a context dateable to AD 350–370 (Clarke 1979, 295–6, fig 86, 436k, pl Ia, grave 323), and others from burials at Butt Road, Colchester belong to period 2, *c* AD 320–450 (Crummy 1983, p 32, fig 34, 559 and 634; p 33, fig 34, 806; p 34, fig 36, 1348 and 1419). In the Doncaster area, there is a further example from the Sandtoft site (Samuels and Buckland 1978, fig 7, 3, not described in the text).

Objects of Glass

33. The greater part of a bead, in dark blue glass with irregular marvered yellow pattern. 26mm in diameter and 12mm deep.
RB/11.1WMB/L.4. (Fig 20, 33).
The type is essentially Iron Age, occurring for example at Meare Village East, Somerset (Coles 1987, fig 3.19, G2), although with less complex pattern. Guido (1978, Group 1) regards the type as dating to *c* 50 BC – AD 50, and an example from a late 1st or early 2nd century AD Roman context in Carmarthen (James 1978, fig 9, 35) is described as a 'survival'.

34. Glass bead.
RB/- unstratified. (Fig 20, 34).

35. Half of a small glass bead. 9mm in diameter and 4mm deep.
RB/- unstratified. (Fig 20, 35).

36. Fragment of a clear glass bracelet of Price (1988) type 2.
RB/- unstratified. (not illustrated).
Dated by Price (*op cit*) to the late 1st to early 2nd century.

Object of Bone

37. Fragment from a cylindrical bone toggle, decorated with a longitudinal line and groups of parallel lines, burnt. The object is probably part of what Waugh and Goodburn (1972, 149) have identified as a bone hinge (see also Greep 1998, 283).
RB/WMB/L.5a. (Fig 21).

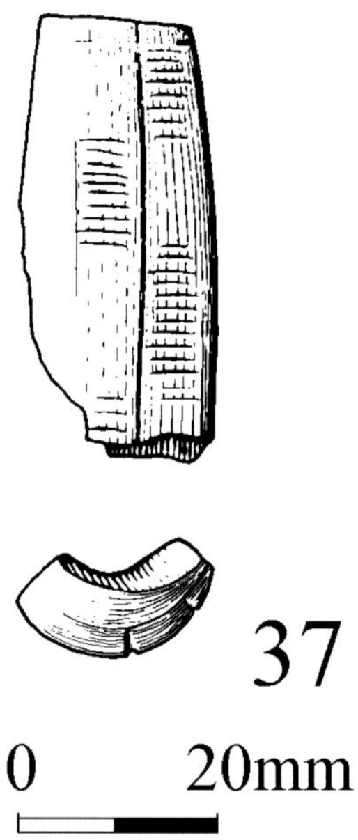

Figure 21. Part of a decorated bone toggle, calcined, from Rossington Bridge. Drawing: M. Durrant.

Wood

Large amounts of worked and unworked wood were recorded from the Rossington site but, in the absence of conservation facilities, all, apart from the three figured items, were allowed to dry out and were either disposed of, or are no longer in a condition to provide useful information.

38. Double-sided wooden comb, with coarse teeth along one side, and a finer set opposite. Now in two pieces, a central section, and an outer one with a wide curved end piece. Outer section: length 42mm, height 55.5mm, inner section: length 33.6mm, height 37mm.
RB/WMB/L.6 (peat). (Fig 22).
An example of a boxwood comb is illustrated amongst the

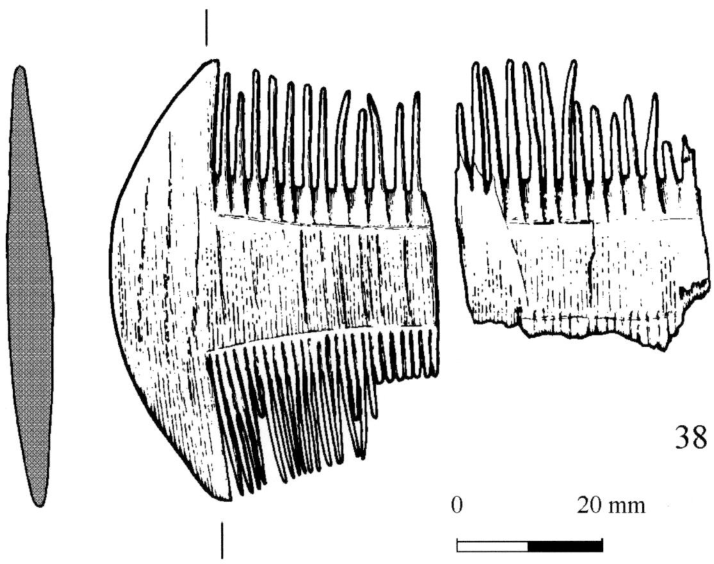

Figure 22. Wooden two-sided comb from the peat at Rossington Bridge. Drawing: M. Durrant.

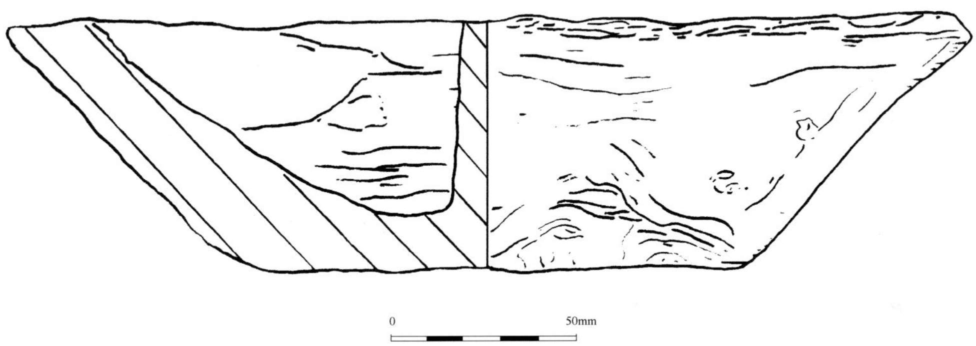

Figure 23. A complete two partition wooden trug from Rossington Bridge. Drawing: P.I. Buckland.

late 1st and 2nd century finds from the fort at Newstead, with a note that a second example came from pit LXXIII (Curle 1911, 311, pl XCIII, fig 33); other examples are noted from Portchester, from a well, filled in by the middle of the 4th century (Cunliffe 1975, 262, fig 137, 322 – the wood is not specified) and from Shakenoak, Oxfordshire, descried as a virtually complete boxwood comb found in a context dated to the first half of the 3rd century (Brodribb *et al* 1978, 110, fig 46, 1).

39. Rough wooden trug, rectangular and divided into two compartments. Length 190mm, depth 50mm. RB/8.1WMB/L.5a. (Fig 23 and Pl 27).

40. Rectangular softwood block. ? palette (Pl 28). RB/–/L6.

Leather Items (Fig 24)

Much of the large amount of leatherwork recovered from Rossington Bridge had been allowed to dry out, and is in a very poor state of preservation. An attempt had been made to treat the more obvious items by induration with carbowax, although this has been marginally successful. The treated pieces have all lost their documentation during the process but from the site notes it is evident that all come from layers 5, 5a and 6.

1. Right sole of a shoe, single thickness leather, with holes for about fifty studs, now lost. Length *c* 245mm. Compare Rhodes (1980, fig 59 and p 105, 107) for varied patterning of hob nails found on Roman shoes and discussion.

2. Left sole, or insole from a shoe or sandal, a little damaged. Present length *c* 243mm.

3. Insole of a shoe or sandal, for right foot, poorly preserved at the toe end. Length *c* 175mm.

4. Insole for shoe or sandal, for right foot, damaged. Length 170mm.

5. Fragment of a *carbatina* with part of loop. The remains of stitching along the lower side suggest that it may have been patched at a later stage of use, cf the near complete item, 13, below. Size 75 × 30mm.

6. Uncertain fragment with edges indicating stitching, possibly part of an insole. Length 150mm.

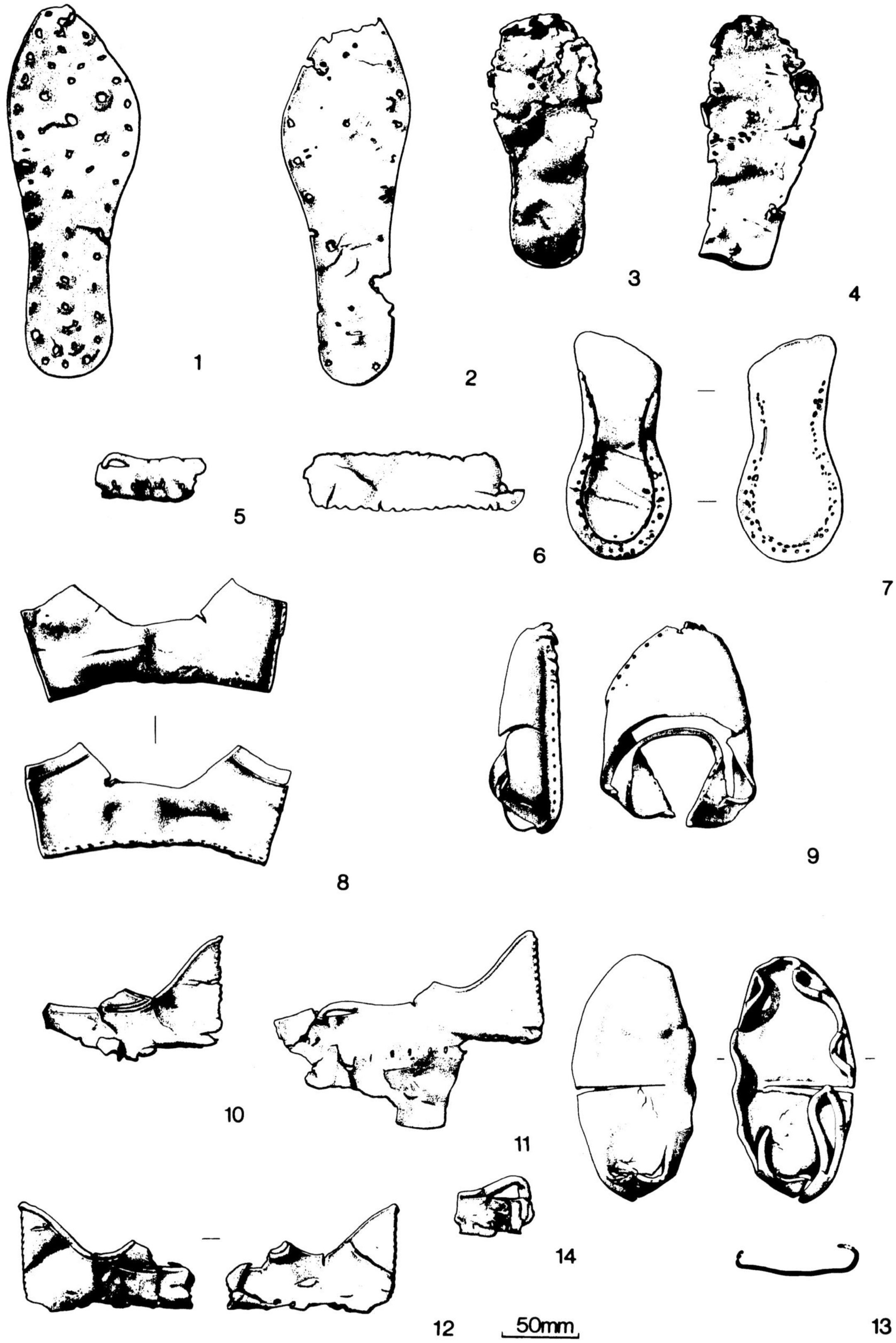

Figure 24. Leather shoes and sandals from the river bed at Rossington Bridge, 1956–1961. Drawings: M. Durrant.

7. Insole of a sandal, with marking out line around the heel and instep on the underside, most of the toe section is lost. Length *c* 150mm. Compare the example with similar marking out lines from Billingsgate Buildings, London (Rhodes 1980, 117, no 628, fig 66, 67).

8. ?Heel stiffener with stitching holes along the sides and lower edge, and incised decoration on part of upper edge. This decoration may suggest that it was part of another shoe which had been reused. The irregular cut out section may also be part of a later adaptation. Width 176mm, height 71mm.

9. Fragment of shoe, cut up for reuse?, with the original stitching holes evident around lower edge. Width 104mm, length 136mm, height 48mm.

10. Heel and part of side of *carbatina* with remains of incised patterning along the upper edge and remains of stitching holes along the heel seam. This may belong with item **12** below. Length *c* 120mm, height at heel *c* 75mm.

11. Part of sole, side and heel section of a carbatina, with remains of only one incomplete side loop. The stitching line at the back of the heel and traces of decoration along the upper edge are similar to that on items 10 and 12. The line of holes at the edge of the sole section, as on nos **5** and **14**, suggest that the piece has been patched. Length *c* 180mm, height at heel *c* 75mm. For examples of *carbatinae* with patched soles, see the pieces from Scole, Norfolk (Adams 1977, 207, fig 88, 1, 6).

12. Heel section and part of side of *carbatina*, almost identical to item **10** above, to which it may belong. The double thickness leather is clearly identifiable. As **11**, the stitching holes along the edge of the sole suggests that it may have been patched at a later date. Length *c* 115mm, height at heel *c* 72mm.

13. *Carbatina*, almost complete, for the right foot of a child. There are two loops along each side, with larger loops at the ankle, one of which is damaged. The slit across the sole may not be original. Length 145mm. This example shows clearly the construction of this simple and economical form of foot gear, cut out of a single piece of leather, with a T-shaped seam at the back making a snug fit for the heel. Similar examples of the type are noted from London (Wheeler 1930, 106, pl XLIV,3), Bar Hill (Keppie 1975b, 59–64, especially fig 20,13–16, 18, and fig 21, 28–30) and Scole in Norfolk (Adams 1977, 207, fig 88, 1–5). **13a-e**, not illustrated, are further examples of the same type of child's *carbatina* in varying states of preservation.

14. Fragment of the heel section of a *carbatina* with part of ankle loop, and a crude line of stitching along the edge of the sole, similar to **5** above. Size 52 × 38mm.

15. Part of the heel section of a *carbatina* with incised decoration and a cut out pattern of triangles, remains of three ankle loops and a line of stitching holes for the seam at the back of the heel. Maximum length 112mm, height 52mm. The decorative cut out pattern can be compared with the elaborate pieces discovered in London (Wheeler 1930, 121–128, especially fig 68, 646, 647, 649, 652, 654, 658 and fig 70, 645 and 660, with useful discussion of the type). (not illustrated).

16. Part of the heel section of a *carbatina* of simpler style than **15** above, with plain rectangular cut out pattern. There are remains of one complete and two damaged ankle loops, and a small section of the sole. The line of stitching holes for the heel seam is evident. (not illustrated).

Textile Impression from Rossington Bridge
J.P. Wild

The corner of a building tile carries a very faint negative impression, covering about 3cm², of a plain weave cloth. It appears as if a piece of fabric had been held parallel to the surface of the tile and allowed to touch it lightly in places:

System (1) spin direction uncertain, *c*5 threads per cm, wide spaced.
System (2) probably z-spun, *c*18 threads per cm.
System (2) covers (1) to a large extent.

Cloth impressions are relatively common features on Roman tile, but the body of evidence is still too small to enable us to explain how they got there. The Rossington impression could be from clothing.

Objects of Stone

Fragments of at least three beehive and 10 rotary querns have been recovered from the Rossington Bridge site, although the fragmentary nature of the material makes it difficult to be certain of the number. One, or possibly two, are in Mayen lava, while the remainder are of what is conventionally termed Millstone Grit, although one probable source, the Wharncliffe Rock, lies at the base of the Coal Measures, west of Sheffield (Wright 1988). Buckley and Major (1990; 1998) provide recent discussion of the dating of querns in Yorkshire in their reports upon material from the villa at Dalton Parlours and the fort at Castleford respectively.

1. The greater part of a ?topstone of a rotary quern, 520mm in diameter and 50mm thick, in a coarse grit from the Millstone Grit Series. The central hopper is large, 108mm in diameter, and rounded. The upper surface shows traces of fittings, perhaps as in the Stibbington example (Swan 1984, pl 14) to take lead weights to balance it. The wear pattern on the upper surface suggests that the object has been modified for a secondary function, probably as a potter's kick wheel, or perhaps was originally intended for that purpose.
RB/- no data. (Fig 25, 1).

2. Fragment of a ?shallow trough, probably from the bottomstone of a rotary quern in a medium grained felspathic sandstone from the Millstone Grit Series. The wear pattern of shallow grooves on the inside appears to be concentric, but the surface lacks any polish, as would result from grinding cereals, although the inner surface of the lip is highly polished, perhaps the result of the use of a smaller, poorly fitting topstone. As the pair of quernstones would rely on spilling the ground flour over the edge of the lower stone, there would a considerable disadvantage in allowing the lower to become trough shaped and an alternative use is perhaps to be sought.
RB/- no data. (Fig 25, 2).
See, for example, the small stone trough from the Norton kiln site (Swan 1984, pl 11).

3. Fragment of a large ?bottomstone of a rotary quern in a light grey Millstone Grit. The upper surface shows a series of concentric grooves as **2** above.
RB/- no data (37). (Fig 25, 3).

4. The greater part of the topstone of a rotary quern in a light grey grit from the Millstone Grit Series, 410mm in diameter and 45mm thick at the centre, where the hopper hole is 40mm across. The grinding surface is pecked with no evidence of use. Perhaps a kick wheel as suggested for **1** above.
RB/- 'potter's hut'. (Fig 26, 4).

5. As **4** above, 410mm in diameter and 60mm thick at the edge of the central hopper, which is 44mm in diameter.
RB/4/S, from the stokehole to kiln 4. (Fig 26, 5).

6. Topstone of a beehive quern, 270mm in diameter, in a coarse arkosic grit from the Millstone Grit Series. The concave grinding surface has been pecked out as a small basin, 145mm across, around the feeder hole. The wear pattern is irregular and not a result of grinding. The stone has been broken/ retrimmed for its secondary use, and the hole for the insertion of the handle, 45mm deep by 25mm across, has been broken.
RB/4/S, from the stokehole to kiln 4. (Fig 27, 6).

7. Large block of light grey gritstone from the Millstone Grit Series. The shallow grooves and pockmarks on the upper surface are unsmoothed and probably reflect the initial working of the block. Possibly the underside a large bottomstone of a quern or millstone, although there is no wear and all the edges are broken.
RB/27/- no data (36). (Fig 27, 7).

8. Small segment of the edge of a topstone of a rotary quern, perhaps 500mm in diameter and 60mm deep. The surface is well finished with slight evidence of pecking and a regular rim. The grinding surface is heavily glossed from use. The rock is a hard light grey medium-grained sandstone with much decayed feldspar, from the Millstone Grit.
RB/4/S.2 (24) from the stokehole to kiln 4. A joining fragment is unstratified (30). (Fig 28, 8).

9. Small segment from a topstone of a rotary quern, probably about 300mm in diameter, in a hard, light grey grit from the Millstone Grit Series.
RB/- no data (Fig 28, 9).

10. Section of the rim and hopper of a quern, 400mm in surviving external diameter at the top and 195mm in depth. The collar, lightly defined by pecking is 20mm deep. Although there is some gloss from use on the grinding surface, pecking from trimming is still evident. In a hard, light grey grit from the Millstone Grit Series.
RB/- no data. (Fig 28, 10).
This distinctive form is paralleled by a more complete profile from Castleford (Buckley and Major 1998, fig 104, 14).

11. Segment of a flat rotary quern, 600mm in diameter and 45mm thick, probably a topstone, in a dense vesicular lava with evident large phenocrysts; probably from the Mayen quarries of the Middle Rhine (cf Peacock 1980). The grinding surface retains its radial surface grooves, at 15mm centres, but the outer surface and top are smoothed by wear, probably through use as a potter's kick wheel.
RB/- (58). No data. (Fig 28, 11).

12. Broken fragment of a rotary quern with a series of radial grooves on upper surface leading in towards the hopper, in a light grey grit from the Millstone Grit Series.
RB/- (35). No data. (Fig 29, 12).

13. Drift pebble of a fine grained sandstone with three shallow longitudinal grooves worn into one surface and a smooth, hemispherical cup into the other. Of uncertain use, although it is possible that the cup-shaped hollow represents use as a pivot stone for a potter's wheel, cf **18** below. RB/5-6/L. (Fig 29, 13).

14. Drift pebble of quartzite, well polished on the flat face, perhaps a burnishing tool.
RB/4-5/S.2, the stokehole to kilns 4 and 5. (Fig 29, 14).
Several other examples of quartzite pebbles from the Drift of this general form occur elsewhere on the site, see **16** and **19** below.

15. Irregular piece of Lower Magnesian Limestone, with a conical pit, 10mm across worn in one face. Despite the present softness of the stone, the smoothly worn nature of the pit suggests a regular circular motion, perhaps the pivot of a potter's wheel (cf Swan 1984, pl 13), although not of sufficient size to be associated with the querns perhaps used as kick wheels.
RB/5-6L/- (49). (Fig 29, 15).

16. Drift pebble of a fine grained sandstone, smoothed and polished by use on both flat faces, presumably as a burnisher.
RB/- no data. (Fig 30, 16).

17. A small piece from the cutting edge, burnt, and a further fragment from the body of a Neolithic polished axe, the latter having a flattened surface where it has been used as a burnisher. A thin section shows that this piece belongs to Group VI, the Langdale axe factories in the Lake District.
RB/17.1/L.5a (54). (Fig 30, 17).
Swan (1984, 52) notes the use of stone axes as modelling tools on kiln sites at Rushden, Northamptonshire, Hevingham, Norfolk, and the Derby Racecourse kilns, as well as in the Central Gaulish samian industry. Webster (1999, 18) notes part of a Group VI axe, 'reused, possibly by a potter' from Water Newton. The Derby piece, the butt of an axe also of petrological group VI, has been published by Dool (1985, fig 95, 64).

18. Fragment, 90 × 45 × 75mm, of a Millstone Grit quern with red ochre (7.5R 3.8) on the grinding surface. The piece has presumably been used for grinding pigment for paint on such vessels as 112. A large block of red ochre was also recovered from layer 5a.
RB/16.1/L.5a. (Pl 29).

19. Flat pebble, of a hard, medium grained sandstone from the local Drift; one face is smoothed and polished, perhaps by use for burnishing.
RB/- no data. (Pl 30).

Not illustrated

Bottomstone of a beehive quern, 300mm in diameter across the slightly convex grinding surface and 145mm high. The seating for the pivot is 25mm in diameter and 35mm deep and the grinding surface retains its radially pecked grooves. Rossington Bridge Pumping Station 1965, found during the erection of a new power line.

Two fragments of rotary quern in Millstone Grit, the one 95 × 115 × 35mm and the other 100 × 90 × 35mm.
RB/-(45) and (46).

As above, from a quern of about 460mm diameter.
RB/- (29).

Two fragments from a small rotary quern.
RB/9.1/L.5.

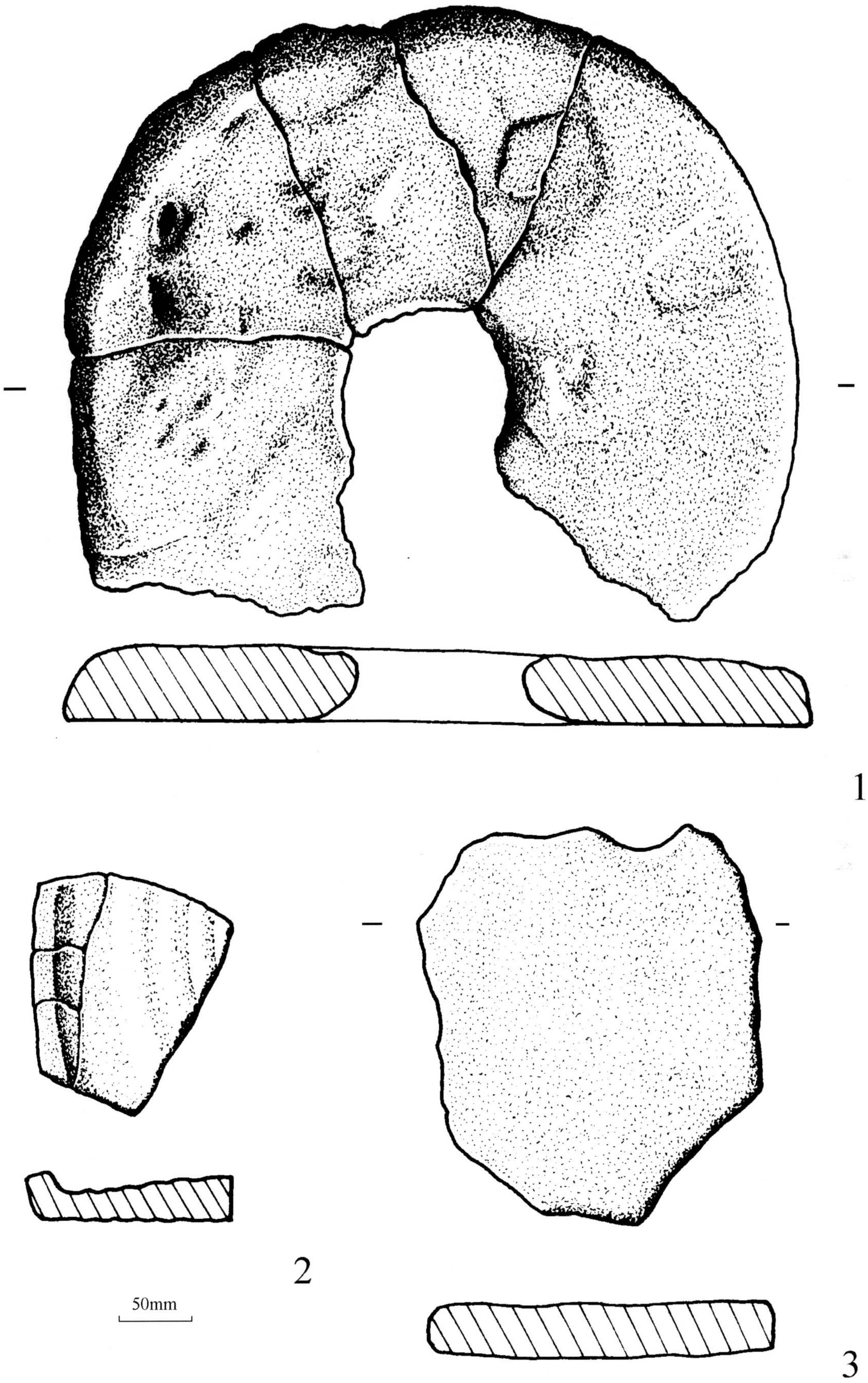

Figure 25. Quern or potter's kick wheel (1), and other stone from Rossington Bridge. Drawings: M. Durrant.

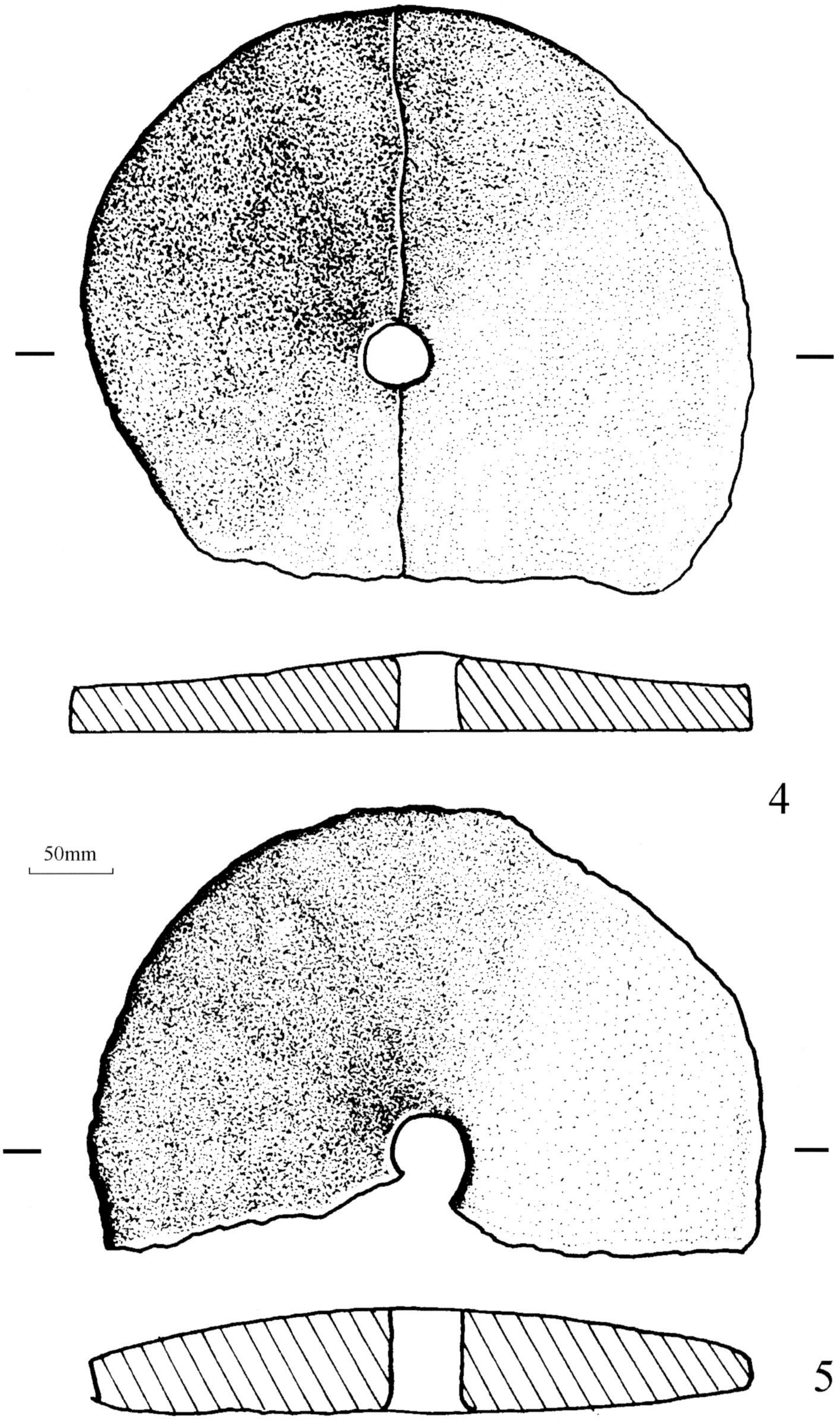

Figure 26. Two Millstone Grit rotary querns from Rossington Bridge. Drawings: M. Durrant.

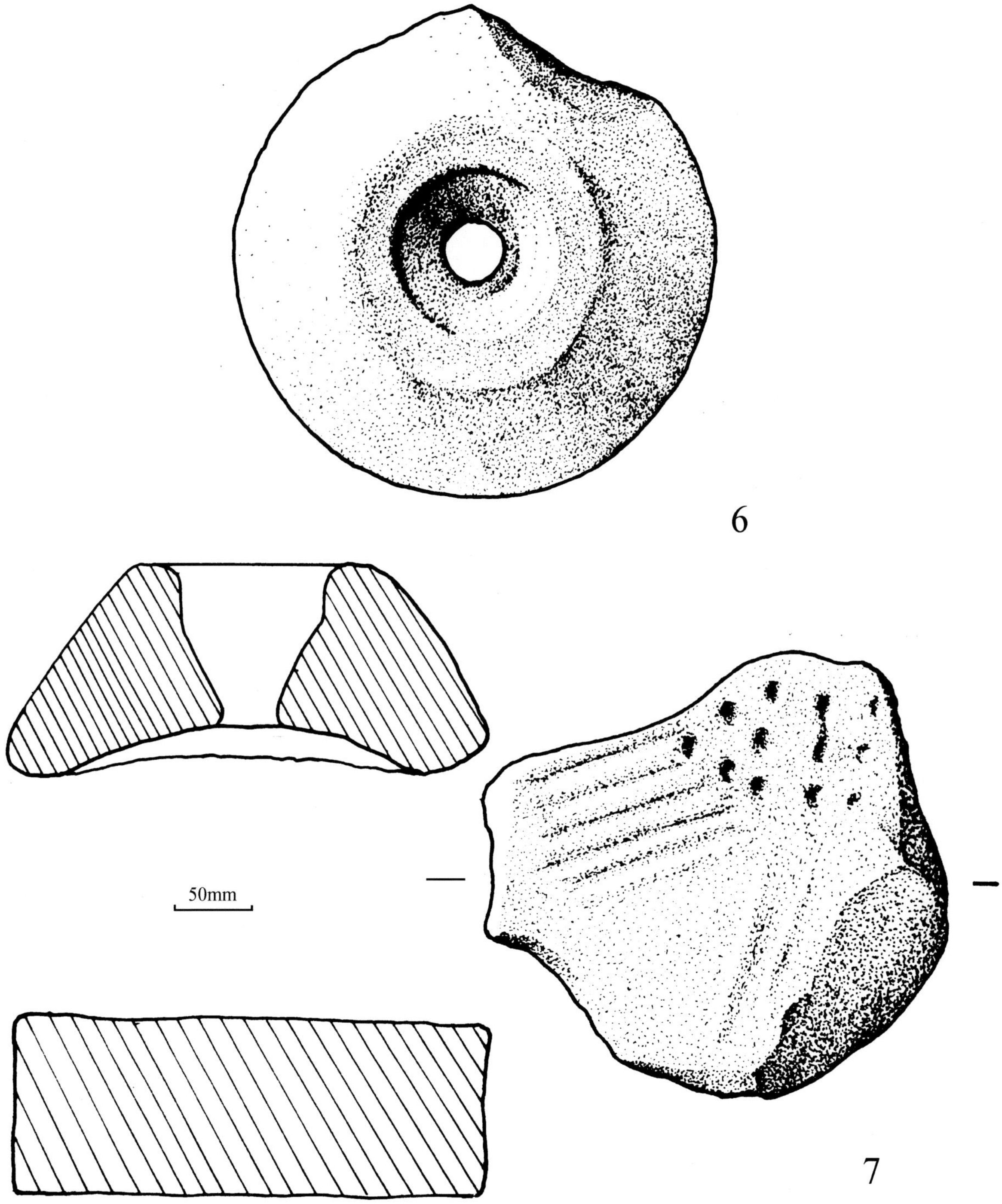

Figure 27. Beehive quern in Millstone Grit and worked stone from Rossington Bridge. Drawings: M. Durrant.

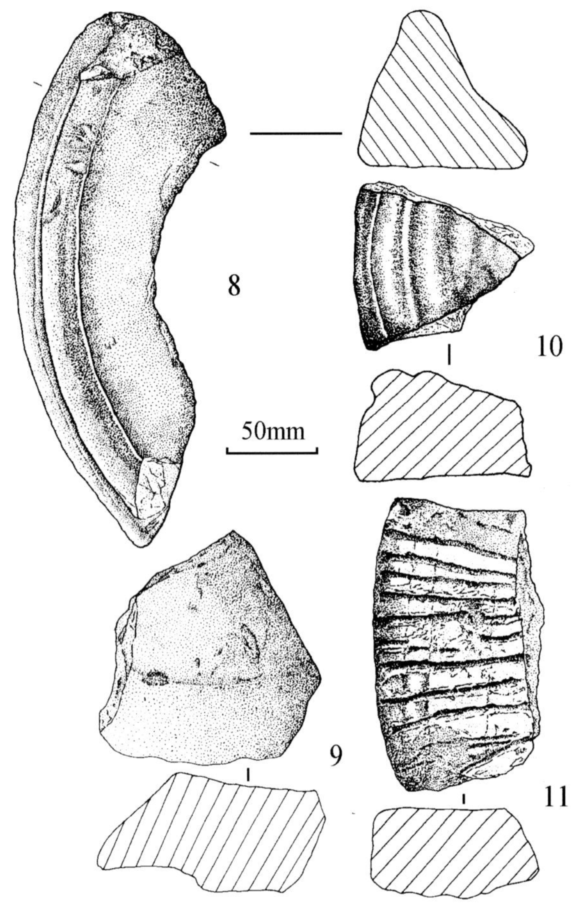

Figure 28. Quern fragments from Rossington Bridge. Drawings: J. Minter.

Small fragment of Millstone Grit quern, 60 × 55 × 30mm. RB/13.1/L.4 (57).

Irregular fragment of Millstone Grit, probably a quern fragment, 90 × 70 × 30mm. RB/- 'burnt area' (55).

Fragment of a beehive quern, 125 × 80 × 80mm, in a brown gritstone, partly burnt to red. The wear on the grinding surface suggests some secondary use after breakage. RB/- (25).

Triangular fragment of a pinkish white ?burnt, fine-grained sandstone, 95 × 50 × 26mm, probably from the Coal Measures. No evident wear pattern but certainly a manuport. RB/21.1/L.3 top. (2).

Burnt and shattered fragments of a block of micaceous sandstone, probably from the Coal Measures, 55mm thick, with tool marks on one surface and the other ground flat. Probably not a quern. RB/8.1/L.5a dark sand. (63).

Much decayed, amorphous fragments of a Mayen lava quern, possibly part of **11** above. RB/K4/S, the stokehole to kiln 4.

Head *et al* (1997, figs 12.4 and 5) have published two further beehive querns from a site east of Rossington village (SK 590978), suggesting a source in the Rivelin Grit, west of Sheffield, where Wright (1988) has located manufactories. There are additional examples from the area in Doncaster Museum (Magilton 1977), but flat rotary querns are relatively uncommon in the region away from the more Romanized sites.

'Roman' Coals from Rossington Bridge near Doncaster
E. Bradburn

This report records the examination of a number of pieces of coal and cannel found in an excavation at Rossington Bridge about 4 miles south-east of Doncaster. Some slag-like material found with the coals was also examined.

The pieces of coal, about 20 in all, and not much more than 20mm square, and one piece of cannel, were submitted by Mr. Gilmour of the Doncaster Museum. The samples were found in association with pottery in excavations made as a result of the discovery of Roman remains in a trench dug from the pumping station at Rossington Bridge to the River Torne during 1956. The specimens were at a depth of about 8ft (2.4m) in sand and gravels of a previous bank of the River Torne.

The coal includes a variety of petrographic types including cannel. A small portion of coal was removed from three of the larger pieces, perpendicular to the bedding, and this was crushed to give a composite sample of about 3 grams. A portion of the cannel was treated separately. Some of the powdered coal was embedded in

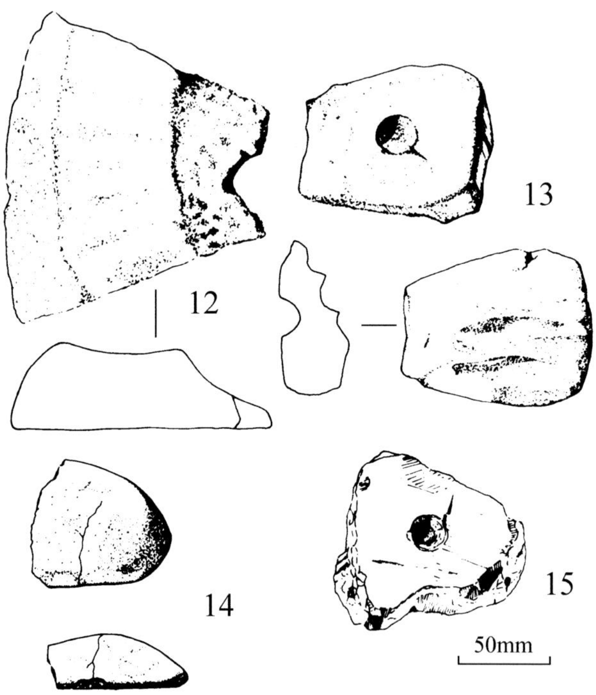

Figure 29. Objects of stone, including pivot block, probably for a potter's wheel from Rossington Bridge. Drawings: M. Durrant.

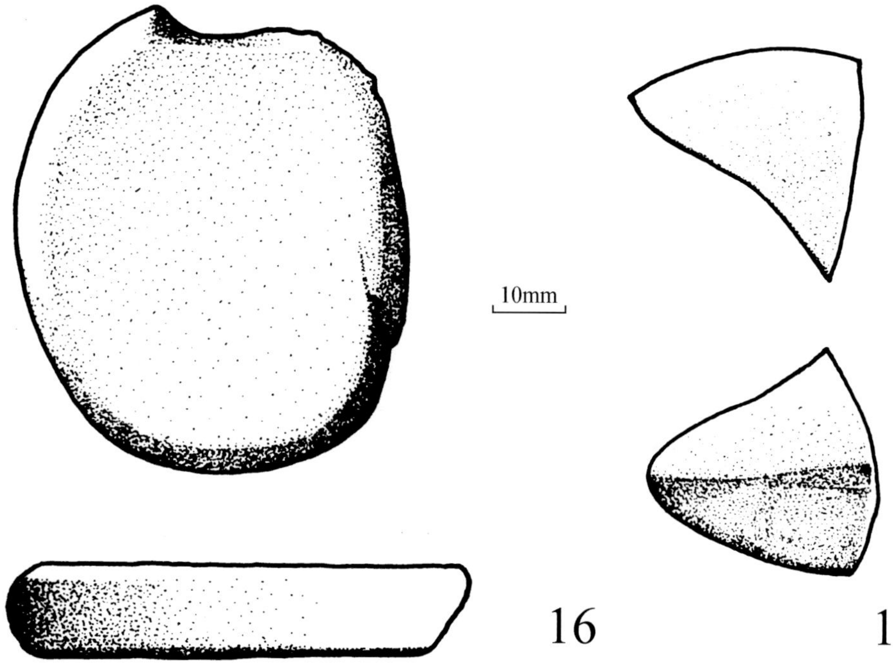

16 17

Figure 30. Drift pebble utilised as a burnisher, and part of a neolithic polished axe re-used as a burnisher, from Rossington Bridge. Drawings: M. Durrant.

resin and polished so that measurements of reflectance could be made on the bright coal to determine the approximate carbon content. A further portion of the coal was macerated with fuming nitric acid to isolate the spores. The cannel coal proved difficult to macerate, but prolonged treatment gave results. The sample was analysed for moisture and chlorine contents and the coking power of the coal was determined in the Gray-King apparatus.

Results

Moisture a.d.	4.2%
Chlorine	0.04%
G.K. coke type	B/C
Carbon	84.1% (by reflectance)

Microspore analysis – a varied assemblage of microspores was obtained from the 3g sample of coal. The assemblage included several specimens of each of two species, *Dictyotriletes bireticulatus* and *Endosporites globiformis* that indicate that the coal probably originated from that part of the Middle Coal Measures sequence between the Clay Cross and Mansfield Marine bands. The evidence from the other species does not conflict with this view.

The assemblage from the cannel coal mainly comprised one species *Densosporites sphaerotriangularis*.

Discussion

The microspore assemblage indicates that the coal came from a seam between the Clay Cross and Mansfield Marine bands. The species found were more heterogeneous than those found in an all-bright coal and indicated that the seam contained dull bands. It is suggested, therefore, that the coal came from one of the Hazel-Barnsley-Swallow Wood group of coals. Coals of this age, and with the rank indicated by the above physical and chemical properties, outcrop extensively in the Yorkshire Coalfield, to the west of Rossington, although the course of the River Torne does not intersect any of the seam outcrops in question so that the possibility of the coal having arrived in the alluvium to Rossington Bridge is ruled out. Coals of this rank and age occur in other coalfields, but the spores provide no evidence on this point. Whilst there is no evidence of the use of coal in pottery manufacture (Swan 1984), it is not infrequent on Roman sites (Smith 1997), and pieces have been recorded from a roughly contemporary pit in the civil settlement in Doncaster (Smith 1986).

Slag Material

Several pieces of slag material were found with the coal. One of these looked and felt like coke in the hand specimen, but microscopic examination showed it to be a glassy slag with a bubble structure. Three of the pieces had a red coloration, indicative of iron compounds and resembled clinker. One piece of slag had some dense, glassy material attached, possibly a piece of pottery. A further piece was a burnt, sandy shale.

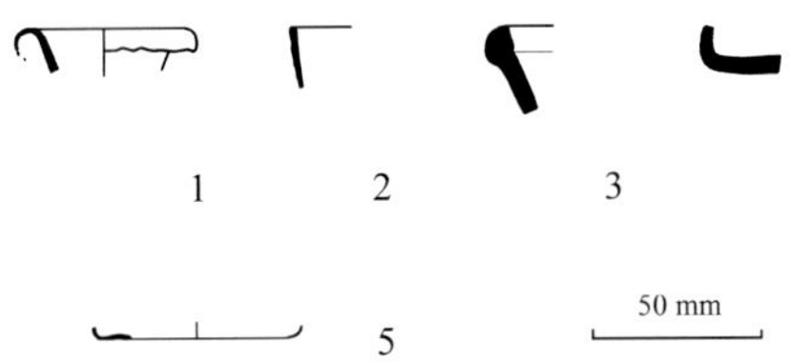

Figure 31. Glass vessels from Rossington Bridge, 1957–1961.

Glass Vessels (Fig 31)

1. Out-turned rim of glass bottle in a transparent light green glass and several shards, including basal piece. Some melted glass may be from this or similar vessels.
RB/- unstratified.
2. Rim of a small beaker or bowl, diameter indeterminate, in a dark green translucent body.
RB/9.1/L.4
3. Rim of a glass vessel, possibly a flagon, diameter indeterminate.
RB/- Unstratified.
cf Verulamium (Charlesworth 1972) fig 76, 20, AD 150–160.
4. Sherd from the base of a cylindrical glass bottle.
RB/- unstratified.
5. Base of glass vessel.
RB/10.1/L.4

Object of Fired Clay (Fig 32)

A lozenge-shaped object, probably a loom or thatch weight, 120mm by 100mm and 58mm thick. All edges are rounded and the ? top is flat, 40mm across. The two shorter sides of the lozenge have central roughly semi-circular grooves, 8mm across, made before firing. The fabric is a very hard, slightly sandy light brownish grey (2.5Y 6/2) with some darker greyish brown (2.5Y 5/2) surface, and is indistinguishable from that used for some of the kiln furniture. RB/4/S, the stokehole to kiln 4. The type is essentially Iron Age, appearing, for example, at Maiden Castle, Dorset (Wheeler 1943, fig 100, 1) and Verulamium (Wheeler and Wheeler 1936, fig 26, 1), although these are pierced rather than grooved. Examples also occur in Claudio-Neronian deposits at the military works depot at Longthorpe, near Peterborough (Wild

Figure 32. Rossington Bridge: lozenge-shaped baked-clay loom weight from kiln 4 stokehole.

1987, fig 30, 171–174), and in Neronian to Flavian contexts at Old Winteringham, Lincs. (Stead 1976b, fig 123, 211); the Rossington piece may relate to pre-Flavian occupation associated with the vexillation fortress, south of the river.

The Pottery
Introduction

In addition to the rather indifferent quality of excavation at Rossington Bridge, the finds have suffered subsequently. Most of the material was bagged, unwashed, on the site, and the necessary excavation record made in either ink or pencil on the outside of the bag. Only a few items were recorded in a finds book, which was rapidly abandoned, and some of the more impressive pieces were labelled directly, again unwashed, in Indian ink; others were merely pulled out to show visitors and thereby lost any documentation. Doncaster's old museum had no facilities for finds processing, and only one sink. The finds were dumped into a basement already overflowing with pottery from rescue excavations at Cantley and in Doncaster; much of the documentation fell victim to damp and mice. The move in 1963 to the new museum in Chequer Road was accomplished by dumping all the finds into cabinets in its basement, with an inevitable further loss of information. In the early 1970's, one of us (PCB), with a group of local volunteers, began the processing of over a tonne of unwashed, unsorted finds in the Museum collection. All unlocalised kiln material was disposed of, buried deeply in a Council land-fill site in Balby, and undecorated body sherds were similarly discarded. The excavator, John Lidster, had shown the samian to B.R. Hartley and B. Dickinson and some of the mortaria to K.F. Hartley at various times in the 1960's, and this at least allowed reference to some of the industry's archaeologically more significant products (eg Hartley 1975). Preliminary sorting also meant that the importance of the site in black burnished ware (BB1) production was also noted (eg Farrar 1973; Gillam 1976; Williams 1977). A concerted examination only began as part of the publication work upon excavations in Doncaster over the past decades (Buckland and Magilton 1986). An interim review of south Yorkshire Roman pottery production appeared in 1980 (Buckland *et al* 1980), and two minor kiln sites, Branton and Blaxton, have been published (Buckland 1976; Buckland and Dolby 1980). The Rossington material was examined as part of a doctoral thesis at Nottingham (Samuels 1984) and a basic rim count was carried out as part of this. The application of more 'sophisticated' techniques of assessment (cf Orton 1989) was considered inappropriate in view of the state of the assemblage. Samuel's counts have since been revised to enable comparison with previously published groups from south Yorkshire kilns, and the type series (Table 3) follows that adapted by Buckland (1976) from Cregeen's (1957) earlier work, although several of the sub-groups are insufficiently differentiated in Samuels' original (1984) table to be listed separately.

Rim counts of material from Rossington Bridge

J. Samuels

Table 3. Rossington Bridge Pumping Station (Kilns 1–5 and layers in WM trench and baulk)

Type	K1	K2	K3	K4	K5	K4/5	L2	L3	L4	L5	L6	L7	L8	U/S	Total
A	5	16	8	11	–	13	1	5	7	4	2	–	–	10	82
B	2	19	8	10	4	17	–	11	41	194	25	1	–	270	602
C(a)	26	48	13	19	4	21	–	46	70	301	34	2	6	476	1066
C(b)	2	7	–	–	–	–	–	18	19	9	–	1	–	3	59
D	1	6	9	10	–	2	1	11	16	25	4	–	1	54	140
E(a)	98	137	16	64	4	37	4	57	195	391	80	5	6	897	1991
E(b)	–	–	2	6	–	6	1	1	8	–	–	1	–	22	47
E(c)	–	1	4	–	–	–	–	4	4	29	4	–	–	4	50
F	–	–	2	3	–	3	–	7	5	21	–	–	–	55	96
G(a)	–	–	2	4	–	2	–	1	1	2	1	–	–	8	21
G(b)	2	14	4	8	–	3	–	2	6	15	4	–	–	20	78
H(a)	–	–	–	–	–	–	1	3	7	8	–	–	–	6	25
H(c-d)	26	112	21	49	2	12	–	31	56	113	12	1	1	395	831
J	–	–	–	–	1	–	–	1	–	–	–	–	–	3	5
K	–	2	–	–	–	–	–	1	–	1	–	–	–	1	5
L	–	2	2	–	–	–	–	1	7	10	2	–	–	25	49
Totals	162	364	91	184	15	116	8	200	442	1123	168	11	14	2248	5147
Dales	?	–	–	–	–	–	8	2	1	1	–	–	–	18	29
CCW	–	1	–	–	–	–	2	2	2	–	4	1	–	15	27

Table 4. Rossington Bridge Farm kilns 1 and 2.

Type	*RBF/K1*	*RBF/K2*	*RBFK/1/2*	*RBF U/S*
A	–	*1*		*1*
B	*3*	*3*	*7*	*1*
C(a)	*37*	*35*	*25*	*31*
C(b)	–	–	*1*	–
D	*3*	*4*	*2*	*6*
E(a)	*94*	*74*	*94*	*147*
E(b)	*13*	*6*	*8*	*10*
E(c)	–	–	–	–
F	*3*	*4*	*2*	*2*
G(a)	*1*	*1*	–	*1*
G(b)	*1*	–	*4*	*1*
H(a)	*1*	–	–	–
H(c-d)	*10*	*18*	*13*	*14*
J	–	–	–	–
K				
L	*4*	–	–	*5*
Totals	*170*	*146*	*156*	*219*

Types : A – mortaria. B – shallow dishes with plain or bead rim. C(a) – lipped dishes. C(b) – lipped bowls. D – beakers (including parisian). E(a) – jars (including BB1 cooking pots. E(b) – lid-seated jars. E(c) – jars with rusticated decoration. F – large jars. G(a) – flagons. G(b) – narrow-necked jars. H(a) – colanders. H(c-d) – large bowls. J – cheese presses. K – imitation samian forms. L – lids.

Samian ware from Rossington Bridge
B. Dickinson

Table 5. Minimum number of stratified samian vessels and their suggested date.

Layer	*No. of vessels*
3	
Early Flavian	*2*
Early 2nd Century	*4*
Antonine	*7*
Late 2nd – early 3rd Century	*6*
4	
Antonine	*20*
Late 2nd – early 3rd Century	*1*
5 & 5A	
Late 1st – early 2nd Century	*15*
Antonine	*58*
Late 2nd – early 3rd Century	*2*

Layer 3

Form 31, Central Gaulish. Early to mid-Antonine.
RB/11.1/L.3.
Dish or bowl, Central Gaulish, very worn both inside and out. Antonine.
RB/12.1/L.3.
Form 31R, East Gaulish. Late 2nd- or early 3rd-century. RB/12.1/L.3.
Form 31, Central Gaulish. Antonine.
RB/14.1/L.3.
Form 29 rim, South Gaulish. Early-Flavian.
RB/15.1/L.3.
A scrap, from Les Martres-de-Veyre. First half of the 2nd century.
RB/15.1/L.3.
Form 31, East Gaulish. Antonine.
RB/15.1/L.3. A sherd, from RB/16.1/L.3, is probably from the same vessel.
Form 27 and a decorated scrap, South Gaulish. Flavian or early-Trajanic.
RB/16.1/L.3.
Form 37, a bowl fragment and a flake, Central Gaulish. Antonine.
RB/16.1/L.3.
Form 18/31, burnt, Central Gaulish. Pre- Antonine.
RB/17.1/L.3.
Forms 31 and 33, Central Gaulish. Antonine.
RB/17.1/L.3.
A Central Gaulish scrap. Hadrianic or early-Antonine.
RB/21.1/L.3.
An East Gaulish (?) scrap. Hadrianic or Antonine.
RB/23.1/L.3.
A Central Gaulish scrap. Antonine.
RB/24.1/L.3.
Central Gaulish ware of the Antonine period, with forms 31 (2) and 33 (2).
RB/25.1/L.3.
Form 33, East Gaulish, if samian. Late 2nd- or early 3rd-century.
RB/25.1/L.3.
Form 18/31R, Central Gaulish. Antonine.
RB/27.1/L.3.
Forms 31 (2) and 79 or Ludowici Tg, Central Gaulish. Mid- to late-Antonine.
RB/27.1/L.3.

Layer 4

Four fragments, three perhaps from the same form 31 and a footring, also from a dish. All Central Gaulish and Antonine.
RB/7WMB/L.4.
Form 37 base, Central Gaulish. Antonine.
RB/8.1/L.4.
Forms 30 (burnt), 31, 37 and a scrap, Central Gaulish. Antonine.
RB/8WMB/L.4.
A rim sherd, East Gaulish. Late 2nd- or early 3rd-century.
RB/8WMB/L.4.
An Antonine group of Lezoux ware, with three residual sherds from Les Martres-de-Veyre. The forms include 18/31 or 31, 31 (at least 4) and 37, probably in the style of Cinnamus ii.
RB/9.1/L.4.
An Antonine group, probably all from the latter half of the period, with forms 31, 33, 43 and a scrap.
RB/10.1/L.4.
Form 30 or 37 rim, burnt, Central Gaulish. Antonine.
RB/11.1/L.4.
Form 33, burnt, stamped P VL IM by Paullus iv of Lezoux (die 5b). The faint stroke between and V presumably comes from a scratch on the die. Paullus's general site record (a pottery shop of the 140's at Castleford, the Birdoswald Alley, Binchester, Camelon, and the Rhineland) and the predominance of forms 18/31 and 27 in his plain ware suggest a date *c* AD 135–160.
RB/11.1/L.4.

Forms 30 or 37 (rim), 31 (2) and a scrap, Central Gaulish. Probably all Antonine.
RB/12.1/L.4.
Form 31R, Central Gaulish. Mid- to late- Antonine.
RB/12WMB/L.4.
Form 37, Central Gaulish, with scroll decoration. The leaf is probably *Rogers* H70 used, perhaps exclusively, by Iullinus ii. *c* AD 160–190.
RB/12WMB/L.4. cf example also from Layer 5a.
Form 37 sherd.
RB/25.1/L.4, join to RB/25.1/L.5. Forms 18/31R and 31 (with two rivet-grooves), Central Gaulish. Antonine.
RB/25.1/L.4.

Layer 5

Form 31, burnt, Central Gaulish. Mid- to late-Antonine, plus a small Central Gaulish flake, Antonine. RB/7.1/L.5.
A mid- to late-Antonine group, all Central Gaulish, with forms 31 (several), 31R, 37, 79 and Curle 15 or 23.
RB/7WMB/L.5.
Forms 31 (2), 79/80 and a scrap, Central Gaulish. Mid- to late-Antonine.
RB/8.1/L.5.
Form 37, Central Gaulish. In the style of Cinnamus ii, with an acanthus (*Rogers* K12) and his characteristic hollow-bead terminals to the panel borders. *c* AD 150–180.
RB/8.1/L.5.
Form 37, Central Gaulish, with other sherds in RB/9.1/L.5 (2, one burnt), RB/9WMB/L.5 and RB/10WMB/L.5a. The T- tongued ovolo (*Rogers* B206) was used by members of the Quintilianus i and Paternus v groups of potters. The eagle (D 987), Pudicitia (D 540), dolphin (D 1050, apparently with a rosette replacing the broken tail- fin), column (*Rogers* P3), festoon (*Rogers* F15) rosette (similar to *Rogers* C143) and astragalus were all used by Laxtucissa, but the ram's-horn motif is more characteristic of the Quintilianus group. This bowl is either a late product of that group or an early product of Paternus or one of his associates. *c* AD 145–170.
RB/8.1/L.5.
Form 37, with the characteristic leaf of Cettus of Les Martres-de-Veyre (*Rogers* J144) and a lion, which he also used (S. and S. 1958, pl 141, 5, 10, 16 etc). *c* AD 135–160.
RB/8WMB/L.5.
Forms 31, 33, 37 (2, one in the style of the Cerialis ii - Cinnamus ii group), 38 and several scraps, Central Gaulish. Early- to mid-Antonine.
RB/8WMB/L.5.
Scrap, Central Gaulish (?), with a rivet-hole. 2nd-century.
RB/9.1/L.5.
Two burnt fragments of form 18/31 (Tq), Central Gaulish. Hadrianic-Antonine.
RB/9.1/L.5.
2 sherds, 1 burnt, of form 37 bowl, see RB/8.1/L.5 above.
RB/9.1/L.5.
Form 37 (2), Central Gaulish, one perhaps by Cinnamus ii. Antonine.
RB/9.1/L.5.
An Antonine group, all Central Gaulish, with forms 31, 31R and 37. Decorated pieces worthy of note are:

i. Two joining fragments from a bowl with wide panels containing hares (D 950A and its reverse) and a narrow panel with a caryatid (D 656). All used by Criciro v and Divixtus i, as were the beaded ring- terminals. *c* AD 135–170.
ii. A bowl with Cinnamus ii's ovolo 2 (*Rogers* B231). *c* AD 150–180.
iii. See RB/8.1/L.5 above.
RB/9WMB/L.5.

Form 37, in the style of Drusus i (x-3) of Les Martres-de-Veyre. *c* AD 100–120.
RB/10.1/L.5.
Forms 18/31, 37 (in the style of Cettus) and a scrap, from Les Martres-de-Veyre. Hadrianic or early- Antonine.
RB/10.1/L.5.
Forms 18/31 or 31 (2), 37 and a cup footring, Central Gaulish. Hadrianic or Antonine.
RB/10.1/L.5.
Form 37, Central Gaulish, with a leaf used by Banuus and Casurius ii (*Rogers* H69). *c* AD 160–190.
RB/10.1/L.5.
Form 31 or 31R, East Gaulish, stamped (MARCV)SF by Marcus vwi of Rheinzabern, where the die (2a) is known. Like many Rheinzabern potters, Marcus can only be dated by his forms. These include 31R, 32, 39 and Ludowici Tb, suggesting that he worked in the late 2nd or early 3rd century.
RB/10.1./L.5.
An Antonine group, with forms 30 or 37 (rim), 30 (3 fragments, burnt, one joining a sherd in RB/12.1/ L.5), 31 (at least 7), 33 (1 or 2, slightly burnt), 37 (2) and 38 (flange), Central Gaulish and form 33, East Gaulish. One form 33 is stamped M[, almost certainly by Mercator iv (MERC M, die 8b, known at Lezoux). This stamp is nearly always on forms 79 and 79R, and has been recorded from Catterick. *c* AD 160–190.
RB/11.1/L.5.
Forms 30 or 37 base and 33 (burnt), Central Gaulish. Antonine.
RB/11WMB/L.5
Form 31R, Central Gaulish. The stamp, I TII I, is not known elsewhere. This may be a retrograde stamp of Iullinus ii of Lezoux, botched by the die-cutter, but it is more likely to be the work of a Iatenus (with an accidental stroke through the T) or a Iafenus. Mid- to late-Antonine, in any case.
RB/11WMB/L.5.
Form 37, from Les Martres-de-Veyre. Almost certainly by Drusus i (X-3), in view of the uneven row of beads and the faint zone of beaded circles below it. *c* AD 100–120.
RB/12.1/L.5.
Forms 31, 33 (burnt) and 30 (from the bowl in RB/11.1/L.5), Central Gaulish. Antonine.
RB/12.1/L.5.
Two joining fragments of form 33, stamped CESORINI by Censorinus ii of Lezoux, where the die (4a) is known. This stamp appears on both plain and decorated ware. There is one example on form 80. Another, on form 33, comes from a group of burnt samian of *c* AD 170 at Tac (Hungary). There is no central, external groove on this sherd. *c* AD 160–190.
RB/12.1/L.5.
Form 37, with an ovolo used by many Rheinzabern potters (Ricken-Fischer (1963), E23). Late 2nd- or early 3rd-century.
RB/12.1/L.5.
Form 81 (?), Central Gaulish. Antonine.

RB/16.1/L.5.
A burnt scrap. Undatable.
RB/17.1/L.5.
Form 37 (grooved for a rivet), in the style of one of the potters who supplied moulds to Medetus and Ranto. The fabric could have come from either Les Martres-de-Veyre or one of the Ligonne workshops at Lezoux. For repeated saltires, cf S and S (1958), pl 30, 365, from Chesterholm. *c* AD 110–130.
RB/25.1/L.5 Further sherd in RB/24.1/L.4. (With another rim sherd in L.5).

Layer 5a

Form 31 (2) and two scraps, Central Gaulish. Antonine.
RB/7.1/L.5a.
Form 37, Central Gaulish, with alternating wide and narrow panels. The beaded rings at the base of the borders are diagnostic for Criciro v and Divixtus i, and Criciro used the hare in the wider panel (0 2129A). One of the narrow panels almost certainly contains one of the caryatids which both potters used. Too little survives to be sure who made this bowl, but a range *c* AD 135–170 should cover the possibilities.
RB/7WMB/L.5a.
Forms 33 and 37, Central Gaulish. Antonine.
RB/8.1/L.5a.
Form 37, Central Gaulish, with a freestyle scene. The ring-tongued ovolo (*Rogers* B103) was used by several Lezoux potters, including Advocisus and Divixtus I. This bowl is more likely to be by the former, since Divixtus rarely, if ever, used freestyle decoration. The animals include two lions (probably 0 1497J and D 740). The lioness (D 795) is on a stamped bowl of Advocisus from Aldborough. *c* AD 160–190.
RB/8.1/L.5a.
Form 37 and a dish, Central Gaulish. Probably Antonine.
RB/8WMB/L.5a.
Flake, from Les Martres-de-Veyre, grooved along the fabric, as if for a folded-over feature. Early 2nd century.
RB/9.1/L.5a.
Form 31, Central Gaulish. Antonine.
RB/9.1/L.5a.
Form 33, East Gaulish. Antonine or later.
RB/9WMB/L.5a.
Form 18/31. from Les Martres-de-Veyre. Hadrianic or early-Antonine.
RB/10WMB/L.5a.
A joining rim sherd from the bowl in RB/8.1/L.5.
RB/10WMB/L.5a.
Form 31, riveted, Central Gaulish. Early- Antonine.
RB/10WMB/L.5a.
Forms 18/31 or 31, 30 or 37 (rim), 33 (burnt), 37, a jar and two scraps, Central Gaulish. Antonine.
RB/10WMB/L.5a.
Form 37, Central Gaulish, with a hunting scene. The lion (D 740) and *bestiarius* (D 631) both occur on a stamped mould of Aunus from Lezoux, and the leaf (*Rogers* H151) is on a bowl in his style, also from Lezoux (Coll. Oswald-Plicque, at Durham). *c* AD 140–165.
RB/10WMB/L.5a.
Forms 33, 37 and 38, Central Gaulish. Antonine.
RB/11WMB/L.5a.
Form 18/31, from Les Martres-de-Veyre. Trajanic or early-Hadrianic.
RB/12WMB/L.5a.
Form 18/31–31, burnt, Central Gaulish. Hadrianic or early-Antonine.
RB/12WMB/L.5a.
Several scraps, probably all Central Gaulish and Antonine, form 37, perhaps from the bowl in L4.
RB/12WMB/L.5a.
Form 18/31 or 31, Central Gaulish. Hadrianic or Antonine.
RB/13WMB/L.5a.
Form 37, South Gaulish, with a trident-tongued ovolo. Flavian-Trajanic.
RB/16WMB/L.5a.
Form 31, Central Gaulish. Antonine.
RB/16WMB/L.5a.
Forms 18 (burnt) and 37, South Gaulish. 1st-century and Flavian, respectively.
RB/17WMB/L.5a.
Form 37, Central Gaulish, with scroll decoration. Hadrianic or Antonine.
RB/17WMB/L.5a.

Layer 6. (Peat)

Form 37, from Les Martres-de-Veyre, perhaps with Cettus's small s-motif across a bead-row. Late- Hadrianic.
RB/13.1/L.5a.
Form 37, Central Gaulish.
RB/16.1/L.5a.
Form 31, stamped [B N]OLVCCI by Banoloccus of Central Gaul, presumably Lezoux. This stamp appears on forms ranging from 18/31 and 18/31R to 80. His work occurs in Antonine Scotland and in a pit-group of the 150's at Alcester. *c* AD 145–170.
RB/12.1/L.5a.

Burnt area

Form 31R, burnt, East Gaulish. Antonine or later.

River bed

Form 37, South Gaulish, with one of M. Crestio's ovolos and a coarse cable border. *c* AD 80–100.

Unstratified Material

An East Gaulish (?) scrap. Antonine or later.
RB/13.1/-
Two East Gaulish scraps, one the footring of a dish or bowl. Antonine or later.
RB/14 WMB/-
An East Gaulish scrap. Late 2nd or early 3rd century.
RB/28.1/-
Form 37, Central Gaulish. Hadrianic-Antonine. Perhaps from the same bowl as RB/K3.2/-.
RB/G3.2/-
Form 33, Central Gaulish. Antonine.
RB/K2.1/-
A rim fragment (form 30 or 37), Central Gaulish. cf RB/G3.2/-.
RB/K3.2/-
Form 31R, Central Gaulish. Mid- to late-Antonine.
RB/L.2.2/-
Form 31R, East Gaulish. Late 2nd- or early 3rd-century.
RB/O/-
Form 31, East Gaulish. Hadrianic-Antonine. Probably from the same dish as RB/T3.1/-

RB/O2/-
Form 37 base, South Gaulish. Probably Flavian.
RB/Sl/- and RB/S2/- See also RB/2.0.3/-, RB/S3/-, RB/T3.l/- See 02.
Five fragments of form 37, Central Gaulish. The ovolo (*Rogers* B32) and chevron wreath were both used by X-6 and occur together on bowls in his style from Lezoux (S and S (1958), pl 75, 15) and London (BM). The latter also has the beaded rosettes. This bowl is related stylistically to such potters as Mapillus, Pugnus ii and Tittius. The inside of the base is very worn. *c* AD 125–150.
RB/2.0.3/-, E2.2, S1 and S2.
Form 31, stamped GIPPIM by Gippus of Lezoux (die 2b). No other examples of this stamp have been recorded. His commoner one has been noted in the Aquincum Hoard, and in a group of burnt samian of *c* AD 170 at Tac (Hungary), but some of his rouletted dishes are on the borderline between forms 18/31R and the fully-developed 31R. The tight circle round the stamp is unusual. *c* AD 155–180.
RB/8J/gravel.
Form 33(?), Central Gaulish. Hadrianic or Antonine.
RB/10L/-
Form 37, Central Gaulish, with a panel with an astragalus impressed vertically and another with a column (*Rogers* 3) by a member of the Paternus v group. Albucius ii, Q. I. Balbinus or Stanfield and Simpson's (1958) Servus I are the most likely candidates, in view of the fine astragalus borders. *c* AD 150–180.
RB/11C/- RB/11L/-
i. Form 37, from Les Martres-de-Veyre. A freestyle scene, with a leopard (D 799) and cornucopiae. Probably from a mould by one of the potters who supplied Medetus and Ranto. Trajanic or early-Hadrianic.
ii. Form 38, Central Gaulish. Early-Antonine.
iii. Form 37, Central Gaulish. Antonine.
iv Two scraps, Central Gaulish. Probably Antonine.
v. Jar (form 72 etc), with 'cut-glass' decoration, Central Gaulish. Second half of the 2nd century.
Form 31 (2), Central Gaulish. Antonine.
RB/12/- RB/17/-
i. Form Curle 15 or 23, burnt, Central Gaulish. 2nd-century.
ii. Form 37, Central Gaulish, with scroll decoration. Hadrianic or Antonine.
Form 37, Central Gaulish, with panels: 1) Vine-scroll (*Rogers* M4) over a leafy spray (*Rogers* H117). 2) Single festoon, with a dog (D 934) and leaf (probably *Rogers* J162), over another dog (D 915). The single-bordered ovolo (*Rogers* B28), seven-beaded rosette (*Roger* C280) and setting-out line, which here coincides with, and takes the place of, the border below the ovolo, suggest that this bowl is by Quintilianus i. All the details except the vine-scroll appear on his signed or stamped bowls, and the scroll is on several bowls almost certainly by him. *c* AD 125–150.
RB/18R/-

Unlabelled unstratified Vessels

Material ranging from the Flavian or early-Trajanic period to the late 2nd or early 3rd century. The bulk of it is Lezoux ware of mid- to late-Antonine date, but there are three sherds of South Gaulish ware and one from East Gaul. The forms represented are:

South Gaul forms 18 and 37 (2). Flavian or early-Trajanic.
Les Martres-de-Veyre form 37, in the styles of Cettus (2?) and a potter who supplied moulds to Donnaucus.
Central Gaul Forms 18/31R, 27, 31, 31R, 33, 37, including bowls in the styles of the Cerialis ii-Cinnamus ii group, Cinnamus ii, Divixtus i, Paternus iv, and three bowls by Paternus v or one of his associates. All Hadrianic-Antonine to the late 2nd century, probably all from Lezoux.
East Gaul form 31, late 2nd- or early 3rd-century.

Mortaria
K.F. Hartley

Apart from the fabrics produced on the site, (Fabrics 1 and ?4), a number of alien vessels occur; their fabrics are included in the following list:

Fabric 1 Rossington Bridge

Hard, orange-brown fabric, sometimes with grey core; texture varies dependant upon the size and amount of inclusions. Majority have fair amount of sub-angular quartz, sparse red-brown and rare black inclusions. Some are coarser textured with frequent quartz inclusions. Trituration grit consists of soft, dark, red-brown ?haematite, a result of the oxidation of ironstone (siderite mudstone) during firing, quartz and some sandstone. All vessels probably had a cream slip, although it does not always survive. Many of the mortaria are burnt to various shades of brown and black; some also show severe waster cracks and some sherds show distortion.

Sarrius mortaria: Fig 35, 1, 5, 7, 12, 13, 15 and 16.
All stamps are from the same die (die 4), variously impressed. Fig 33, 1 and 2 show the impressions upon vessels **1** and **13** respectively.

Of the 15 examples, all stratified vessels are from either kiln 4, or the waster tips (Layers 5 and 5a); 3 are either unstratified or lack sufficient data.

Sarrius/Setibogius mortaria: Fig 35, 3.
A single vessel, impressed with both stamps (Fig 33, 3), comes from the stokehole to kiln 4.

Sarrius/Secundua mortaria: Fig 35, No 8.
A single vessel, bearing both stamps impressed close together (Fig 33, 4), is recorded as from 'wicker fence, working floor'. The site records add little to this, other than the fact that this feature must have been sufficiently downslope to have been wholly waterlogged (see Pls 17 and 18) and must therefore lie within layers 5–6.

Secundua mortaria: Fig 35, 10, 24 (stamp Fig 33, 5), and 26 (stamp Fig 33, 6).
Of the four examples, 2 are from kiln 4, 1 from the waster tips (Layer 5a) and 1 unstratified.

Diccia mortaria: Fig 35, 22 and 23 (stamps Fig 33, 7 and 8 respectively).
Two vessels are noted from kiln 4, one within the chamber, and one, **22,** from kiln 1.

Figure 33. Mortarium stamps from Rossington Bridge, 1956–1961: Local potters. Drawings: P.I. Buckland.

Virrinus (VBRN) mortarium: Fig 35, 21 (Fig 33, 9). Although unstratified, the vessel is an evident waster, implying manufacture on the site. This potter also worked at Cantley, kiln 24 (Cregeen 1957).

Illegible stamp ?*HBIX*: Fig 35, 6 (Fig 33, 10) and 25. One example occurs unstratified over kilns 4–5, and the other in Layer 6, downslope from the kilns.

Trademark *54*: Fig 35, 3 (Fig 33, 11).

Two examples, one, fragmentary, labelled kiln II (= Rossington Bridge Farm kiln 2), and the other unstratified from the main Rossington Bridge site.

Trademark *55*: Fig 35, 9 (Fig 33, 12)
A single example, labelled P.5, presumably from Peg 5 (= kilns 4–5), but no other data.

Trademark *57*: Fig 35, 18 (Fig 33, 13).
A single example from the waster tips (RB/13.1/L.6).

Trademark *56*: Fig 35, 27 (Fig 33, 14).
A stamp of the type more usually applied to parisian ware (see below Table 6 DL1 , and p 59), impressed twice across the flange; unstratified.

There is some variation in fabric. Vessel **19** (type 16) and two joining base sherds, all unstratified, differ from the norm in being harder and finer textured and in having a very thick grey core with few tiny inclusions of quartz and red brown fragments. No **19** has lost most of its trituration grit, but the other vessel has abundant, hard blackish (haematite) trituration grit, which is dark red when scratched; there is no quartz. Vessels **9** and **17**, the former unstratified over kilns 4–5 and the latter from layer 6, are in varying shades of drab pale to dark grey fabric, with a fair amount of quartz inclusions. Trituration grit is mainly opaque quartz pebbles, up to 5–7mm, and occasional soft red-brown and black fragments. The slip is now reduced to black all over but was presumably intended to be cream. These two mortaria differ superficially from Fabric 1, but it is likely to be the result of unintentional reduction during firing; both probably come from unexcavated kilns.

Fabric 2 Midlands or Rossington Bridge

A cream to brownish-buff fabric, sometimes with a pinkish core and a slightly powdery surface; common inclusions of fairly well-sorted quartz, occasional red-brown ?sandstone and ?haematite, black and white fragments. Trituration grit red-brown ?sandstone and haematite and quartz. The soft dark red material (?haematite) incorporated in this fabric has not been noted in mortaria made at Mancetter or Hartshill, and is only very common in vessels made at Rossington Bridge, where it also appears in the lid-seated jars from kilns 4 and 5 (**217–223**). The normal clay used at Rossington, Cantley, Branton, etc produced a distinctly pink – or orange-brown fabric (fabric 1), but these potters did have access to some clay which was suitable for making the white slip commonly used on the mortaria, so there is no reason why they should not have produced an occasional mortarium in a cream fabric.

Sherds from at least four vessels, all from the stokehole to kilns 4–5, suggesting an association with Sarrius.

Fabric 3 Midlands

Cream fabric, differs from Mancetter-Hartshill (Fabric 4) in being coarser, with more granular texture, frequent fairly well-sorted inclusions of quartz, ill-sorted red-brown and black fragments (up to 3mm. Trituration grit is a very mixed assemblage: quartz, sandstone, feldspar, ?metamorphic rock. Buff slip present.

Several sherds, probably from the same pot, from layer 5 (9WMB).

An unstratified base has been included in this fabric, but it differs in being buff-cream with a slight powdery surface and smaller quartz inclusions. Trituration grit includes opaque coloured quartz and soft, red-brown fragments.

Fabric 4 Mancetter-Hartshill

Hard, fine-textured, slightly micaceous, cream fabric; few inclusions of quartz, sparse red-brown and black fragments and clay pellets. Texture may vary and be slightly coarser with moderate quartz inclusions. Trituration grit, after *c* AD 150, mainly hard red-brown or blackish refired pottery fragments, sometimes with occasional quartz and sandstone. The infrequent earlier vessels normally have a mixed trituration grit containing a high percentage of quartz and sandstone. Vessel **344**, an unstratified mortarium of DOCCAS, and a further unstratified piece have ill-sorted grits, up to 5mm, and a higher percentage of opaque quartz than refired pottery fragments.

Sarrius (Die 3) mortarium: Fig 52, 348, stamp (Fig 34, 1). Unstratified.
Icotasgus (?Die 5) mortarium: Fig 51, 347, stamp (Fig 34, 2). One example from layer 5a and another unstratified.
Gratinus (Die 1) mortarium: Fig 51, 345, stamp (Fig 34, 3). Two examples, one from layer 5a, the other unstratified.
Doccas (Die 5) mortarium: Fig 51, No. 344, Stamp (Fig 34, 4). Unstratified.
Other rims: Figs 51–2, 343, 349–354, 356–358.

Fabric 5 Lower Nene Valley

Hard, fine textured fabric, usually greyish-cream but here discoloured throughout by burning; few inclusions of tiny quartz, larger (1mm) sparse, red-brown and 'chalk' fragments. Trituration grit is of black iron slag.

Fig 52, 359 , from RB/9.1/L. 4 – *c* AD 230–300.

Fabric 6 Crambeck

Fairly fine-textured fabric, frequent inclusions of fairly well-sorted tiny quartz, very sparse orange-brown fragments. Trituration grit tiny (2mm) black iron slag. The two fragments, one from layer 3 (RB/16.1/L.3), the other (Fig 52, 360) from the 'upper peat' (RB/13–14/peat), are probably from the same vessel, but the fabric of both has been softened and discoloured to brownish-buff from the normal off-white by chemical weathering.

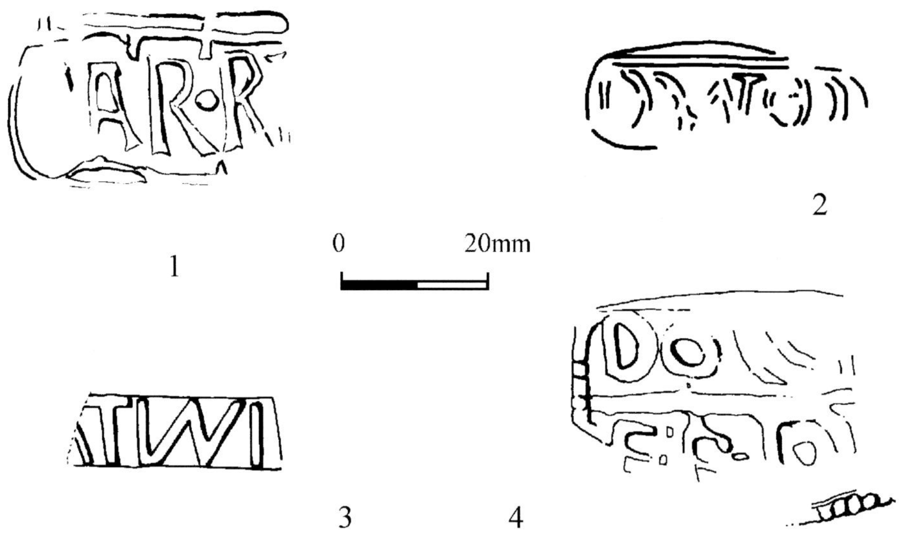

Figure 34. Mortarium stamps from Rossington Bridge 1956–1961: non-local vessels. Drawings: P.I. Buckland.

Fabric 7 Aldborough, Castleford or Lincoln

Hard, fine-textured greyish-white fabric; few inclusions of quartz and black fragments. Trituration grit (2–3mm) mainly quartz with some ?flint or chert. The fabric of the single vessel, from the stokehole to kiln 4, is probably discoloured from an original cream by burning.

Fabric 8 Source unknown

The fabric is discoloured to pale brown, inclusions barely visible at ×10 magnification; a few tiny quartz and red-brown fragments. Trituration grit brown iron slag? The single sherd is unstratified.

Fabric 9 Northern France

Fine textured fabric with frequent tiny inclusions of quartz and red-brown fragments. Trituration grit mainly flint with some quartz. The fabric is normally cream coloured, but these pieces (Fig 51, 342) have been badly discoloured by chemical weathering before fracture. The one example (Gillam 238, AD 65–100) is from the base of the stratigraphy, layer 6, and forms one of a small group of late 1st century vessels.

Description of vessels (Fig 35)

1. Type 1, 320mm in diameter, burnt grey throughout. Medium grey (N4) fabric with scattered quartz temper; moderate red (5R 4/6) outer layer and light olive grey (5Y 6/1) surface, with patchy very pale orange (10YR 8/2) slip and angular multicoloured trituration grit, including rock fragment of ?Millstone Grit and large, to 6mm, ironstone fragments.
   RB/4/S.2 (stokehole to kiln 4).
2. Type 1, with stamp of S]ARRI(VS), (Fig 33, 1). Gritty reddish orange (10R 6/6) fabric, with patchy very pale orange (10YR 8/2) slip, and scattered subrounded to angular trituration grit, grey (N5) core to rim. A cracked and distorted waster.
   RB/9.1/L.5 plus an unstratified joining sherd.
3. Type 2, with part of stamp of SETIBOGIVS, approximately 320mm in diameter. An atypically pale, greyish pink (5R 8/2) fabric, much abraded, but with oxidised ironstone (haematite) trituration grit, and therefore almost certainly a Rossington product.
   RB/4/S.2 (stokehole to kiln 4).
4. Type 3, with trademark stamp, (Fig 33, 4), 310mm in diameter. Light grey (N6) fabric with scattered quartz and many sublinear voids, moderate orange pink (10R 7/4) outer layer and similar (5YR 8/4) poorly slipped surface, with temper showing through; no trituration grit survives.
   RB/14–15WMB/- unstratified.
5. Type 4, with part of the margin of a stamp of SARRIVS, 310mm in diameter, in a grey (N6) fabric with patchy very pale orange (10YR 8/2) slip and multicoloured angular to subrounded grit.
   RB/4/S.2 (stokehole to kiln 4).
6. Type 5, with an illegible stamp ? HBIX, (Fig 33, 10), in a hard reddish orange (10R 6/5) fabric with grey (N7) core and little evident quartz temper; off white (10R 8/7) slip over oxidised surface and angular red to black ironstone trituration grit, with occasional quartz.
   RB/4–5/X (unstratified over the kiln group 4–5).
7. Type 6, with stamp of SARRIVS, in a gritty dark grey (N3) fabric with abraded white slip; overfired and badly cracked.
   RB/4/K (within kiln 4).
8. Type 7, with stamps of SARRIVS and SECVNDVA, (Fig 33, 4) impressed close together; fired grey (N6) throughout, with white (10YR 8/2) patchy slip and medium quartz temper; a small quartzite pebble, to 7mm occurs in the broken section.
   RB/- ('wicker fence, working floor').
9. Type 8, with trademark stamp (Fig 33, 12). Light grey (N7) fabric, with darker (N4) core and rather scuffed surface slip; temper of angular quartz, with numerous linear voids evident in the fresh break. the slip has burnt to an off-white on part of outer surface. Scatter of crushed, large, angular trituration grit, including crushed pottery and some quartz.
   RB/4–5/- (kiln group 4 and 5).

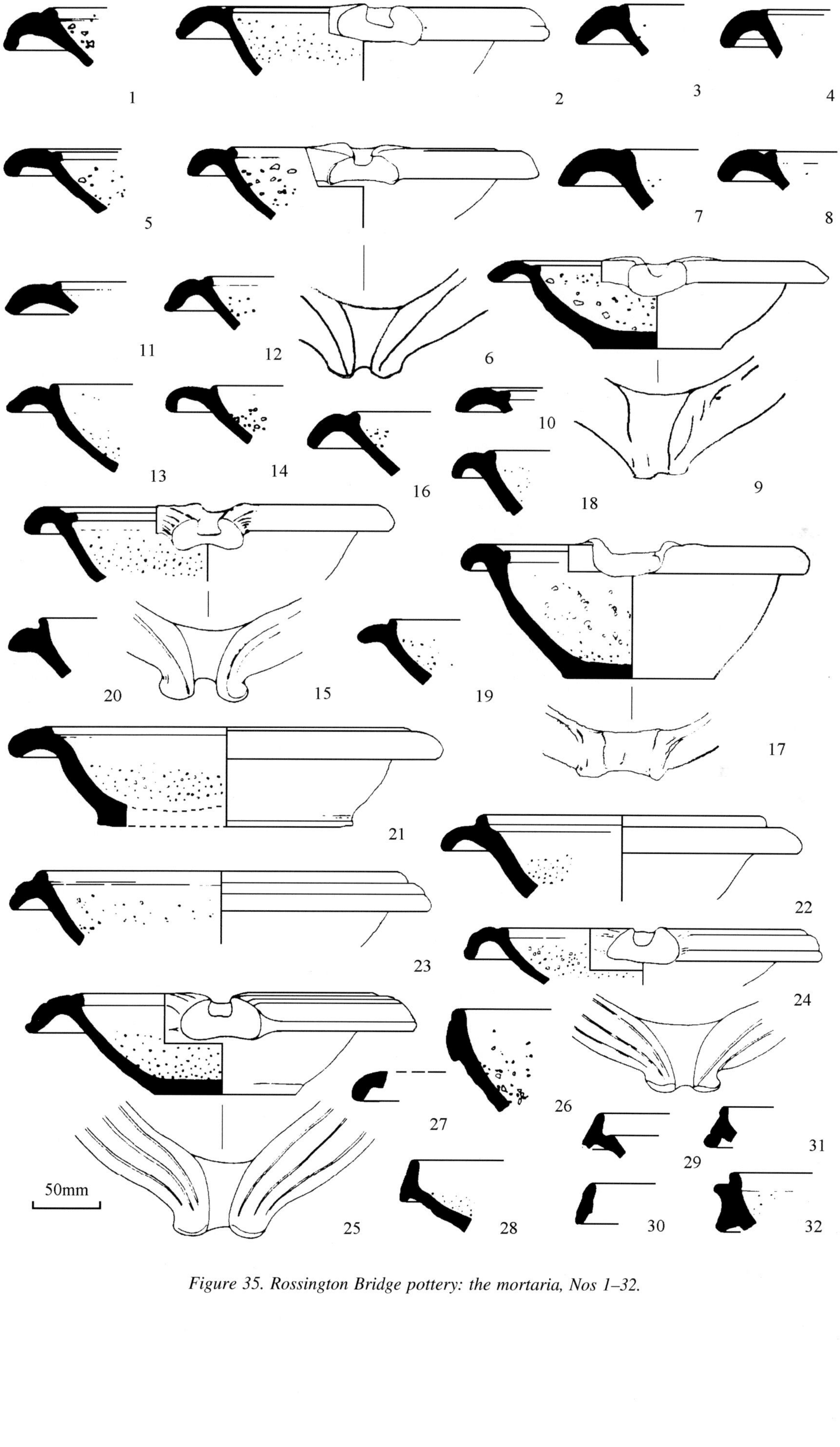

Figure 35. Rossington Bridge pottery: the mortaria, Nos 1–32.

10. Type 8, with stamp of SECVNDVA, diameter indeterminate, in a grey fabric.
RB/4/S.1 (stokehole to kiln 4).

11. Type 9, diameter indeterminate, in a hard, medium grey (N5) fabric with traces of pale yellow (10YR 9/6) slip; other examples have the stamp of SARRIVS.
RB/4/S.1 (stokehole to kiln 4).

12. Type 10, with stamp of S]ARRI(VS), moderate reddish orange (10R 6/6) fabric, with light grey (N7) core and thin, very pale orange (10YR 8/2) slip; scattered subrounded quartz and ironstone trituration grit, to 5mm.
RB/7.1/L.5a and RB/9.1/L.3.

13. Two sherds, probably from the same mortarium, Type 10, with stamps of SARRIVS, (Fig 33, 2), S]ARRI and SARR[I either side of the spout, in a grey fabric.
RB/K4–5/-, over kilns 4 and 5, and RB/11/L.5–6- ('by timber').

14. Type 11, 300mm in diameter, with part of spout as **15** below, in a gritty moderate reddish orange (10R 6/6) fabric with light grey (N7) core with very pale orange (10YR 8/2) slip.
RB/1.1/L.5a, and a further sherd in RB/5/S (stokehole to kiln 5).

15. Type 12, with stamp of S]ARRI(VS), moderate orange pink (5YR 8/4) fabric with light grey (N6) core and light greyish orange (10YR 8/4) slip; scattered angular to subrounded quartz trituration grit.
RB/7.1/L.5a

16. Type 13, with stamp of S]ARRI(VS), gritty moderate reddish orange (10R 6/6) fabric with grey (N6) surface and very pale orange (10YR 8/2) slip and medium quartz and ironstone trituration grit; surface much cracked in firing.
RB/4/S.2 (stokehole to kiln 4).

17. Type 14, an unstamped vessel; the rim is of varying form, a squared off flange giving way to a more rounded profile part of the way around the vessel. A slightly gritty, grey (N6) fabric with darker (N5) core and reduced, very dark grey (N3), somewhat lustrous slip. The trituration grit is poorly sorted , rather coarse and rounded, largely of quartz, but with some other rock fragments.
RB/9.1/L.6.

18. Type 15, with trademark stamp (Fig 33, no. 13), in a grey (N5) fabric with moderate orange pink (5YR 8/2) surface and traces of white slip; scattered, small angular multi-coloured trituration grit.
RB/13.1/L.6.

19. Type 16, 270mm in diameter, in a light grey (N6) fabric with oxidised moderate reddish orange (10R 6/6) surface, and very pale orange (10YR 8/2) slip; angular black (N1) trituration grit.
RB/- no data, *c* AD 150–200.

20. Type 17, approximately 240mm in diameter, in a fine light grey (N7) fabric with oxidised light red (10R 5/6) surface and white slip.
RB/- , 'P. clay' ? unstratified, *c* 160–200+.

21. Type 18, with stamp of VBRN (Virrinus) (Fig 33, 9), a waster, cracked under the flange and around the base. Hard, medium grey (N6) fabric, with patchy moderate orange pink (5YR 8/4) slip and large, multicoloured trituration g rit.
RB/9.1/L.6 (peat). The rim form and stamp also occur at Cantley kiln 24 (Cregeen 1957, fig 1, 7).

22. Type 19, with stamp ..]CIAF, possibly DICCIA F(ECIT) (Fig 33, 8), in a rather gritty light grey (N6) fabric with traces of white slip and angular, dominantly quartz trituration grit.
RB/1/K (interior of kiln 1).

23. Type 20, with stamp of DIC(CIA) (Fig 33, 7), fabric as **22**, but with subrounded trituration grit.
RB/4/- (over kiln 4).

24. Type 21 mortarium, with stamps of SECVNDVA, SECVN[DVA on right and SEC]VNDVA on left of spout (Fig 33, 5), in a moderate reddish orange (10R 6/6) fabric with pale red (10R 8/2) core and off white slip; angular to sub-rounded quartz and ironstone trituration grit.
RB/8.1/L.5a.

25. Type 22, greater part of a mortarium, stamped to either side of spout with an illegible stamp, as Fig 33, 10. HBIX, light brown (5YR 6/4) fabric with grey (N5) core, sparse medium quartz temper and brown to pale brown (10YR 6/2) surface, slipped over rim; trituration grit multicoloured, including rounded pebbles to 5mm of ironstone and quartz.
RB/10WMB/L.6.

26. Type 23, with stamp of SEC]VNDVA, upside-down on wall-sided rim (Fig 33, 6), 250mm in diameter. Slightly gritty dark grey (N4) to light brown (10YR 6/4) fabric, with thin white (10YR 8/2) slip and multicoloured grit, largely of red fired ironstone, but with some subrounded quartz. RB/4/S.2 ('under clay floor', the earlier phase of the stokehole to kiln 4).

27. Not typed, a flange fragment, diameter indeterminate, with a divided rectangle type parisian stamp impressed twice across the flange (Fig 33, 14). Light grey (N7) fabric, with moderate reddish orange (10R 6/6) outer layer and thin very light grey (N8) slip.
RB/- unstratified.

Vessels **28–32** are in the same fabrics as the previous vessels but appear to relate to later production.

28. Type 25, with sloping collar, intermediate between wall-sided and hammer-head in form, and unstamped. Light brown (5YR 5/6) fabric, with grey (N6) core and very pale orange (10YR 8/2) slip and small, angular ironstone grit. RB/9WMB/L.4. The form is 3rd or 4th century, although the fabric suggests local manufacture.

29. Type 25 variant, unstamped and diameter indeterminate. Moderate reddish orange (10R 6/6) fabric with abraded white slip.
RB/- unstratified. The form is again 3rd or 4th century.

30. Type 26, collared rim in three zones, diameter indeterminate, in a fine orange pink (5YR 7/4) fabric with light grey (N7) core and patchy white slip.
RB/- no data.

31. Type 24, a hammerhead rim, approximately 260mm in diameter, divided into three zones, the central one broader, in alight brown (5YR 5/6) fabric with thin very pale orange (10YR 8/2) slip.
RB/10.1/L.4 *c* AD 180–250.

32. Type 27, an unusual form, 300mm in diameter, in a gritty light grey (N6) fabric with light greyish orange (10YR 8/4) slip and scattered small ironstone trituration grit.
RB/7WMB/L.3. Probably a 4th century vessel; the fabric could be local, and may belong with the small amount of material hinting at some later production on the site. The form is reminiscent of Crambeck type 8 (Corder and Birley 1937)

Discussion

SARRIUS, SETIBOGIUS and SECUNDUA *(Figs 36–9).*

The 15 stamps from 11–14 mortaria in Rossington Bridge fabric are all from the most commonly used die of Sarrius, the most prolific of all British potters stamping mortaria during the 2nd century. The vast majority of his recorded stamps (112) were made in the Mancetter-Hartshill potteries, where at least 116 more stamps have been recorded. Two other mortaria in Rossington fabric were found with stamps of Sarrius, but each also had the stamp of one other potter, Setibogius and Secundua respectively, impressed close by. This clearly indicates some kind of association with Sarrius, but the relative numbers of stamps representing each potter shows equally clearly that most of the mortaria were stamped only with the name of Sarrius. Four other stamps of Secundua from three vessels were also found and also one of Setibogius. There is no indication that any other potter's name was present on these mortaria, and this is certain for the one mortarium of Secundua where the stamps from both sides survive.

Two mortaria of Secundua are known from Corbridge (Birley and Gillam 1948, 190 and fig 2, 501, mistakenly conflated with the stamp of another potter and read as Securus). A mortarium with stamps of Sarrius and Setibogius impressed close together is known from Catterick village (Croft-Andrew collection 1930), and stamps of Setibogius alone are recorded from Adel in Leeds and Halton Chesters (Hartley 1960); a faint stamp from Ilkley may also be one of his. All of the above mortaria are in Rossington Bridge fabric with the single exception of that of Setibogius from Halton Chesters, which may have been made in the Mancetter-Hartshill potteries, although it is not in any of the common fabric variants.

Sarrius is exceptional not only in the extent of his production but also because he opened up a workshop at Rossington Bridge and yet another in Scotland, probably close to Bearsden in the western sector of the Antonine Wall (Breeze, in prep). This fabric is also red-brown, and he used the same die. Until all of his relevant mortaria have been re-examined, the exact distribution of his Rossington Bridge products will remain in some doubt. However, mortaria in red-brown fabric with stamps from the die represented at Rossington Bridge and Bearsden have been noted from Aldborough, Castleford, Cantley (1–2), Doncaster, and Rossington Bridge (11–14) in England, and Balmuildy (2), Bearsden (28 stamps from *c* 20 vessels) and Camelon on the Antonine Wall. Stamps from a die never used in the Midlands, and thus appearing only on red-brown mortaria, have been noted from Birrens, Carlisle and Corbridge. These mortaria also require re-examination, but a fragmentary stamp found at Doncaster (Buckland and Magilton 1986, 146, fig 33, 10), although from a different die, is so close to the Carlisle stamp that it is almost certainly from another, quite similar die of Sarrius. If this is the case, then all three dies would have been used at Rossington Bridge.

These two dies were used only in the north, but the die represented at Rossington Bridge and Bearsden was also the one most commonly used in his main workshops in the Mancetter-Hartshill potteries. Two kilns used by Sarrius have been excavated at Mancetter, and his work is recorded from Hartshill so he may also have had a workshop there.

Sarrius' date is assessed from the abundance of his work at forts on the Antonine Wall, its absence from Pennine forts unoccupied *c* AD 120–160, his rim-forms and his probable association with Iunius at one of his Mancetter kilns. A stamp from Verulamium is dated *c* AD 155–160 (Frere 1972, fig 146, 35), and one from a Period 1a deposit at Birdoswald suggests that he was at work before AD 140 (Birley 1930, 187, no 2, 'with illegible stamp'). The evidence points to his overall activity lying within the period AD 135–170. One can reasonably assume that his production in the north began later than AD 140, perhaps as late as AD 150.

It might be possible to make a case for the die being moved to Rossington and to Bearsden in succession, but it seems more likely that there were three or more identical dies made from a single matrix. The die which is common to the Midlands and the North is the clearest, most detailed and well-developed of his dies, and it is the only one for which a professional die-cutter might have been employed. His probable association with the somewhat later potter Iunius and his rim profiles, not to mention the extent of his output, all strongly indicate that production continued simultaneously in the Midlands and North.

There is no certain evidence to indicate exactly when his Bearsden and Rossington Bridge workshops were active, or whether and to what extent they were contemporary. the rim profiles, however, do give some indication. At Bearsden there are at least 12 individual wall-sided mortaria attributable to Sarrius and 16 other fragments from these or other wall-sided vessels: Rossington has no wall-sided vessels attributable to Sarrius and all of his Rossington mortaria known from other sites are flanged. This does suggest that flanged mortaria were the preferred type in his Rossington workshop; it might also indicate that production started later at Bearsden than at Rossington and continued later. Whilst this chronology might be what one would expect, it should be remembered that Secundua was certainly making wall-sided mortaria at Rossington. It might also be added that Sarrius' Warwickshire workshops did produce wall-sided vessels, albeit on a very small scale.

We have little concrete evidence of the organisation of Sarrius' enterprises. The large output of his workshops in the Mancetter-Hartshill potteries suggests that they continued in production after his two northern workshops were opened. The same die-type was used in all three workshops. The dual stamps of Sarrius with Setibogius

Key to Figs 36–39.

No.	Site	Creamy white fabric	Red-brown fabrics	Creamy white with die 4	Red-brown with die 4
1	Strageath	x		x	
2	Ardoch	x			
3	Camelon	x	x		x
4	Mumrills	x			
5	Rough Castle	x			
6	Croy Hill	x			
7	Bar Hill	x		x	
8	Wilderness Plantation	x			
9	Balmuildy	x	x		x
10	Bearsden		x		x
11	Newstead	x		x	
12	Carzield	x			
13	Birrens	x	x	x	
14	Birdoswald	x			
15	Housesteads	x		x	
16	Corbridge	x	x	x	x
17	Wallsend	x			
18	Carlisle	x	x		
19	Lanchester	x			
20	Old Penrith	x		x	
21	Catterick	x		x	
21a	Catterick Village		x		x
22	Ravenglass	x			
23	Aldborough	x	x	x	x
24	York	x		x	
25	Ribchester	x			
26	Ilkley				x
27	Castleford	x		x	x
28	Leeds				x
29	Cantley	x			
30	Doncaster		x		x
31	Rossington Bridge	x	x		x
32	Manchester	x			
33	Wilderspool	x			
34	Templeborough	x		x	
35	Chester	x			
36	Littleborough	x			
37	Lincoln	x		x	
38	Swineshead	x		x	
39	Meering	x			
40	Little Holland	x			
41	Margidunum	x		x	
42	Little Chester	x			
43	Willington	x			
44	Wisbech	x			
45	Thistleton	x		x	
46	Broughton Lodge	x			
47	Leicester	x		x	
48	Wroxeter	x			
49	Shenstone	x			
50	Mancetter	x			
51	Hartshill	x			
52	High Cross	x			
53	Walker's Heath	x			
54	Tripontium	x			
55	Blant's Green	x			
56	Alcester	x			
57	Sidbury	x			
58	Fengate	x		x	
59	Stonea	x		x	
60	Verulamium	x		x	

Figure 36. Distribution map: all stamps of Sarrius on the (creamy-white) Mancetter/Hartshill fabric.

Figure 37. Distribution map: stamps of Sarrius Die 4 on the (creamy-white) Mancetter/Hartshill fabric.

and Secundua on three mortaria attributable to Rossington shows that they were working in some form of association with him. Both are recorded independently also, the former in a fabric which might be Mancetter/Hartshill (Hartley 1960), but they appear to be very minor potters. Sarrius was clearly something of an entrepreneur, and whilst we cannot know the exact details of how his workshops were managed, it is reasonable to assume that Setibogius and Secundua were deputed by him to run the Rossington Bridge workshop.

Although there can be little doubt that the market being targeted at both Rossington and Bearsden was the army, we cannot know how far and in what way the army was directly involved in the setting up of the workshops. It is possible that the Rossington Bridge workshop is positioned at the northern limit of the territory of the Corieltauvi, and that Sarrius' movement was here restricted to within his own *civitas*, so as to avoid frontier dues, but the workshop near Bearsden is less easily explained without a direct military connection.

Black burnished ware production at Rossington Bridge

Illustrated Vessels in BB1 fabric

Nos 33–45, 47, 50–3, 56–8, 60–4, 67, 69–71, 73–5, 78–80, 85, 88–9, ?93, 106–7, 115–6, 159–60, 172–3, 178–82, ?184, ?188, 191–2, 195, 197, 200–3, ?213, 214–5, 224, 324, 330, 335.

Some preliminary discussion of BB1 production at Rossington Bridge has already appeared (Farrar 1973, 94–5; Williams 1977, 194; Buckland *et al* 1980), but the examination of the whole of the excavated assemblage and comparison with material from the Cantley and Rossington Bridge Farm kilns has necessitated some revision. In all the kiln groups, there is an intimate association between BB1, wheel-thrown grey wares and fine ware products. The heavily eroded sherds from such groups, however, are not ideal for the examination of BB1 production, as, in that state, they are often indistinguishable from wheel-thrown grey ware wasters. Some care has also to be exercised in the use of material from the wastage tipped down the slope (layers 4–6).

Figure 38. Distribution map: stamps of Sarrius Die 4 and Setibogius on oxidised red-brown, white-slipped fabrics.

Figure 39. Distribution map: stamps of Sarrius on oxidised red-brown, white-slipped fabrics.

The considerable quantities of samian, colour-coated and other evident alien products indicate substantial occupation continuing beyond the period of BB1 production, as well as pottery manufacture, and non-local products must inevitably be included amongst the assemblage. These deposits, however, are dominated by obvious wastage and contain sherds both oxidised (cf **172**) and severely cracked, which, as Farrar (1973, 92) has noted with regard to the Dorset BB1 production centres, might indicate firing in clamps, something for which the excavations at Rossington provides evidence (Pl 14).

The fabric is macroscopically often indistinguishable from the Dorset vessels, although one of us (PCB, in Gillam 1976), has been able to pick out probable Rossington pieces in the BB1 from Corbridge, where their presence has since been confirmed by heavy mineral analysis (Williams 1977, 202). Williams (1980) has also shown the presence of Rossington material at Balmuidy, Bar Hill, Bearsden, Castledykes, and Rough Castle on the Antonine Wall.

In recent work at Castleford, however, Rush (2000,98) considered the fabrics macroscopically indistinguishable. The typical fabric is heavily tempered with fine quartz sand, creating a rather hard, if brittle fabric, granular in the fracture, and inevitably resulting in much breakage among the wasters and few full profiles. Larger quartz grains and sometimes small pebbles may occasionally be incorporated in the fabric. The small angular 'plates' of shale, characteristic of much of the Dorset material are, however, absent from the Rossington products. The usual colour is light grey (N5) to grey (N6), rarely black (N3), in the fresh break, although a narrow outer zone, red (2.5YR 5/6) to reddish brown (2.5YR 4/4) or light grey (N6) may exist beneath the burnished surface. The wastage also exhibits considerable numbers of oxidised vessels in a range of colours from light red (2.5YR 6/8) through to red (2.5YR 5/8). Where sufficiently well preserved, the hand-made nature of the vessels is evident, although wheel-thrown 'copies', as with some of the Rossington Bridge Farm vessels (**Fig 54, 20–22**) and the Acacia Road site in Cantley (Buckland and Magilton, in prep), are difficult to isolate in badly abraded assemblages, and similar vessels must occur in the material from the Rossington Bridge kilns.

As the term black burnished indicates, the usual intended finish is a shiny black (N1–2), although some dark grey (N3) vessels were no doubt also traded. The surface colour of waster sherds is very variable, including yellowish-red (5YR 5/6) and red (2.5YR 5/6) oxidised pieces. The individual strokes of burnish tend to run over the curve of the vessel, apart from around handles, decorative features (eg on **115–7**) and bases, where the finish has often been applied transversely, apart from around the margins. Each stroke shows as a slightly concave depression, usually truncated by an adjoining stroke. Occasionally, on the more poorly finished pieces, a slight elevation, rather than ridge of unburnished surface may remain; the latter, however, is uncommon. Bowls and dishes are normally burnished throughout with no reserve zone for lattice as on the cooking pots. The latter are burnished not only above and below the invariably acute-angled lattice zone but also on the base and inside the rim, down as far as the junction between neck and rim; The grey ware 'copies' show similar details, and some confusion with what have been called 'grey burnished' products of such kilns as Lincoln Racecourse (Corder 1950) is probable. In addition, Buckland (in Brassington 1980) has suggested that there may have been some BB1 production at the Derby Racecourse kilns during the 2nd century, and this may provide another of the minor sources in this fabric, although it has not been confirmed by heavy mineral analysis (Williams 1985).

The abraded state of much of the wastage further makes assessment of decoration difficult. Cooking pots were clearly intended to have a broad zone of acute-angled lattice across an unburnished zone, probably applied with the same tool used to apply the burnish. The regularity of this varies considerably (compare **172** and **182**), and some sherds show strokes extending outside the reserve zone towards the base of the vessel. A wavy line, applied to the outside of the neck has been noted on a few cooking pots (eg **215**), but it is uncertain how widespread this practice may have been. Whether some bowls were intended to be plain is also uncertain, but well preserved vessels invariably show acute-angled lattice of variable quality extending from just below the rim to the base. The angle of the lattice, however, is more variable than on the cooking pots. No internal decoration has been noted but the undersides of bases on both bowls and dishes are frequently, although not invariably, decorated, either by scribbling, as on **56**, or by rows of wavy lines as **51–2**. Occasional atypical vessels, as **80**, show a certain exuberance in decoration, perhaps borne of release from the boredom of many thousands of lattice decorated vessels on the part of the potter.

Types B(a) and B(b). Dishes

Shallow dishes with a plain or vestigial bead provide a small proportion of the wastage, and, insofar as it can be ascertained, are entirely in BB1 fabric, whilst bead-rimmed dishes, with a clearly defined bead appear in both fabrics. A basal chamfer is probably characteristic of the grey ware dishes, as **46**, whilst a sagging base is evident on many BB1 examples. It is inevitable that the fragmentary nature of preservation on a kiln site leads to problems in separating bowls from dishes and both forms are included in the rim counts for Type B. Certainly bowls, like **38,** form an appreciable part of the wastage and these also appear to have a basal chamfer. Acute lattice, drawn with varying degrees of care, is likely to have been the norm on this form, although poor preservation has removed it from much of the wastage. Farrar (1973, 88) has pointed out that potters in Dorset do not appear to have finished the rim of their bead rim dishes as clearly as elsewhere and this may be a character useful in separating Rossington products in northern assemblages. Many of the Rossington pieces, clearly in BB1, have a deep, angular groove defining the bead. The majority of vessels fall within the size and depth range typified by **38** and **42**, between 44mm and 72mm deep, and up to 200mm in diameter. The large, shallow platter, represented by vessel **33**, is rare and invariably in BB1, usually with a slightly sagging base. Undersides of bases are burnished, often with scribbled circles as on **56** below.

33. Large, plain rimmed dish or platter, BBl, black (N1–2.5) fabric with lattice decoration on outer surface and three wavy lines on underside of the slightly sagging base, as **51**. RB/-/L.6.

34. Plain rimmed dish, BBl. Dark grey (N3) fabric, with black (N1–2) burnished surfaces.
RB/-/L.5a.

35. Plain rimmed dish, BBl. Black (N2) burnished surface with black (N2) core. Undecorated, with traces of wiping with a ?cloth on the outer surface before firing. The base is slightly raised rather than sagging. RB/-, but probably L.5–6.

36. Bead-rimmed dish, 160mm in diameter, BBl. Grey (10YR 6/1) fabric, with pink (5YR 7/4) to grey (5YR 6/1) burnished surface and lattice decoration.
RB/2/S (stokehole to kiln 2).

37. Bead-rimmed dish, BBl. Gritty very pale brown (10YR 7/4) to light grey (10YR 7/1) fabric, with traces of grey (10YR5/1) burnished surface.
RB/4/S.2 (stokehole to kiln 4).

38. Bead-rimmed bowl, BBl. Gritty grey (10YR 5/1) fabric with grey (N5) and pink (7.5YR 7/4) burnished inner surface. Chamfer well delineated, but outer surface too abraded for any trace of lattice to survive. The vessel is sufficiently deep to be regarded as a bowl, rather than a dish and Gillam's (1976) point about the absence of chamfers from dishes remains valid.
RB/4/S (stokehole to kiln 4).

39. Bead-rimmed dish, diameter indeterminate, BBl. Grey (N6) fabric, outer surface abraded but with traces of lattice decoration.
RB/2/S (stokehole to kiln 2).

40. Bead-rimmed dish, BBl. Dark grey outer surface, lighter core and inner surface.
RB/3/S (stokehole to kiln 3).

41. Bead-rimmed dish, with markedly sagging base. BBl. Light grey (N7) fabric, abraded surfaces although traces of a grey burnished surface survive on the inner surface.
RB/4/S.2 (stokehole to kiln 4).

42. Bead-rimmed dish, BBl. Gritty grey (N5) fabric, with burnished light grey (2.5Y 7/2) surface. There is a slight chamfer to the base on this vessel.
RB/3/S (stokehole to kiln 3).

43. Bead-rimmed dish, BBl. Gritty dark grey (N4) fabric with brown (7.5YR 5/6) outer zone and grey (N5–6) abraded surface with trace of lattice decoration.
RB/2/- (kiln 2).

44. Bead-rimmed dish, 120mm in diameter, BBl. Very pale brown (10YR 7/3) fabric with grey (N5) core and plain burnished surface, very abraded.
RB/2/K (kiln 2 interior).

45. Bead-rimmed dish, with poorly defined bead, 300mm in diameter, BBl. Hard, grey (N5) fabric, well burnished to grey (N6), with slightly obtuse lattice decoration and scribbling, as on **56**, on underside of base. The vessel appears to be not quite circular.
RB/11WMB/L.5a.

46. Bead-rimmed dish, with an evident basal chamfer. Dark grey (N5) burnished surfaces with very faint traces of lattice decoration; grey (N6) core and light grey (10YR 7/2) outer zone; probably wheel thrown.
RB/2/S (kiln 2 stokehole).

47. Bead-rimmed dish, BBl. Light grey (10YR 7/1) fabric with grey (N6) core and grey (N6) to dark grey (N4) burnished surface. Faint trace of lattice decoration on abraded outer surface.
RB/4/S (stokehole of kiln 4).

48. Bead-rimmed dish, 210mm in diameter. Light grey (N7) fabric, with darker (N5) surface.
RB/2/S (stokehole of kiln 2).

Type C(a). Lipped Bowls

The problems of differentiating between bowls and dishes, apparent with the bead-rimmed vessels, is equally acute with the lipped examples, where the rim forms on the shallow dishes, usually about 40mm deep and 160mm in diameter, as **52**, are the same as those on bowls, up to 100mm deep and 270mm in diameter, as **75**. Dishes, with the exception of the atypical form **85**, again lack basal chamfers, whilst most bowls have a marked chamfer and in one case, **84**, apparently not in BB1, this approaches the form of a flat rimmed carinated bowl. Although the material from kilns and stokeholes includes both wheel thrown and hand-made lipped vessels, some forms are restricted to the former category. No **65**, with its stub triangular rim is wheel-made, although other clearly wheel thrown vessels, as **65**, overlap completely in form with BB1 vessels. Where extant, the decoration again consists of varyingly executed acute lattice, applied either in a continuous zigzag or as overlapping inverted chevrons. On some of the larger examples (eg **88**), application is in the form of individual criss-cross strokes. Bases are often decorated on the underside, ranging from circular intersecting scribbles (**56**) to sub-parallel wavy lines (**51–52**). Gillam (1976) has pointed out that the use of inverted chevrons in decoration had appeared on vessels at, for example, Mumrills on the Antonine Wall, before AD 160, and intersecting arcs, absent from the Rossington Bridge material, had appeared by *c* AD 180.

49. Lipped dish, 200mm in diameter, Gritty light brownish grey (2.5Y 6/2) fabric; very badly abraded.
RB/2/K (interior of kiln 2).

50. Lipped dish, diameter indeterminate, ?BBl. Gritty very pale brown (10YR 7/3) fabric; very abraded surfaces with grey (N6) core.
RB/3/S (stokehole to kiln 3).

51. Lipped dish, BB1. Black (N2) burnished fabric, with dark grey (N4) core, decorated on sides and base with wavy lines underneath.
RB/D2.1/-, with **52** below.

52. Lipped dish, BBl. Black burnished fabric as **51**. Lattice decoration on body and wavy lines on underside of base, although the latter is faint against the burnished background.
RB/D2.1/-.

53. Lipped dish, diameter indeterminate, BBl. Gritty light grey (10YR 7/1) surface, with dark grey (N4) core. A much abraded waster.
RB/3/S (stokehole to kiln 3).

54. Lipped bowl or medium sized bowl. Light red (2.5YR6/8) fabric with grey (N6) core.
RB/4/S.1 (below quern in stokehole to kiln 4).

55. Lipped bowl or medium sized bowl, 110mm in diameter. Light grey (N7) fabric with very abraded surfaces.
RB/3/S (stokehole to kiln 3).

56. Decorated base of a BB1 bowl or dish. Black (N2) burnished fabric, with grey (N6) and reddish brown (5YR 7/3) core.
RB/- unstratified.

57. Lipped dish, 200mm in diameter, BBl. Gritty reddish yellow (5YR 7/6) fabric with traces of grey (N5) burnishing surviving on abraded surfaces. The base is apparently chamfered rather than sagging.
RB/2/S (stokehole to kiln 2).

58. Lipped dish, probably BB1. Light grey (10YR 7/1) fabric with darker grey (10YR 6/1) burnished surface. Slight traces of lattice.
RB/4/S.2 (stokehole to kiln 4).

59. Lipped dish. Gritty grey (N6) fabric with traces of burnishing on inner surface.
RB/2/S (stokehole to kiln 2).

60. Lipped dish, 200mm in diameter, BBl. Light yellowish brown (10YR 6/4) outer surface, burnished grey (N6) rim and inner surface; grey (N6) and light red (2.5YR 6/8) sandwich core. Very light traces of lattice decoration on outer surface.
RB/4/S.2 (stokehole to kiln 4).

61. Lipped dish, 190mm in diameter, BBl. Gritty light grey (10YR 7/2) fabric with some traces of darker (N5) burnished surface and very slight traces of lattice decoration on outer surface.
RB/4/S (stokehole to kiln 4).

62. Lipped dish, 190mm in diameter, BBl. Gritty light grey (10YR 7/2) fabric with grey (N5) surfaces.
RB/2/S (stokehole to kiln 2).

63. Lipped dish, BBl. Dark grey (N4) fabric. with lattice

decoration. Burnished on inner surface. Incised scribbling on small fragment of base.
RB/4/S.2 (stokehole to kiln 4).

64. Lipped dish, BB1. Light grey (2.5Y 7/2) fabric with badly abraded grey (N5) surfaces; traces of burnish and very faint evidence of lattice decoration.
RB/3/S (stokehole to kiln 3).

65. Lipped dish, 170mm in diameter and wheel thrown. Grey (N6) fabric with very dark grey (N3) surface. Undecorated.
RB/- unstratified.

66. Lipped dish, 170mm in diameter. Gritty reddish yellow (5YR 7/6) to grey (10YR 6/1) fabric, abraded.
RB/4–5/S (stokehole to kilns 4–5).

67. Lipped dish, BBl. Light grey (10YR 7/1) fabric with traces of burnished surface.
RB/3/S (stokehole to kiln 3).

68. Lipped dish. Light grey (2.5Y 7/2) fabric with patches of darker grey (N5) to light brownish grey (2.5Y 5/2) burnished surface and slight traces of lattice decoration.
RB/3/S (stokehole to kiln 3).

69. Lipped dish, 220mm in diameter, BBl. Grey (N5) fabric, with burnished surface.
RB/2/S (stokehole to kiln 2).

70. Lipped dish, 190mm in diameter, BBl. Dark grey (N4) fabric, with light greyish brown (2.5Y 6/4) core.
RB/2/S (stokehole to kiln 2).

71. Lipped dish, BBl. Grey (N6) fabric, abraded darker greyish brown (2.5Y 5/2) burnished surface and slight trace of lattice decoration. The base would appear to sag, rather than be chamfered.
RB/3/S (stokehole to kiln 3).

72. Lipped dish, 190mm in diameter. Pink (7.5YR 7/4) to light grey (N7) fabric with very abraded surfaces but some traces of burnishing.
RB/4/S.2 (stokehole to kiln 4).

73. Lipped bowl, BBl, 210mm in diameter; Gritty dark grey (N4) and light brown (7.5YR 6/4) fabric, with patchy abraded exterior, and grey (N5) core and reddish yellow (5YR 6/6) inner surface. Very slight traces of lattice decoration.
RB/- unstratified.

74. Lipped bowl, BBl. Dark grey fabric, with black (N1–2.5) burnished surfaces with lattice decoration; underside of base burnished and undecorated.
RB/8.1/L.5.

75. Lipped bowl in BBl. 240mm in diameter, with chamfered base. Grey (N5) fabric, with burnished light red (2.5YR 6/6) surface and lattice decoration; traces of scribbling on underside of base.
RB/- Peg 8, under clay floor. A further example, from RB/7.1/L.5a, has a much more irregular lattice.

76. Lipped bowl, 175mm in diameter. Light grey (2.5Y 7/2) fabric, with abraded surfaces.
RB/2/S (stokehole to kiln 2).

77. Lipped or medium sized bowl. Hard, brownish grey (2.5Y 6/2) fabric, clearly wheel thrown.
RB/2/S (stokehole to kiln 2).

78. Lipped bowl, BBl. Gritty, light red (2.5YR 6/6) fabric with grey (N5) core and darker (N4) surface with lattice decoration.
RB/- unstratified.

79. Lipped bowl, 200mm in diameter, BB1. Grey (N6) fabric, with light grey (10YR 7/1) to reddish yellow (7.5YR 8/6) abraded surfaces.
RB/2/S (stokehole to kiln 2).

80. Lipped bowl, probably BB1. Exterior surface pale brown (10YR 6/3), darker grey (N4) core and interior surface; reddish yellow (7.5YR 6/8) sandwich layer. Badly fire-cracked.
RB/2/S (stokehole to kiln 2).

81. Lipped bowl. Light grey (2.5Y 7/2) fabric, with darker greyish brown (2.5Y 5/2) burnished surface and core. The fabric is much less gritty than the BB1 vessels.
RB/1/S (stokehole to kiln 1).

82. Lipped bowl. Light grey (N7) fabric with darker (N3) core and traces of surface.
RB/2/S.1 (stokehole to kiln 2).

83. Lipped bowl, probably medium-sized as **277** below, but with very irregular lattice decoration. Hard grey (N5) fabric, with darker (N3–5) surface, burnished on top of rim and to top of lattice.
RB/25.1/L.3.

84. Carinated bowl with flat lip; grey (N5) to pale yellow (2.5Y 7/4) fabric smoothed on the outer surface on lower part of vessel.
RB/- ('Peg 8, under clay floor').

85. Lipped and carinated dish, BBl. Hard, dark grey (N4) to black (N2) fabric, pale brown (10YR 6/8) on rim and patches on exterior surface. Scribbled decoration on base, outer surface and also very faintly on rim. Fabric is probably Rossington Bridge, but form and decoration is unusual.
RB/8.1/L.5b. (One example only).

Bowls with grooved lip (Type C(b)) and straight-sided flanged bowls (Type C(c))

The origins of the flanged bowl and the date of its arrival in the north of Britain have been the subject of much debate. Its morphological development as the more effective base of a casserole, consisting of a bowl and dish combination, has been effectively argued by Gillam (1976). In an overall review of the sources of pottery reaching northern military sites, he (Gillam 1973) favoured a date between AD 180 and 210 for the first appearance of the true flanged bowl, truncated conical in profile with a clearly defined flange, although examples do occur earlier. The piece from Birrens (Robertson 1973, fig 83, 18) is now matched by similar vessels from late Antonine Exeter (Bidwell 1979, fig 65, 167–168), and a Durotrigan source seems probable. A bowl with grooved lip in a BB1 fabric appears in deposits of early Antonine date at Castleford (Rush 2000, fig 64, 346), and a few examples in BB1 occur amongst the Rossington Bridge wastage. A kiln site with both earlier and later domestic occupation is not the place to base arguments for dating, but it may be significant that only one flanged bowl is recorded from Layer 5a (**92**) and that this piece, with its curved walls resembles the example published from 2nd century Birrens. Furthermore, the Rossington Bridge Farm assemblage, with its evident links with the Pumping Station kilns, also lacks flanged bowls among the wastage; the one flanged piece (Fig 54, 11) does not belong to this type. Bowls with grooved lip appear to have been made in both BB1 and wheel thrown grey ware at Rossington,

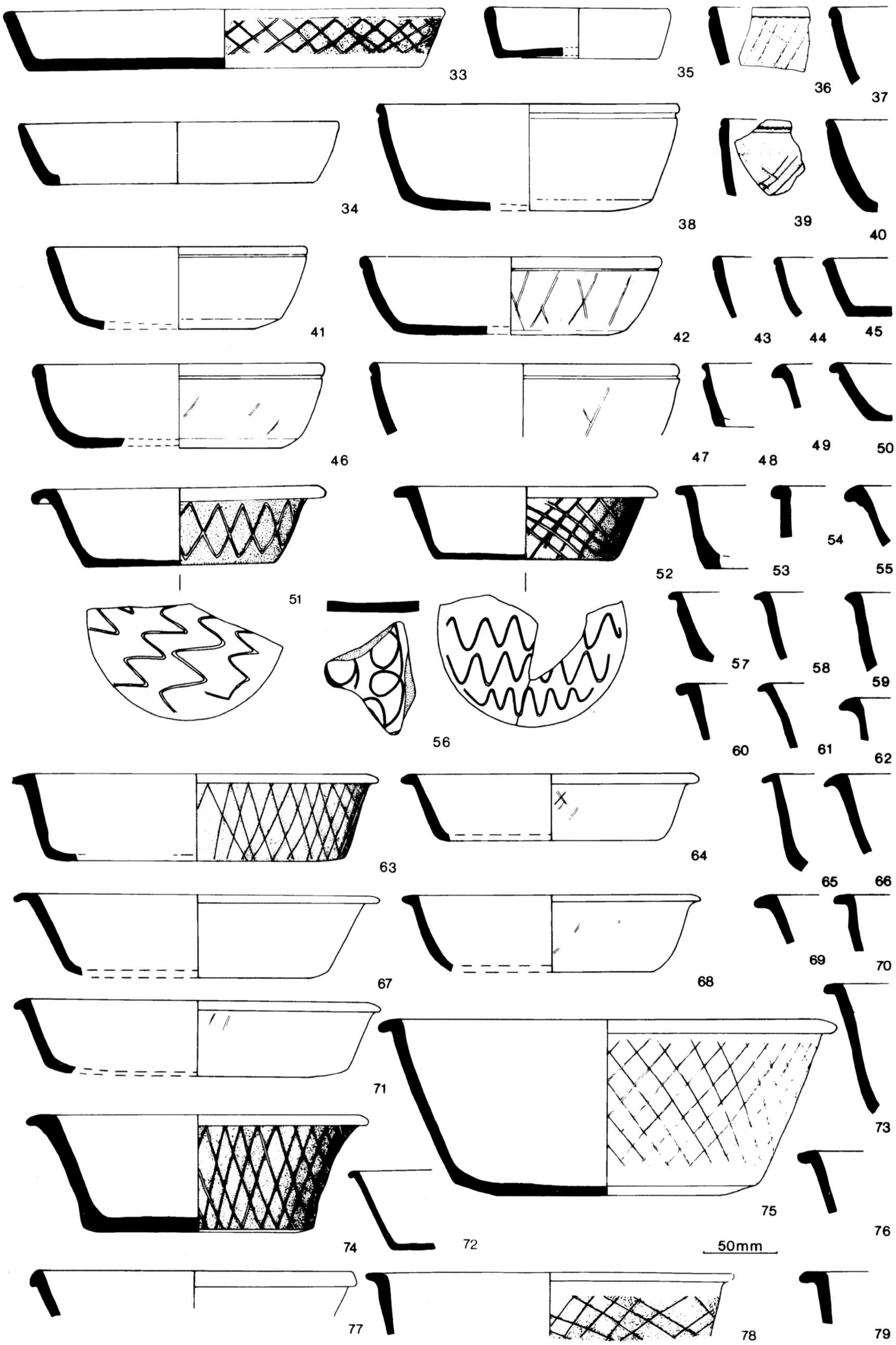

Figure 40. Rossington Bridge pottery: dishes and lipped bowls, Nos 33–79.

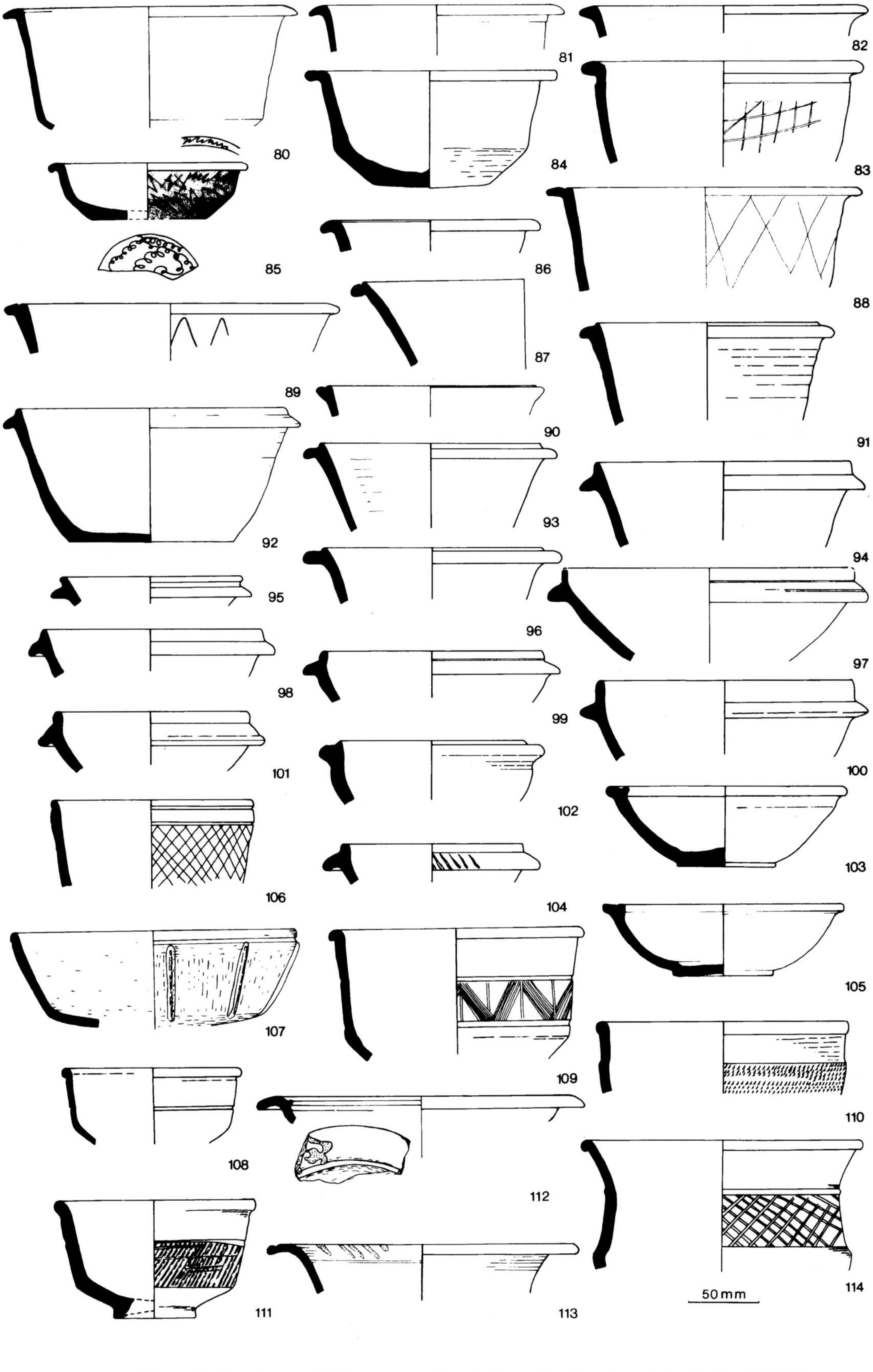

Figure 41. Rossington Bridge pottery: lipped, flanged and carinated bowls, Nos 80–114.

but the evidence for later production of flanged bowls is currently equivocal, the few examples in layers 3 and 4 in local fabrics being equally likely to have come from other Cantley kilns to the occupation site.

86. Bowl with grooved lip. Hard, grey (N6) fabric with darker grey (N5) burnished surface. Wheel thrown.
RB/7WMB/L.4.

87. Bowl with grooved lip. Hard, light grey (N7) fabric with darker (N5) surface, with metallic lustre. Wheel thrown and a finer fabric than that used for BB1; the vessel has been slightly distorted in firing.
RB/12–13C/L.5a.

88. Bowl with grooved lip, BB1. Black (N2) burnished surfaces, with very dark grey (N3) core and light lattice decoration.
RB/-/L.5.

89. Bowl with grooved lip, BB1. Dark grey (10YR 4/1) fabric with black (N2) burnished surface and lattice decoration.
RB/10WMB/L.5.

90. Bowl with grooved lip / straight sided flanged bowl. Gritty grey (N6) fabric with darker grey (N5) surface, partly oxidised to reddish yellow (5YR 7/6).
RB/2/S (stokehole to kiln 2).

91. Straight sided flanged bowl. Dark grey (N4) surfaces over a light grey (N7) core. Hard fabric with slightly burnished surfaces. Wheel thrown.
RB/7WMB/L.3.

92. The greater part of a straight sided flanged bowl. Wheel thrown, in a hard light grey (N6) fabric with a linear burnished grey (N5–7) surface. The vessel, distorted in firing, is undecorated and the base clearly string cut.
RB/15–16/L.5a (One example).

93. Straight sided flanged bowl, ?BB1. Black (N2) burnished surface with grey (N5) core. Some sooting under the rim; fabric as **89**.
RB/- unstratified.

94. Straight sided flanged bowl. Light grey (2.5Y 7/2) surface with grey (N6) core, burnished irregularly inside and out. As **87**, and wheel thrown.
RB/15WMB/L.3.

95. Straight sided flanged rim in a light grey (N8) fabric with patchy darker (5Y 4/1) surface.
RB/1/K (interior of kiln 1). Although figured with the bowls for comparison, the small diameter and angle of these sherds suggests that they belong to a narrow necked jar. The form was made in black burnished ware at Ower in the Isle of Purbeck (Farrar 1977, nos 33–4), where the type is tentatively assigned to the 4th century. The Rossington vessel, however, appears to come from kiln 1.

96. Straight sided flanged bowl. Light brownish grey (2.5Y 6/2) to dark grey (N3) surfaces, with light grey (N6) core.
RB/9.1/L.4.

Type C(e). Segmental Flanged Bowls

Amongst the vessels made in small numbers at Rossington, are a number of segmental flanged bowls. Some, like **97** and **100**, approach the more competent imitations of samian form 38 in shape (**325–326**) in shape, whilst others (eg **101**) may be better regarded as lids. Unlike later production at Cantley (Buckland and Magilton, in prep), there appears to be no standard form and, although fabrics can be matched closely in the kiln wastage, most stratified examples come from the later layers 3 and 4 and local, rather than Cantley, production must remain open to doubt.

97. Segmental flanged bowl. Grey (N6) fabric, with grey (N5) to very dark grey (N3) surface, burnished on the outside.
RB/10WMB/L.5.

98. Segmental flanged bowl. Dark grey surfaces with silvery sheen, light grey core.
RB/-/L.3/4.

99. Segmental flanged bowl. Pink (5YR 7/5) oxidised fabric with pale red (10R 5/4) slipped surface.
RB/- unstratified.

100. Segmental flanged bowl. Light brown (7.5YR 6/2) smoothed surfaces with grey (N6) core.
RB/15.1/L.3.

101. Segmental flanged bowl. Light red (2.5YR 6/8) oxidised fabric with grey (N5) core. Gritty fabric as that of the mortaria.
RB/- unstratified.

102. Segmental flanged bowl. Black (N2) surface, burnished over rim, with red (2.5YR 4/6) core.
RB/-/L.3.

103. Segmental flanged bowl. Light brown fabric with a few grit inclusions; patches of sooting on rim.
RB/- unstratified.

104. Segmental flanged bowl. Greyish brown (10YR 5/2) surfaces and pale brown (10YR 6/3) core. Unusually fine and hard fabric, similar to **113** below; very pale brown (10YR 8/3) slipped decoration on flange.
RB/9WMB/L.3 (one example).
This vessel has much in common with the later Cantley products (Buckland and Magilton, in prep), 3rd – early 4th century.

105. Segmental bowl with slightly kicked base. Brown fabric.
RB/- unstratified.

Type C(f). Other bowls

This group is again represented by forms of which there tends to be few examples, and the ones figured are in fabrics which would not be out of place among the Rossington products, **106–7** and **115–6** being in BB1. The girthed and carinated bowl **114** presents a surface feature which appears characteristic of many of the Rossington finer grey ware vessels, in that the surface has been vitrified to form a lustrous silvery grey sheen. Bryant (pers comm) has suggested that this is a result of wood ash acting as a flux on the surface of the vessels leading to almost a glaze. It has not been noted in any of the other south Yorkshire kiln groups, either as a result of poorer preservation of wastage, or because there was something slightly different in the late stages of firing in at least one Rossington kiln.

106. Vessel with beaded rim and deep groove below bead, BB1. A hard grey (N5) fabric with dark grey (N4) surfaces and metallic lustre. Very finely incised lattice decoration.
RB/11.1/L.5. (A further undecorated example comes from RB/10WMB/L.5a.)
Although figured with the bowls and insufficiently complete to show a handle, these vessels are probably tankards of Gillam (1970) type 181. The form is more widespread in

oxidised fabrics from the Severn Valley kilns (eg Chester (Carrington 1977) fig 10.2, 36, Birrens (Robertson 1975) fig 66, 28, and Old Kilpatrick (Webster 1977) fig 11.2, 29), but occasional reduced examples occur. *c* AD 120–200.

107. Bead-rimmed bowl with applied vertical ribs, BB1. Gritty grey (N5) fabric with darker (N4) burnished surface, vertical lines of burnishing evident between ribs.
RB/13C/L.6 (peat). (One example).
This is one of the more esoteric pieces from the site which serves to emphasise the direct Durotrigan connection. The type derives from the bowls with pedestal base and applied ribs of Dorset (cf Maiden Castle (Wheeler 1943) no 182, from the 'War Cemetery'). In the late 1st century, examples were reaching Exeter (Bidwell 1979, nos 119–120), and the Rossington example could be an early import associated with the vexillation fortress. Its form, however, close to Exeter (Holbrook and Bidwell 1992) fig 17, 112, dated *c* 125–140/60, suggests influence from the bead-rimmed dish and local manufacture is more probable.

108. Bowl, cf samian form 37. Very dark grey (N3) surfaces with weak red (2.5YR 4/2) core, metallic lustre on outer surface and lighter patches on inside.
RB/8WMB/L.5a.

109. Carinated bowl. Grey (N5) surfaces with metallic lustre and chevron decoration between grooves; light grey (N6) core.
RB/2.2/-. (One example).

110. Hemispherical bowl, cf samian form 37. In a hard reddish yellow (5YR 6/6) fabric with grey (N6) core. Burnished on neck and rim. Rouletted decoration.
RB/16.1/L.5a. Doubtfully a Rossington product.
The type is widespread; Manchester (Webster, 1974 no 120) provides a close parallel, although in a grey fabric. Two examples from the Antonine fort at Mumrills (Gillam, 1960–1, fig 15, 82–3) are in an oxidised fabric.

111. Carinated bowl in an oxidised light reddish brown (5YR 6/4) fabric with grey (5YR 6/1) core; rouletted diagonal decoration and traces of burnish.
RB/16.1/L.6 (peat).

112. Segmental bowl, in a hard, slightly gritty oxidised reddish yellow (5YR 6/6) fabric with reddish brown (2.5YR 4/4) painted decoration.
RB/11WMB/sand.
The fabric suggests that this is a Rossington product and a further example, from RB/5-6WMB/L.5a, has been distorted in firing. Another waster of this type occurs at Blaxton (Buckland and Dolby 1980, no 217). An example from kiln 1 (RB/1/K), lacking the internal bead and perhaps related to samian form 36, has a grey slip, probably refired from an oxidised original. The type was made in large numbers in the later Cantley kilns (Buckland and Magilton, in prep). cf the similar example, in a finer fabric, from Doncaster (Buckland and Magilton, 1986, fig 35, 87), associated with a coin of AD 154–5. The type was also made at the Derby Racecourse kilns (Brassington, 1971, fig 7) during the 2nd century.

113. Rim of a campanulate bowl with beaded lip, in an oxidised light red (2.5YR 6/6) fabric, similar to **104** above and **328** below, with light reddish brown (5YR 6/3) burnished surface and traces of red (2.5YR 5/6) painted decoration on inside of rim.
RB/10WMB/L.5a.
cf Brough-on-Humber (Wacher 1969) fig 64,290, although this is in a grey fabric, late 2nd – 3rd century.

114. Carinated bowl in a fine dark grey (N6) fabric with light grey (N3) core and burnished lattice decoration over a lustrous surface.
RB/l0/L.6 (peat).
The fabric suggests a Rossington product, but the form, ultimately probably derived from Cam 83 (Hawkes and Hull 1947, pl LV), appears earlier; cf Great Casterton (Corder 1954) fig 2, 2, where the parallel with Jewry Wall (Kenyon 1948) fig 25, 16 is invalid, and Brough-on-Humber (Wacher 1969) fig 57, 103, early 2nd century. The form was also made in the Derby Racecourse kilns (Brassington 1980, fig 14, 373).

115. Bowl, BB1, similar to **107** above. Black burnished surfaces and grey (N5) core. Decorated with finger tip impressions and nipples, apparently hand-made and probably part of **116** below. A fragment of flint in the temper suggests that this may not be a local product.
RB/D2-1/-.

116. BB1, as **115** above. Black fabric, abraded on surfaces but traces of burnishing remain. Fingertip impressions and nipple decoration on body of vessel.
RB/12WMB/L.6.

Relief Decorated Pottery
V. Rigby

1. The stamp-decorated wares – Parisian Ware

Philip Corder (1956) coined the term 'Parisian Ware' for a group of vessels in a fine-grained, grey ware, with a smooth, burnished finish, and decorated with impressed stamps, which had been found during his excavations at Brough-on-Humber, and elsewhere in Yorkshire. At that time, there was just a single example from south of the Humber, a bowl from Mablethorpe, Lincolnshire. Subsequent fieldwork and research south of the estuary has resulted in a more impressive concentration of finds, including at least three possible production centres at Roxby/Dragonby, South Humberside, Market Rasen, Lincolnshire, and Rossington Bridge, South Yorkshire (Rigby and Stead 1976, 181–187). As a result of these discoveries, the term Coritanian, or, more recently, even Corieltauvian (Tomlin 1983) Ware might have been rather more appropriate than Parisian Ware; however, it is the accepted term, and until all the production centres have been discovered, and their products exhaustively analysed, it seems unnecessary to change.

Research into stamp decorated wares from south Lincolnshire and East Anglia has helped to define Parisian Ware and place it in its context as a regional variation, with its own preferred vessel forms, fabrics and motifs, within a range of decorative techniques which were current in the late 1st and 2nd centuries AD in eastern England, north of the Thames (Elsdon 1982; Rodwell 1978; Perrin 1980; Rigby 1986). It has been known for over three decades that impressed stamps were combined with other incised techniques by potters working at West Stow, Suffolk (West 1989), and, from the range of examples found on other settlements in the region, several other production centres followed suit.

Besides making vessels with incised decoration, there is evidence from West Stow for the use of 'Makers' Marks' impressed centrally on the upper base of platters and bowls, possibly as a production control strategy (Rigby 1998). A number of settlements in what might be termed the 'Eastern Stamp-Decorated Ware Zone', for example, Baldock, Hertfordshire, Ashton and Duston, Northamptonshire, Scole, Norfolk, and Grandford, Cambridgeshire, demonstrate that both stamp-decorated wares and stamp-decorated vessels were made at a large number of different production centres, in the same period *c* AD 90–180. It may be significant in elucidating any complex trading patterns which could have developed within this broader region that a stamp from a maker's mark used by a potter working at West Stow, Suffolk, was found on the fort site at Doncaster (Rigby 1998); presumably stamp-marked products were traded as far afield as stamp-decorated vessels. Other new Stow products have been identified at Wereham, Norfolk, Brandon, Suffolk, Colchester and Mucking, Essex.

Stamp-decorated wares are not entirely unknown in western and southern Britain, although, with the exception of the late colour-coated products of the Oxfordshire (Young 1977) and New Forest potteries (Fulford 1975), they were not common. Small sherds from three identical vessels have been found at Chichester, Shoreham and Littlehampton, Sussex (Rigby 1989, fig 16.4, 82). Stylistically, they belong to the London-Essex region, Rodwell Group 2A, 2C-D, but the fabrics are different (Rodwell 1978, figs 7.3, 7.5–7). It remains to be seen whether they prove to be precursors of an extensive stamp-decorated tradition in southern Britain, or whether they were traded from the 'Eastern Stamp-decorated Ware zone'. Certainly an increasing number of vessels decorated with incised patterns are being identified, so that it is not beyond the bounds of possibility that the technique of stamping was introduced south of the Thames also (Green 1976, fig 25, 60–1).

Rather than being seen as a uniquely decorated range of Roman pottery, parisian ware can now be viewed as a regional variation within a much more widespread trend to produce pottery decorated with incised patterns and motifs, and also stamped with makers' marks. Much effort has been expended in trying to establish its origins, and, in the absence of close continental parallels, a staged and devolved development has been proposed, with imports from northern and central Gaul being propounded as prototypes for forms and motifs (Rigby and Stead 1976). Elsdon (1982) has suggested that there was some degree of continuity between Iron Age stamp-decorated wares and Roman products, particularly in the Humber area; however, none of the arguments is convincing and there is little evidence of a pre-Roman stamp decoration in the north Nottinghamshire and south Yorkshire region.

In fact, those seeking Gaulish origins for parisian ware in particular have now been richly rewarded in an area hitherto only briefly mentioned, namely Aquitania, south-western Gaul. In their monograph on the pottery from the Bordeaux area, M.-H. and J. Santrot published a group of stamp-decorated beakers which could have derived from any site around the Humber, including Rossington Bridge (Santrot and Santrot 1979, 135–6, type 263). The fabric description fits that of the metallic blue-grey, sandwich ware common in Group Bii at Rossington and examination of the vessels confirms this. Stamp-decorated beakers were found at the Roman pottery of Soubrain, Charente, and here too the fabrics are recognisably 'parisian'. The dating evidence is somewhat insecure, but appears to extend from the second half of the 1st to the mid-2nd centuries AD (Santrot and Santrot 1979, 130). As Henig (1998) has pointed out for samian ware, the ultimate source for parisian forms are metal, pewter and silver tableware, but it is perhaps through these Gallic pottery intermediaries that the origins of parisian ware are to be found. Master potters may have migrated into the area or even skilled slaves brought in. Aquitanian contacts are well attested by the inscription set up by a merchant from Lincoln and York upon his safe arrival in Bordeaux (Ottaway 1993, pl 31). Even in this scenario, a slight question mark remains over the stamp-decorated wares found at Rossington Bridge – are all local products, or are some actual imports?

There are about 70 sherds of stamp-decorated ware belonging to 31 different vessels from Rossington Bridge. Most vessels are represented by no more than a single sherd, and many have such abraded edges and surfaces that they must have suffered a long, varied and disturbed history after their initial discard. The most complete vessels, **122**, **142** and **145**, are in better condition and therefore seem to have suffered less disturbance, and so perhaps provide more reliable archaeological evidence. No distorted, bloated or spalled stamped wasters have been identified, and no stamp-decorated vessels were found as part of an abandoned kiln load, although the most complete example, **142**, was probably found in the stokehole of kiln 3. About one half of the remaining sherds were found in the stokeholes of kilns 3, 4, and 5, while the remainder were more or less unstratified. The hypothesis that these stamp-decorated wares were manufactured at Rossington Bridge therefore depends entirely upon the evidence of the stamps, forms and fabrics, and such evidence can never be absolutely conclusive, unless the sample is a very large one.

The range of pattern motifs (Table 6 and Fig 42) is very restricted when compared with settlements of Old Winteringham and Dragonby, south Humberside (Rigby and Stead 1976, 181–187; Elsdon 1982, figs 9–11). There is only one complex, composite motif, made up from two different elements, die DC 1: the remaining six motifs are amongst the most commonly found simple, single shapes used in stamp-decorated wares – rings, rosettes, single-strand cord impressions, diamonds, geometrically infilled rectangular lozenges and 'fern leaves'.

The identification of individual dies depends on having a range of complete clear and legible stamps, and therefore it can be greatly affected by the depth of the impression, shape of the vessel and degree of surface abrasion: the worn and fragmentary condition of some stamps from Rossington Bridge has hindered die identification. From the surviving evidence, it appears that a remarkably small number of pattern dies, between 10 and 13, have been employed – two rosettes (DR1–2), one diamond (DD1), three geometrically infilled rectangles (DL1-3), one fern-leaf (DF1) and anything from one to four single cord impressions (DC1–3(?4)). The query about the latter total is due to the fragmentary nature of the stamps and the differing depth of the impressions; two examples, **124c-d**, almost certainly represent two different dies, while the remaining pair are uncertain, although probably were made with die DC1).

Generally, two or three motifs of different basic shape were combined, either in individual horizontal bands around the vessel, like **122**, **143–145**, or grouped into alternate, vertical stripes, like **121**, **123**, **126**, **130–1**. In addition, diamond-shaped 'stab' impressions were incorporated into the design, either as vertical stripes, **135**, single bands, **125**, or in a broad, horizontal zone, **149**. Table 7 summarises the association of different motifs and dies. It demonstrates that they can be separated into two mutually exclusive groups, A and B, but whether the division represents the work of different potters, or workshops, or periods of production, or any combination of these, remains uncertain.

Stamp Group A – Nos 121, 123, 126, 130–2. Dies DD1, DL2–3 and DR1

This small group of seven vessels is decorated with only four dies, representing three different motifs – rings, diamonds and two different geometrically infilled rectangles (DR1, DD1, DL2–3). There are five vessels of the same basic shape, a wide-bodied, cordoned beaker, and in the same basic fabric, a fine-grained smooth clay matrix with a scatter of darker clay pellets up to 1mm in length. All are abraded with the result that little or nothing remains of the original surface finish, and some stamp impressions have been affected. The sherds from two remaining vessels are in better condition, with the original dark burnished finish surviving sufficiently to make it impossible to distinguish the clay pellets in the matrix of hand specimens. Not only do the fabrics appear different, but so are the forms. The more complete example, **121**, is a typical poppyhead beaker in shape, complete with a cordon at the base of the neck, while **132** appears to have a high and rounded shoulder, although the sherd is too small for classification.

The find-spots for sherds in Group A are varied and scattered, but include the stokeholes of kilns 3 and 4. The sherds from these particular contexts are so abraded that they must have been kicked about at the ground surface for a long period before their final deposition, and therefore their presence in or near kilns cannot be anything other than accidental, and is scarcely conclusive evidence when trying to identify the kiln or kilns in which the stamp-decorated vessels were fired. Given their condition, it is not beyond the bounds of possibility that these stamp-decorated sherds are derived from imported or traded vessels supplied to a settlement at Rossington Bridge, rather than being produced in one of the workshops there. Such an interpretation does, however, require that the evidence has been affected by a more than usually wide range of unknown factors for the die evidence suggests a single source of origin, with no more than two potters working in a single workshop.

Stamp Group B – Nos 122, 122a and b, 124d, 125, 125a, 134–5, 135a, 142–5, 147, 149a and 150. Dies DT1, DF1, DL1, DO1, DR1 and 2 and DS1 and 2

The larger group comprises sherds from 16 related vessels, decorated with seven dies, representing six different motifs. Only two motifs – rings and geometrically infilled rectangles – also occur in Stamp Group A, the remaining four – rosettes, single strand cords, a composite square and fern-leaves – are peculiar to stamp group B. Further variation was achieved by incorporating 'stab' impressions into the decorative patterns of four vessels, **125**, **135**, **122b** and **149a**, and circle segments into one, **143**.

Stamp group B can be sub-divided into five and nine associated vessels using the two rosette dies, which never occur on the same vessels. In group Bi, the simple rosette, die DR1, occurs with the geometrically infilled rectangle die DL1, but never with the fern-leaf, DF1. The complex rosette of group Bii, die DR2, occurs with the fern-leaf, die DF1, but never with the geometrically infilled rectangle, DL1. The two sub-groups, Bi and ii, are not mutually exclusive, for rectangular stamps and fern-leaves alternate on the same flask, **142**. At present it is not apparent whether the sub-groups are actually significant in production or chronological terms, or simply an accident of archaeological sampling, which will be corrected when the sample size is increased.

Six sherds are decorated with single strand cord impressions, **124**, **124a-d** and **150**. On one vessel, this motif was used with the simple rosette, die DR1, and the infilled rectangle, DL1, while on a second only the rosette and the cord occur; however, both clearly belong to the group Bi potter or workshop (**125** and **150**). Three of the remaining sherds are decorated solely with single strand cord impressions, and unfortunately they are too small and the impressions too fragmentary for a certain die-link with group Bi to be established. The final example combines cords and rings, but is too fragmentary for any classification. At the early Roman pottery at Keston,

Table 6. Stamps used on Rossington Bridge parisian ware.

Motif	Name	Abbrev.	Examples (vessel nos.)
	Stab impression (149)	S (DS1-2)	122b; 125; 127; 192; 149; 149a; 151
	Single ring (121)	DO1	121; 122; 122a; 122b; 124c; 126; 130; 131; 132; 145; 149; 149a
	Double diamond (123)	DD1	123
	Rosette 1 (135)	DR1	125; 125a; 135; 135a; 150
	Rosette 2 (147)	DR2	144; 147
	Divided rectangle 1 (125)	DL1	91d; 125; 125a; 134; 142; 143; ?149; 27 (mortarium)
	Divided rectangle 2 (121)	DL2	121; 123; 123a; 132; ?149a
	Divided rectangle 3	DL3	126; 130; 131
	Fernleaf 1 (122)	DF1	122; 122a; 122b; 142; 144; 145; 147; ?149
	Single strand cord or twine impression (124)	DT1	124; 124a; 124b; 124c; 124d; 150
	Composite motif 1 (134)	C1	134

Kent, single strand cord impressions were made with the notched edge of a disc of fired clay which had been rotated between the thumb and index finger (Philp *et al* 1991, fig 44).

Group Bi has a unique addition to its range of motifs and dies, a name stamp, used in combination with simple rosettes, die DR1, and 'stab' impressions on a wide-bodied and carinated vessel, **135** (Fig 43). The reading and interpretation of the stamp is discussed on p 63, and rather than being the name of the potter who made the pot, or owned the workshop, or both, it appears to be a re-used oculist's stamp, so that its function on the pot was probably purely decorative rather than production control, information or advertising.

In contrast to the decorative use of the functional oculist's stamp, one of the stamp group Bi dies, the infilled rectangle DL1 was used in the traditional place of the maker's mark, namely stamped across a mortarium rim (Fig 35, 27). At Rossington Bridge, it is the most commonly found die of its type, occurring on at least six

Table 7. Concordance of stamps and vessels from Rossington Bridge Pumping Station.

No.	Cont.	S	DR1	DT1	DO1	DL1	DC1	DF1	DR2	DL2	DD1	DL3	F	Frm	Cond.
27	u/s					2G							O	Mo	1s -w
122	u/s				H			H					M	Po	6s - f
122a	u/s				H			H					M	Ro	1s w
122b	u/s	H			H			H						Ro	1s w
124	u/s			5+G									H	La	1s g
124a	u/s			B									M	La	1s w
124b	u/s			X									H	La	1s g
124c	u/s			Z	H								F	Ro	1s w
124d	u/s			4+H		I							F	Ro	1s vw
125	K3/S	2V	2H			I								Wb	
125a	u/s		2H				I							Ro	1s
127	K4–5/S	B											H	Wb	ls f
134	K3/S					I	I						P	Cb	ls w
135	7.1/L.5a	V	4V										F	Wb	1s f
135a	K3		4+G										H	Ro	1s
142	K3/S					2G		I					M	Fl	20+ f
143	u/s					H							H	La	1s g
144	u/s							H	2H				M	Ro	1s f
145	u/s				H			H					M	Fl	10+ s f
147	u/s								H	H			M	Ro	1s f
149	K3/S	B			H	?I		?I		?I			P	Ro	1svv w
149a	u/s	H			H								H	Ro	1s f
150	-/L.4		X	2G									F	?	1s f
151	K2/S	P											H	La	1ss w
121	7.1/L.5a				H					Z			F	Cl	1s w
123	K3/S				3V					I				Po	
123a	u/s									I	3G		P	Wb	1svv w
126	K4-5/S				3V							I	P	Wb	3svv w
130	K4/S				2V							I	P	Wb	1vv w
131	K4/S.2				4G						I	I	P	Wb	1 w
132	-/L.5				H					Z			F	Cl	1 w

Context: L. = layer; K = kiln; S = stokehole; u/s = unstratified.
Stamp data (S – DL3): B = impressions arranged to form a wide, continuous horizontal band; G = groups of impressions; H = a single horizontal row of impressions; P = impressions arranged in shaped panels; V = a single vertical row of impressions; X = insufficient evidence for arrangement; Z = impressions arranged in a zigzag pattern; I = individual impressions.
Fabrics: O = oxidised; M = metallic grey; H = hard, fine and sandy; F = fine and smooth; P = fine, pelleted clay.
Forms: Mo = mortarium; Po = poppy head beaker; Ro = rounded and closed; La = large, rounded and closed; Wb = wide-bodied beaker; Cb = cordoned beaker; Fl = flask; Cl = closed form.
Number of sherds and condition: f = fine; g = good; w = worn; v = very; vv = extremely worn.

closed vessels in reduced fabrics. Such a find is open to differing interpretations. A single group Bi or Bii potter or workshop could have produced both stamp-decorated beakers and flasks in reduced fabrics and mortaria in oxidised, cream slipped wares. However, there need have been no significant connection, for the mortarium workshop may have reused an accidentally acquired pattern stamp for just a short period of time. An intrinsically less likely explanation is that the maker of stamp-decorated wares fortuitously acquired a mortarium maker's mark of precisely the correct dimensions and shape to match his existing range of pattern dies.

The range of vessel forms in stamp group Bi and Bii may also prove to be mutually exclusive, and to divide along the same lines as the stamps, but, at present, there are too few complete examples to be certain. The recognised beaker forms are definitely different, stamp group Bii including a high proportion of round-bodied, narrow-necked flasks. While the twofold division of group B by stamps and forms stands, fabrics provide a rather different and more complex picture. At least four superficially different fine-grained fabrics are represented in both stamp groups Bi and Bii, and two are also present in group A: they are the pelleted fabric most common in Group A, and the fine sandwich fabric with a metallic blue-grey surface finish, which predominates in Group Bii. One vessel, **149**, cannot be placed in either group A or B. The pelleted fabric and ring-stamps of this globular, closed vessel suggest group A; however, the 'stab' impressions and arrangement of the stamps suggest group B. A third motif, overstamped by the rings, could solve the problem, but is too fragmentary for definite recog-

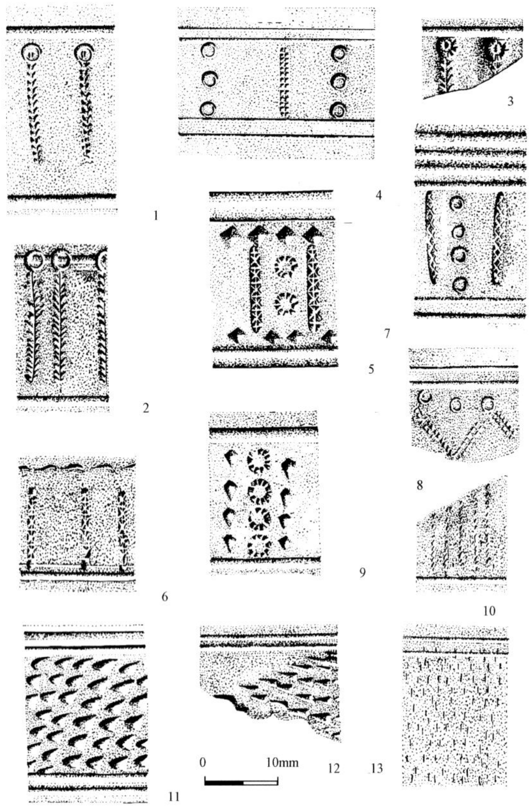

Figure 42. Stamps used on parisian ware vessels. Drawing: M. Durrant.

nition – it could be a fern-leaf from group B, or a geometrically infilled rectangle from either group A or B.

The differing associations of dies and forms in group B suggest that two potters may have been working in the same workshop, and that they had occasional access to the same dies. While the fine sandwich ware with the metallic blue-grey finish may have been the preferred fabric for stamp decorated wares in the group B workshop; other clays could be substituted at will, for whatever reason. It may possibly represent imports from Bordeaux with actual local products being confined to the other, less accomplished fabrics.

While the stamps systematically divide group A from B, the evidence provided by the forms and fabrics is by no means as clear-cut. Certainly, much of group A hangs together well in terms of stamps and forms, with the wide-bodied multi-cordoned beaker form, seemingly exclusive to it. The version of group Bi has no more than a single, broader cordon at the base of the neck. Similarly the poppyhead beaker, with a single, narrow cordon at the base of the rim, is represented by variants differing in detail in groups A and Bii. Again, flasks appear most numerous in group Bii, but the most complete example, **142**, straddles the divide between Bi and Bii, and **132** in stamp group A appears flask-like in size and shape.

The absence of complete fabric specialisation within the three major groupings is typical of Roman pottery production at all levels. Although each workshop may have had a preferred fabric in terms of clay mixture, preparation and finish, with predictable firing results, other clays could be substituted for any number of reasons. Season changes in humidity and temperature could clearly affect clay and filler during preparation, and at Rossington Bridge, for example, naturally tempered pelleted clay may have been seasonally preferred to a homogeneously fine-grained matrix.

Study of the stamp-decorated wares from Rossington Bridge suggests that two workshops were involved, A and B, and that the latter may also have produced other specialist products, in particular, stamped mortaria. The concentration of both workshops upon beakers is a typical 'parisian' regional idiosyncrasy, as is the frequent use of the fern-leaf motif in group B. The production of truly narrow-necked flasks is, however, somewhat unexpected for they were not in common use in northern Britain in the 2nd century AD.

2. Roller-stamped Wares

The Aquitanian influence at Rossington Bridge is not just confined to the fine-grained smooth fabric and stamp-decorated wares. Roller-stamped wares were commonly produced there in a wide variety of different vessel shapes and fabrics, from fine grained smooth to coarse grained sand-tempered cooking pots. The majority of the Rossington pieces come from the two kilns on the south side of the river Torne at Rossington Bridge Farm (Fig 54). Sporadic finds of Roller-stamped Wares have been made in the 'Eastern Stamp-decorated Ware Zone', at St. Albans, Hertfordshire, Colchester and Chelmsford, Essex, Tripontium and Mancetter-Hartshill, Warwickshire, where it was also produced, Leicester, Margidunum, Nottinghamshire, and Rossington Bridge. Part of a hard clay roller stamp has been identified on the site of the early Roman pottery at Eccles, Kent, although no related decorated vessels were found (Detsicas 1974, fig 8, 3). The range of fabrics suggests that a number of different sources were involved, but none appears to be a definite import.

The poor condition of the Rossington sherds makes it difficult to work out the repeat pattern of the roller stamp, but it clearly does not match directly any of the published stamps from Aquitaine (Santrot and Santrot 1979). Despite the variation (Fig 44), it appears that only one die has been employed. The most clearly impressed example, (Fig 44, 5) from the Rossington Bridge Farm kilns, suggests a narrow stamp, approximately 10mm, across with a pattern consisting of four concentric circles flanked by a vertical line and upward pointing chevrons. There is no doubt that this is the same die as used on the small sherds of an indented beaker from the Pumping Station site (Fig 44, 1–2). It has been suggested that the

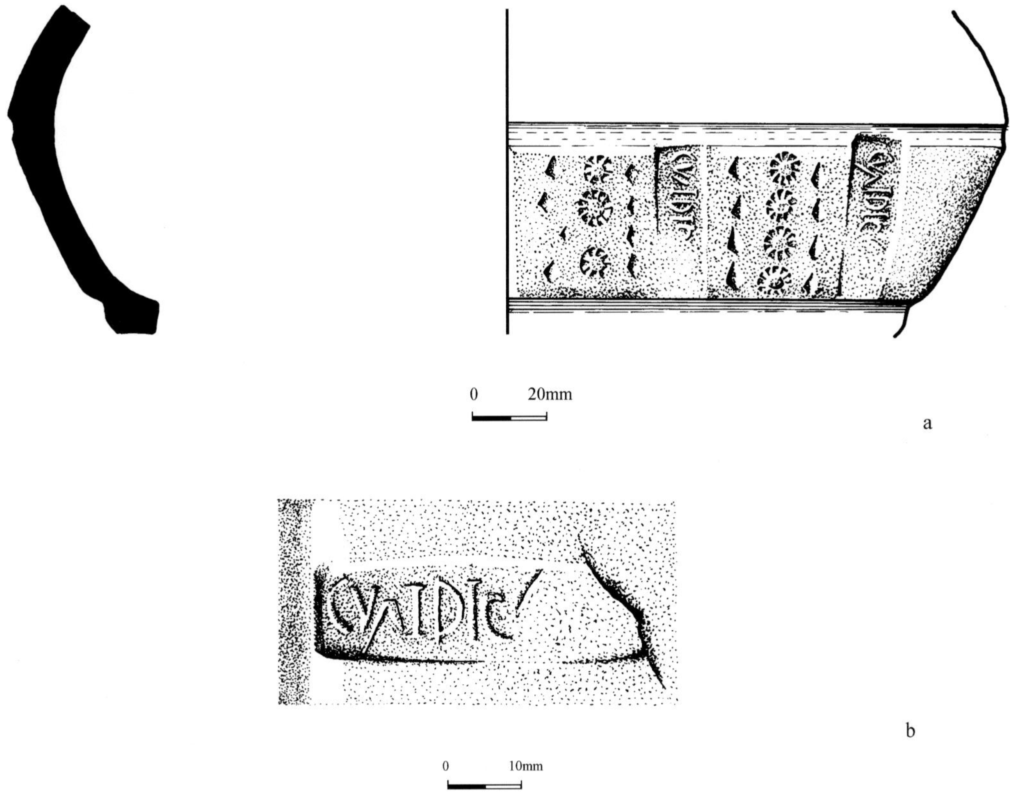

Figure 43. Globular beaker (No 135) with stamp of C VAL DIC[.. . Drawing: M. Durrant.

same roller-stamp can be detected on sherds from Mancetter-Hartshill and some sherds from Rossington, but the condition of the latter precludes definite identification. Not unnaturally, the examples from Leicester (cf Kenyon 1948, fig 27, 36) and Tripontium (Cameron and Lucas 1969, fig 16, 152) do appear to be Mancetter-Hartshill products, since the latter was clearly a local source of pottery for these sites. The jar in an orange fabric from the Derby Racecourse kilns (Brassington 1971, fig 10, 196) may be a local product, although the drawing of the stamp is very similar to the Rossington die. The source of the Margidunum vessels (Oswald 1952, pl XIX, 3 and 6) is uncertain, since the fabrics are not described, but the die appears very close to the Rossington one.

3. Barbotine Decoration

One vessel, Fig 46, **117** and Fig 45, is decorated with a duck motif applied 'en barbotine'. The significance of a single example cannot be estimated, but it may indicate that barbotine techniques were well within the repertoire of potters working at Rossington Bridge, in which case, the most obvious products would have been poppyhead beakers of Gillam (1970) types 70/71, in parisian fabrics. It may represent a new line which was tried out but found no market. Clearly decorative techniques, which either cut down into the surface or built it up in relief, could be and were used by the same workshop (Rigby 1989).

117. Carinated bowl? Black (N2) surfaces smoothed on exterior, with dark grey (N4–5) core. Swan or duck and two blobs in applied clay.
RB/-/?L.6.

118–157. Parisian ware vessels, plain and decorated.

118. Rim of a poppy-head beaker, diameter indeterminate. Dark grey surfaces with grey core.
RB/-/?L.3

119. Rim of poppy-head beaker, diameter indeterminate. Dark grey (N4) surfaces with silvery sheen and light grey (N6–8) sandwich core.
RB/8L/-.

120. Rim of poppy-head beaker. Dark grey abraded surfaces, light grey and grey sandwich core.
RB/4/S.1 (stokehole to kiln 4).

121. Greater part of poppy-head beaker with vertically applied stamps (Fig 42, 4), between groups of three impressed circles below groove on girth; stamps DL2, divided rectangle, and single ring DO1, probably the same die as used on vessels 126, 130–1. Very dark grey (N3) surfaces, highly burnished on the exterior, light grey (N7) and grey (N5) sandwich core. Stamp Group B.
RB/7.1/L.5a.

122. Part profile of a poppy-head beaker with impressed 'ears of corn' stamps below circles (cf Fig 42, 2) on body; stamps DO1 single ring, stamped over at least the upper end of fern-

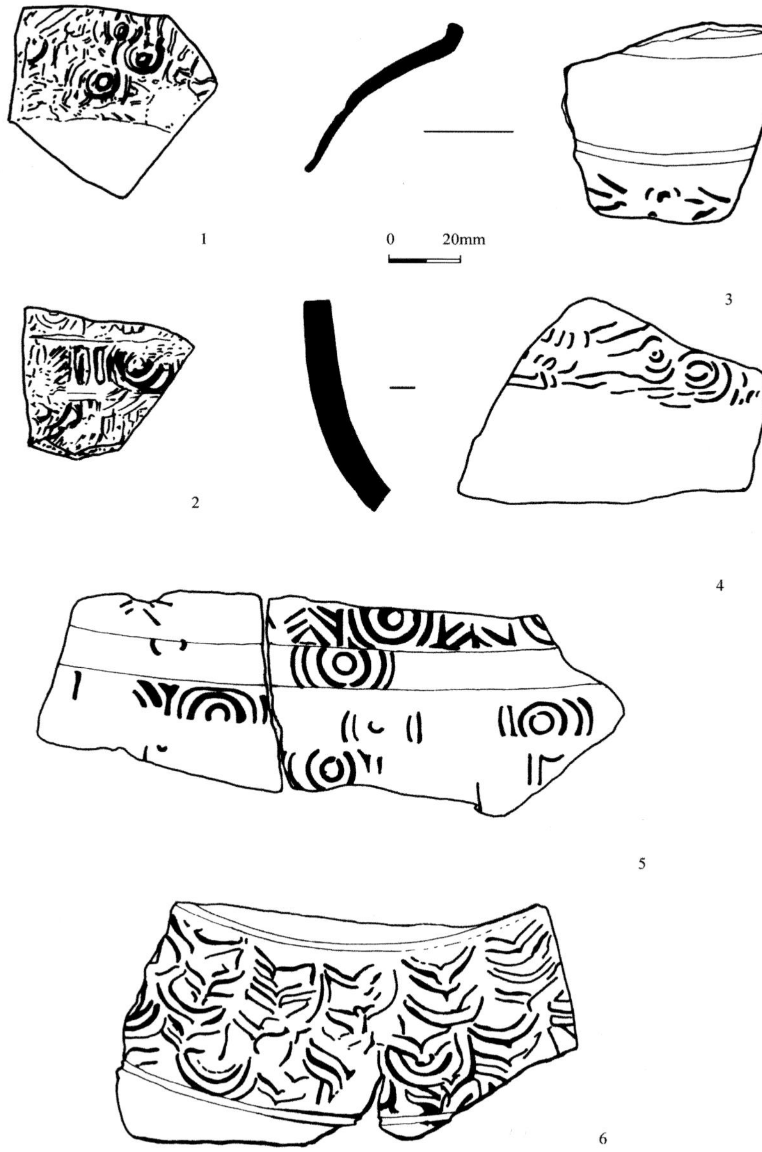

Figure 44. Roller-stamped sherds from Rossington Bridge and Rossington Bridge Farm. Drawing: M. Durrant.

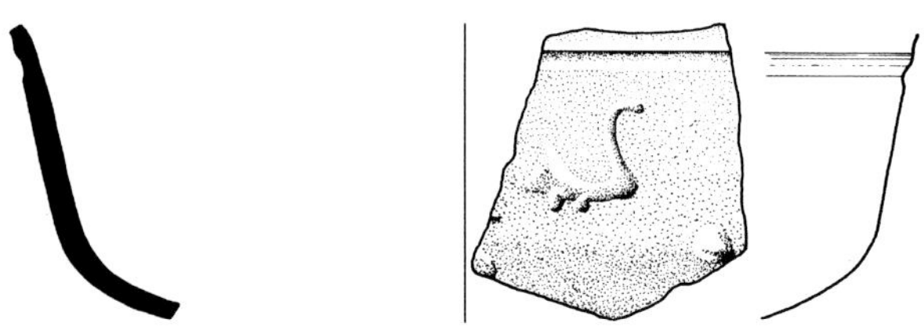

Figure 45. Bowl with barbotined duck motif. Drawing: M. Durrant.

leaf DF1. Black smoothed exterior surface with slight silvery sheen. Grey interior surface and core. Stamp Group A. RB/- Unstratified. **122a** and **b**, not figured, are stamped with the same dies.

123. Sherd from a wide-bodied beaker as **125** below, with impressed groups of lozenges between vertical stamps; divided rectangle DL2, and double diamond DD1 stamps. Black surfaces with traces of burnishing on exterior. Light grey and dark grey sandwich core. Stamp Group B.
RB/3/S (stokehole to kiln 3).
123a, not figured, is a sherd stamped with the same dies.

124. Sherd from a round bodied closed vessel with single strand cord impression, stamp DT1 (Fig 42, 10). A pale brown (10YR 6/3) fabric, with burnished exterior surface, light brown (7.5YR 6/4) interior and dark grey (N6-7) core, fired to a stoneware hardness. Stamp Group A.
RB/17–18R/- Unstratified.

124a-d, not figured, in a hard fine grey fabric, are stamped with die DT2.

125. Wide-bodied beaker with impressed vertical stamps between circular ones with impressed diamond above and below

between cordons (Fig 42, 5); stab impressions S, rosette stamp DR1 and lozenge DL1. Very dark grey (N2) surfaces, burnished exterior with dark grey (N4) core. Stamp Group A.
RB/3/S (stokehole to kiln 3).
125a, not figured, is a sherd stamped with the same dies.

126. Wide-bodied beaker, with vertical stamps between circular ones and multiple cordon above (see Fig 42, 7); Stamps, single ring DO1, from the same die as **130–1**, and divided rectangle DL3. Light grey (10YR 7/2) fabric with traces of burnishing on exterior surface. Traces of grey (N5) surface on interior surface. Slight footring on base. Stamp Group B.
RB/4–5/S (stokehole to kilns 4 and 5).
cf Birrens (Robertson, 1975) fig 76, 30 and 33, the latter an 1/8 scale reconstruction of this vessel; the Birrens sherd is almost certainly a Rossington product.

127. Wide-bodied beaker, with impressed diamonds below multiple cordons (Fig 42, No 11); Grey (N5) surfaces, burnished on exterior below decoration. Light grey (N5–6) core, very hard fabric. Stab impressions S, ?Stamp Group A.
RB/- unstratified.

128. Rim, form uncertain, but cf Winterton (Rigby and Stead 1976, no 29). Grey-brown abraded surfaces over a smooth grey pelleted core.
RB/4/S.l (stokehole to kiln 4).

129. Rim, form probably as **125**, Dark grey (N4) surfaces, smoothed, slightly micaceous exterior surface. A smooth fabric, with white (N8) and grey (N5) sandwich core.
RB/15.1/L.6.

130. Wide-bodied beaker, with single ring stamp DO1, from the same die as on **126** and **131** and divided rectangle DL3. A fine, smooth, light grey pelleted fabric, abraded, with traces of dark grey surfaces. Stamp Group B.
RB/4/S.2 (stokehole to kiln 4).

131. Vessel very similar to **130**, stamped with same dies, but with a different arrangement of motifs. Abraded, in a fine smooth, light grey pelleted fabric with traces of dark grey interior surface. Stamp Group B.
RB/4/S.2 (stokehole to kiln 4).

132. A high shouldered closed vessel, with stamps in a chevron pattern below impressed circles, a single ring stamp DO1, possibly the same die as on **121**, **126**, **130–1**, and divided rectangle DL2. (Fig 42, 8). Abraded, black (N1) surfaces with a fine smooth, light grey and dark grey core.
RB/-/L.5

133. Rim of a wide-bodied beaker. Traces of black surface on exterior, otherwise light grey abraded surfaces with black core.
RB/3/S (stokehole to kiln 3).

134. Cordoned beaker with two types of vertically impressed stamps below grooves and cordons; stamps, divided rectangle DL1 and combined motif C1. Abraded, grey (N5) polished exterior surface, light grey (10YR 7/1) interior surface, and inner zone, with fine pelleted, grey (N5–6) core. Stamp Group A.
RB/3/S (stokehole to kiln 3).

135. Wide bodied beaker, with impressed vertical stamp reading CVALDIC, perhaps an oculist's stamp, applied vertically between stab impressions, S, and rosette stamps DR1(Fig 42, 9 and Fig 43). A smooth, soft dark grey (N4) fabric, with polished black (N1) exterior surface. Stamp Group A.
RB/7.1/L.5a.
Although figured with the Rossington products for comparison, this vessel, despite the equation of the name stamp with that of the mortarium maker DICCIA, is unlikely to be a local product, as the fabric is markedly distinct from all other Rossington parisian vessels. Boon (1983) has drawn attention to the use of oculist's (*collyrium*) stamps on samian vessels from La Graufesenque, and the Rossington piece may be a further example of this.

135a, not figured, a sherd from a second vessel stamped with same rosette (DR1) die, comes from RB/3/-

136. Rim of beaker as **134**. Abraded smooth grey (N6) surfaces with traces of burnishing on exterior, lighter grey core.
RB/4/K.2 (from the interior of kiln 4). A further example in the same group has a light grey (N7) core with oxidised pinkish (5YR 8/6) to light red (2.5YR 6/8) surface.

137. Pedestal base of vessel as **121** or **126**. Abraded grey-brown surfaces with some traces of polishing on exterior. Light grey and black sandwich core.
RB/3/S (stokehole to kiln 3).

138. As **137**. Grey, abraded fabric. Slight footring on base.
RB/- unstratified.

139. Neck of flask similar to **142** below, in a grey fabric.
RB/3/- (from kiln 3).

140. Rim of flask. Grey (N5) surface, over light grey zone and grey (N6) core.
RB/3/- (from kiln 3).

141. Neck of flask probably as form **145** below. Soft 'sandwich' of dark grey (N3) with grey outer zone and traces of polished grey (N4) surface, but very abraded.
RB/- unstratified.

142. Full profile of flask with two rows of vertically impressed stamps (see Fig 42, 1) between grooves; Stamps are divided rectangle DL1, and fern-leaf DF1. Abraded, metallic, dark grey finish over a light grey core. Stamp Group A.
RB/?3/S (probably from the stokehole to kiln 3).

143. Sherd from the body of a large, rounded and closed vessel, probably a flask as **142**, with vertical impressed stamps (see Fig 42, 6) below impressed curved lines; stamps, a divided rectangle DL1, probably from the same die as that used on **125**, but lightly impressed. Very hard fine grey (N5) fabric. Slightly darker (N3–4) outer surface with metallic sheen and polished. Stamp Group A.
RB/17–18/- unstratified.

144. Rounded and closed vessel, probably a flask, similar to **142**, with fern-leaf stamps, die DF1, between circular stamps, die DR2, between grooves. Black surfaces, smoothed on exterior with a metallic sheen; abraded interior surface with grey core. Stamp Group A.
RB/- unstratified.

145. Flask, similar to **142**, with fern-leaf stamps, die DF1, with small ring stamp DO1 stamped over both ends, between grooves (Fig 42, 1). At least 6 sherds from the same vessel but some variation in condition of fabric. Several sherds have a smooth black (N2) surface with a metallic sheen on the exterior; others have the more usual dull black (N2) glossy surface. All have a white (N8) and grey (N6) sandwich core. Stamp Group A.
RB/- unstratified.

146. A globular vessel of uncertain form, with fine stabbed decoration below groove and cordon (Fig 42, 13). Traces of dark grey surfaces over a fine pelleted light grey core.
RB/4/S.2 (stokehole to kiln 4).

147. Large rounded and closed vessel form, perhaps as **142**, with impressed circular stamps, die DR2, stamped over at least

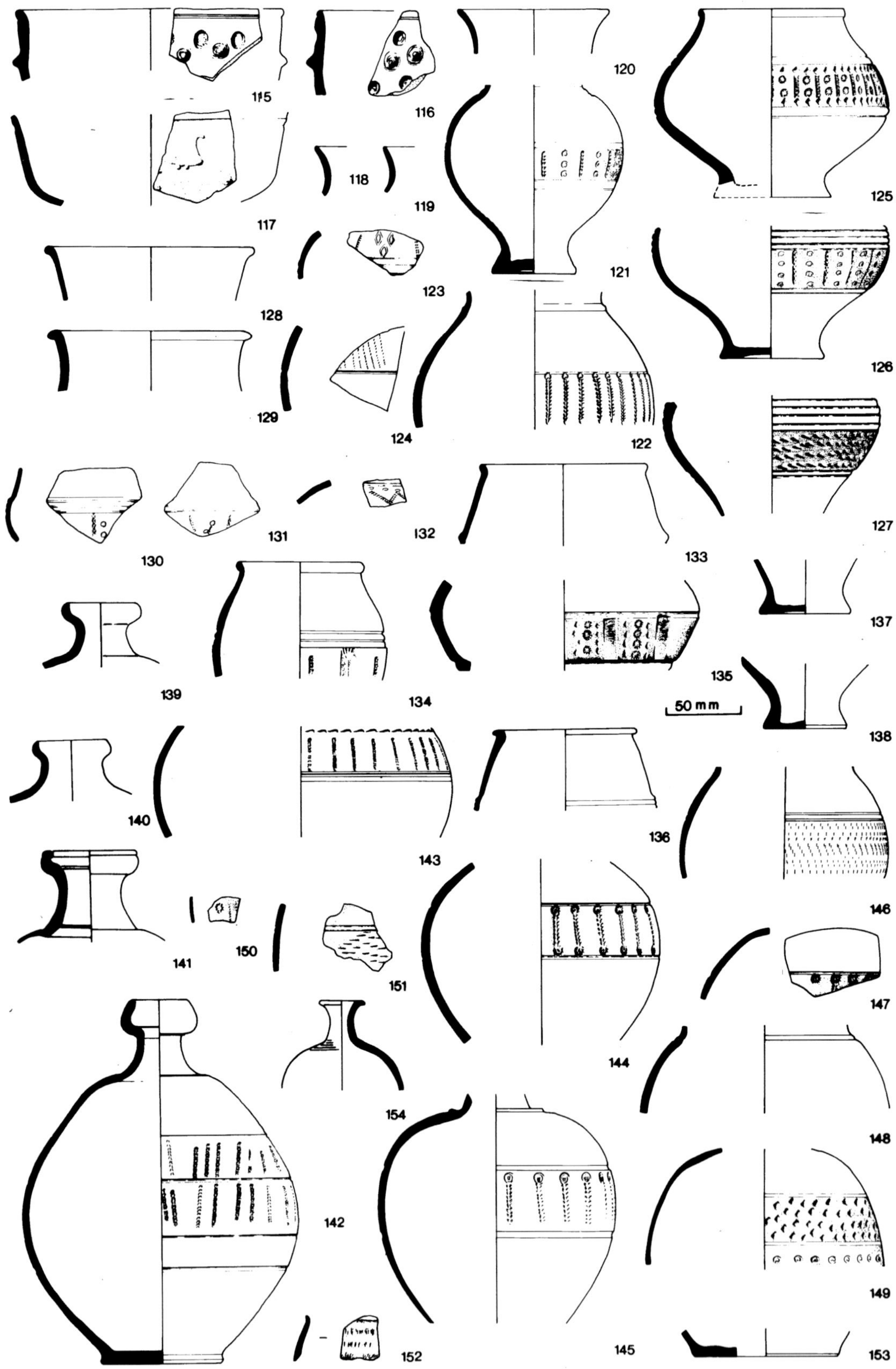

Figure 46. Rossington Bridge pottery: black burnished bowls (Nos 115–117) and parisian fabric vessels, Nos 118–154.

the upper end of fern-leaf DF1, below a shoulder groove (Fig 42, 3). Abraded, dark grey surfaces, grey core. Stamp Group A.
RB/- unstratified.

148. Part of body of plain vessel, perhaps a poppy head beaker. Dark grey surfaces, both with metallic sheen, over a very hard grey core.
RB/-/L.5.

149. Sherd from a rounded and closed vessel form, probably a flask, with stab impressions, S, and single ring, die DO1, stamps over upper end of either a fern-leaf (DF), or lozenge shaped motif (DL). Light grey (N6), fine pelleted fabric with traces of smoothed grey (N6) surfaces over light grey (2.5Y 7/2) outer zone. Very abraded. Fabric contains several black angular grits, maximum size 2mm.
RB/3/S (stokehole to kiln 3).

149a, not figured, is a sherd from a second example, with stab impressions, S, and single rings, DO1.

150. Form uncertain, with impressed rosettes, die DR1 and single strand cord impressions, die DT? Smoothed black exterior surface, over a fine smooth grey core.
RB/-/L.4.

151. Form probably as **127**, with stab impressions below a groove (Fig 42, 11). Oxidised or burnt pink (5YR 7/4) fabric with light red core. RBF/2/S, from the Rossington Bridge Farm kilns to the south of the river Torne, see also **14** (Fig 54) from that kiln group. With the roller-stamped sherds, this vessel provides a link between the two workshops.

152. Sherd with rouletted decoration, form uncertain. Black exterior surface with traces of burnishing. Dark grey interior surface, with light grey and black sandwich core. Fabric fine and smooth but softer than usual.
RB/-/L.3.

153. Base, probably for a vessel as **142**. Dark grey surfaces, except for the base which is light grey, dark grey core, overfired. Traces of wire marks on base.
RB/- unstratified.

154. Bottle, or small flask. Grey (N4) exterior surface, burnished to shoulder; light grey (N7) interior surface and core.
RB/25.1/L.4.

155. Plain beaker, as the stamped parisian vessels **125–126**. Smooth light grey fabric.
RB/- unstratified.

156. Beaker, in the same fabric as the stamped parisian vessels. Smooth dark grey (N4) fabric, burnished to very dark grey (N3) to white (N8) on exterior surface.
RB/4/S.1 (stokehole to kiln 4).

157. Base of small beaker, in the same fabric as the stamped vessels. Dark grey (N3) surfaces with metallic sheen on exterior. Light grey (N7) and grey (N6) sandwich core. Traces of wire marks on partly burnished base.
RB/8.1/L.5a. The form also occurs in a slightly coarser grey fabric with burnished surface.

Type D. Beakers in other fabrics

The small beakers with bead or everted rim in a parisian fabric are matched by a small number of examples in BB1. One, **159**, is sufficiently complete to be certain that it lacked a handle, whilst the much larger example, **160**, has a peg insertion point for a handle of rectangular section, similar to **235** below. Although both these vessels are plain, a further example in a similar fabric has a zone of acute lattice; similar examples are regarded as Antonine by Gillam (1976).

The remaining beakers cover a wide range of forms, distinct from those used in parisian, and are mostly rather coarser vessels. Only the bag-shaped beaker with clay pellet rough casting might be termed a fine ware, deriving ultimately from East Gaulish industries (Symonds 1990), although the Rossington vessel presents a rather simplified everted rim, rather than a true cornice.

158. Small beaker, in the same fabric as the stamped vessels, light grey, with traces of polishing on exterior surface. Fine fabric but containing numerous small black grits. For a probable handle, see **235** below.
RB/4/S.2 (the stokehole to kiln 4).
cf Birrens (Robertson 1975) fig 76, 28, where the fabric is described as 'parisian'. The form continued to be made in the same fabric later in the 2nd century at Blaxton Quarry (Buckland and Dolby, 1980, nos 44–48).

159. A complete small, handle-less beaker with everted rim, similar to parisian and grey ware examples but in the BB1 fabric. Dark to light grey (N1–5) fabric, roughly burnished on the outer surface and rather irregular in form.
RB/- unstratified.

160. Beaker, with everted rim, in a BB1 fabric. Body pierced just below the shoulder of the vessel for the attachment of a rectangular section handle. Light grey (N7) gritty fabric with dark grey (N4) burnished surface.
RB/25.1/L.4.

161. Beaker, BB1. Reddish brown (2.5YR 5/4) to dark grey (N3) surface with grey (N4) core. Burnished on outer surface and inside rim, lattice decoration. Hand-made, a single example of a less common BB1 form.
RB/8WMB/L.5a.

162. Pedestal base of small beaker, in a hard grey (N6) fabric, lustrous, metallic sheen on both surfaces.
RB/8.1/L.5a.

163. Full profile of a bag shaped roughcast beaker, a slightly distorted waster, in a brown (10YR 5/3) fabric, burnished round neck, with clay pellet roughcasting. Cut wire marks on base.
RB/8WMB/L.5a.
Probably a copy of a South Carlton (Webster 1944) product, examples of which occur in the same layer (see **361–363** below).

164. Small beaker or dice box in a hard grey (N5) fabric with metallic sheen on surfaces and lighter (N6) core.
RB/9.1/L.6.

165. Small carinated beaker in a gritty pinkish-grey (7.5YR 6/2) to grey (N5) fabric, decorated on body with incised horizontal groove and irregular burnish.
RB/- ('Peg 8, under clay floor').

166. Small indented beaker, in a very dark grey (N3) fabric, with grey (N5) core; burnished on neck and base.
Joining sherds from RB/15WMB/L.3 and RB/16.1/L.5.

Jars with rusticated decoration

This group is another in which a pedantic statement of its date range has caused several problems. Thompson, both in the Cantley report (1960) and in his publication of the North Hykeham, near Lincoln, kiln (1958), suggested that the type had ceased to be produced by the early years of Hadrian, and the statement has continued to be reiterated (eg Perrin 1990, 269). At Rossington Bridge, sherds of rustic are clearly associated with mortaria of SARRIVS in kilns 1, 2 and 4, and the greater part of a jar was recovered from the stokehole to kiln 2. Sherds also occur among the wastage from Rossington Bridge Farm (Fig 44, 17–18), where there is less possibility for intrusive earlier occupation debris. In the later kilns at Bessacarr (Cantley kilns 40–44), where there is no evidence for other activities or earlier settlement, subdued linear rustication occurs on several vessels. Rusticated sherds are also recorded from the stokeholes to kilns 2 and 3 at Cantley (Annable 1960, nos 313–320). At Doncaster (Buckland and Magilton 1986) two complete rusticated jars, similar to the Rossington vessels (nos 102 and 117) were found in secure mid-Antonine contexts. Swan (1981) has suggested that the south Yorkshire rustic jars are indistinguishable from earlier examples. The rims, however, tend more towards a recurved than everted form and the rustication is crisp and linear. Most examples have a groove delineating the upper edge of the zone of rustication and are burnished above and below. Bases appear to be a simple, well-finished pedestal base and the overall form may be described as pyriform.

167. Complete jar with linear rustication below grooves on shoulder, in a dark grey fabric, with a sooty material adhering to the outer surface.
RB/12.1/L.6 (peat).

168. Jar with linear rustication in a hard grey (N5) fabric with a lustrous silvery surface.
RB/8WMB/L.5a/6.

169. Jar with trace of subdued rustication below groove on shoulder, in a hard grey (N5) fabric with lighter (N7) core, burnished above zone of rustication and on inside of rim; lustrous, silvery sheen to surface.
RB/2/S.1 (L.5) (stokehole to kiln 2).

170. Jar with linear rustication, in a hard, dark grey (N4) fabric with lighter (N5) core, lightly burnished on neck and shoulder.
RB/11.1/L.5. Probably not a Rossington product.

Type E(a) Medium sized jars/cooking pots

Jars with recurved rims form approximately 39% of the total wastage at Rossington Bridge Pumping Station, and 67% of the smaller group from Rossington Bridge Farm. The latter appear to be all wheel thrown, whilst the Pumping Station site is dominated by hand made black burnished ware (Table 8). The eroded condition of much of the wastage makes it very difficult to estimate actual percentages, but Samuels (1984 and Table 8) suggests that about 71% of total jar wastage consists of BB1 vessels, with the contents of kiln 1 including 95 (97%) in this fabric. The majority of BB1 jars are about 170mm high and 100mm in internal diameter (**172**), with a number of larger vessels (**182** and **224**), perhaps to be regarded as storage jars. In form, the Rossington wastage includes forms indistinguishable from Dorset products, although it is perhaps inevitable that, on a site where wheel thrown jars were also made, the range of rim forms includes several variants. The usual form is not a true cavetto (*sensu* Farrar 1973), but recurved and slightly drawn out. There is often a slight offset at the shoulder, a feature shared with some of the grey wares. Lattice decoration, where it survives, is always acute, although of varying quality; Williams' (1977) point about the lattice on Rossington (Gillam (1970) form 133) cooking pots being wider than on Dorset vessels (also quoted as a distinguishing feature in Tomber and Dore (1998, 202)) appears to be of doubtful validity when the whole assemblage is examined. Some, but not all, have a wavy line on the back of the neck (**173** and **215**), where burnish is usually less consistently applied. Outside the reserve zone for the lattice, burnishing is extensive and usually complete on the outside of the cooking pots, including the underside of the bases. Often the application of the burnish has left the surface with a series of sub-linear short facets up to 4mm wide. Burnish is also continued over onto the inside of the rim to the base of the neck. Similar techniques are used in the finishing of the wheel thrown vessels, and, although many of these are in a hard grey fabric, it is often difficult to distinguish the two amongst the kiln wastage. Samuel's counts (Table 8), however, give a clear indication of the dominance of BB1 over wheel-turned products both in the kiln infills and the waster tips; only in layer 4, apparently deposited after the main period of production do the latter dominate. Although Farrar (1981) has urged some caution in the close dating of BB1 on form, there can be no doubt that the Rossington pots belong early in the series in the North, and that production was contemporary with that of the mortaria of Sarrius and his co-workers.

171. Lattice decorated cooking pot, wheel-turned, in a hard grey (N4) fabric with a zone of somewhat irregular burnished acute lattice decoration. A distorted waster.
RB/4/S.l (set into the back wall of stokehole to kiln 4).

172. Complete black burnished cooking pot, BBl, in a red (2.5YR 5/8–6/8) oxidised fabric, burnished on outer surface and on inside of rim and under base; lattice decoration in reserve zone.
RB/16.1/L.5a.

173. Rim of cooking pot, 190mm in diameter, with burnished wavy line on neck, BBl, in a dark grey (N4) fabric with pink (7.5YR 7/4) oxidised surface. This is one of the few examples on which the wavy line survives.
RB/4/S.1 (stokehole to kiln 4).

174. BBl jar rim, 110mm in diameter, in a grey (N5) fabric with reddish yellow (5YR 6/6) outer zone and grey (N5) outer surface, burnished on outer surface and over rim.
RB/4/S (stokehole to kiln 4).

175. BBl jar rim, 190mm in diameter, in a light grey (N6) fabric, burnished on outer surface and rim, to dark grey (N4) and pinkish grey (7.5YR 6/2) surface; faint trace of wavy line on neck.
RB/4/S (stokehole to kiln 4).

Table 8. Numbers of wheel-turned to BB1 cooking pots in the Rossington Bridge kilns.

Type	K1	K2	K3	K4	K5	K4/5	L2	L3	L4	L5	L6	L7	L8	Unstrat.
BB1	95	96	12	49	4	20	–	29	88	292	52	5	5	642
Wheel	3	41	4	15	–	17	4	28	107	99	28	2	1	255

Counts by J. Samuels

176. BB1 jar rim, 150mm in diameter, in a grey (10YR 6/1) to greyish brown (10YR 5/2) fabric with grey (N5) core.
RB/2/S (L.4) (stokehole to kiln 2).

177. Jar rim, 100mm in diameter, in a gritty greyish brown (2.5Y 5/2) fabric with abraded, burnished surface.
RB/4/S.2 (stokehole to kiln 4).

178. BBl jar rim, 135mm in diameter, in a grey (N4) fabric, with very dark grey (N2) to light reddish brown (5YR 6/4) burnished outer surface and over rim, with lattice decoration.
RB/11.1/L.5a.

179. BBl jar rim, 115mm in diameter, in a light grey (2.5Y 7/2) to reddish yellow (5YR 7/6) fabric with some traces of grey (N6) burnishing on outer surface.
RB/4/S.l (stokehole to kiln 4).

180. BBl jar rim, badly fired but traces of a dark grey (N4) surface remain on a light brown (7.5YR 6/4) core.
RB/2/S.l (stokehole to kiln 2).

181. BBl jar rim, 125mm in diameter, in a grey (N5) fabric, with light reddish brown (5YR 6/3) outer zone and black (N2) burnished surface.
RB/11.1/L.5a.

182. Large jar in BBl with dark grey (N4) to light brownish grey (2.5Y 6/2) surface and rim, grey (N5) core, and light grey (N6) outer zone. Outer surface and rim are burnished but untreated in a zone of incised decoration.
RB/9WMB/L.5a.

183. Complete jar, wheel thrown in a soft, gritty very dark grey (5YR 3/1) fabric with dark brown (7.5YR 4/4) core; badly fire-cracked and surface peeling off. No trace of lattice decoration survives.
RB/- unstratified.

184. Jar rim, ?BB1, in a gritty light grey (N7) fabric.
RB/2/S (L.2) (stokehole to kiln 2).

185. Jar rim, in a hard dark grey (N4) fabric.
RB/2/S.1 (stokehole to kiln 2).

186. Jar rim, in a gritty grey (N6) to light grey (2.5Y 7/2) fabric.
RB/4/S.2 (stokehole to kiln 4).

187. Jar rim, 110mm in diameter, in a gritty grey (2.5Y 7/2) fabric with traces of burnished surface on outside.
RB/4/S.1 (stokehole to kiln 4).

188. Jar rim, ?BB1, in a gritty light grey (N7) fabric with traces of darker surface.
RB/4/S.2 (stokehole to kiln 4).

189. BBl jar in a grey (N5) fabric, with darker grey (N4) burnishing on outer surface and over rim, wavy line on neck and lattice on body.
RB/8.1/L.5b.

190. Jar rim, 115mm in diameter, in a light grey fabric.
RB/4/S (stokehole to kiln 4).

191. BBl jar in a light grey (N6) fabric with some darker burnished (N3) and heavily sooted outer surface.
RB/5–6WMB/L.5a.

192. Jar rim, probably BB1, in a gritty dark grey (N5) fabric, burnished outside and over rim.
RB/3/S (stokehole to kiln 3).

193. Jar, 140mm in diameter, in gritty light brownish grey (2.5Y 6/2) fabric, burnished externally and over rim.
RB/4/S (stokehole to kiln 4).

194. Jar rim, in a gritty grey (2.5Y 7/2) fabric with traces of darker surface.
RB/l/S (stokehole to kiln 1).

195. Jar rim, BBl, in a gritty grey (N5) fabric, light grey (2.5Y 6/2) internally.
RB/4/S.2 (stokehole to kiln 4).

196. Jar rim, 145mm in diameter, in a light grey (N6) fabric, with dark grey (N4) surface, burnished on inside of rim, and having a metallic lustre. Probably wheel thrown.
RB/12.1/L.6.

197. Everted rim of small jar. BB1. Smooth, slightly micaceous light grey (2.5Y 7/2) to light reddish brown (2.5YR 6/4) fabric, with traces of burnish; apparently fire cracked.
RB/9WMB/L.5a.

198. Jar rim, in a gritty grey (N6) fabric, with darker (N4) surface. Wheel thrown.
RB/4/S. (below quern in (stokehole to kiln 4).

199. Jar rim in a gritty light grey (2.5Y 7/2) fabric; wheel thrown.
RB/-/L.5.

200. Jar rim, BB1, in a light grey (N5) fabric, with light red (2.5YR 6/8) burnished surface and trace of lattice on body.
RB/12.1/L.6.

201. Jar rim, BB1. Grey (N5) fabric, with darker (N4) burnished outer surface, to inside of rim. Clearly hand-made and rather irregular in form.
RB/21.1/L.3.

202. Jar rim, BB1, in a grey (N6) fabric, with darker (N4) burnished surface.
RB/21.1/L.3.

203. Jar rim, BB1. Hard grey (N6) fabric, burnished on outside and over rim.
RB/12WMB/L.5a.

204. Jar rim in a hard grey (N5) fabric, fired sufficiently to cause surface vitrification.
RB/2/- (L.4).

205. Indented jar rim, in a hard grey (N5) fabric, burnished over rim and to a groove above a reserve indented zone.
RB/11–12.1/L.6 (peat). (One example but a few body sherds of others were recovered, including sherds from a roller stamped vessel, Fig 44, 1–2).

206. Jar rim, 110mm in diameter, in a grey (N5) fabric, with red (2.5YR 5/8) core. Wheel thrown.
RB/12.1/L.6.

207. Jar rim in an oxidised reddish yellow (5YR 7/6) fabric; abraded surfaces with some traces of dark grey (5YR 7/1) burnished surface on outside.
RB/2/-.

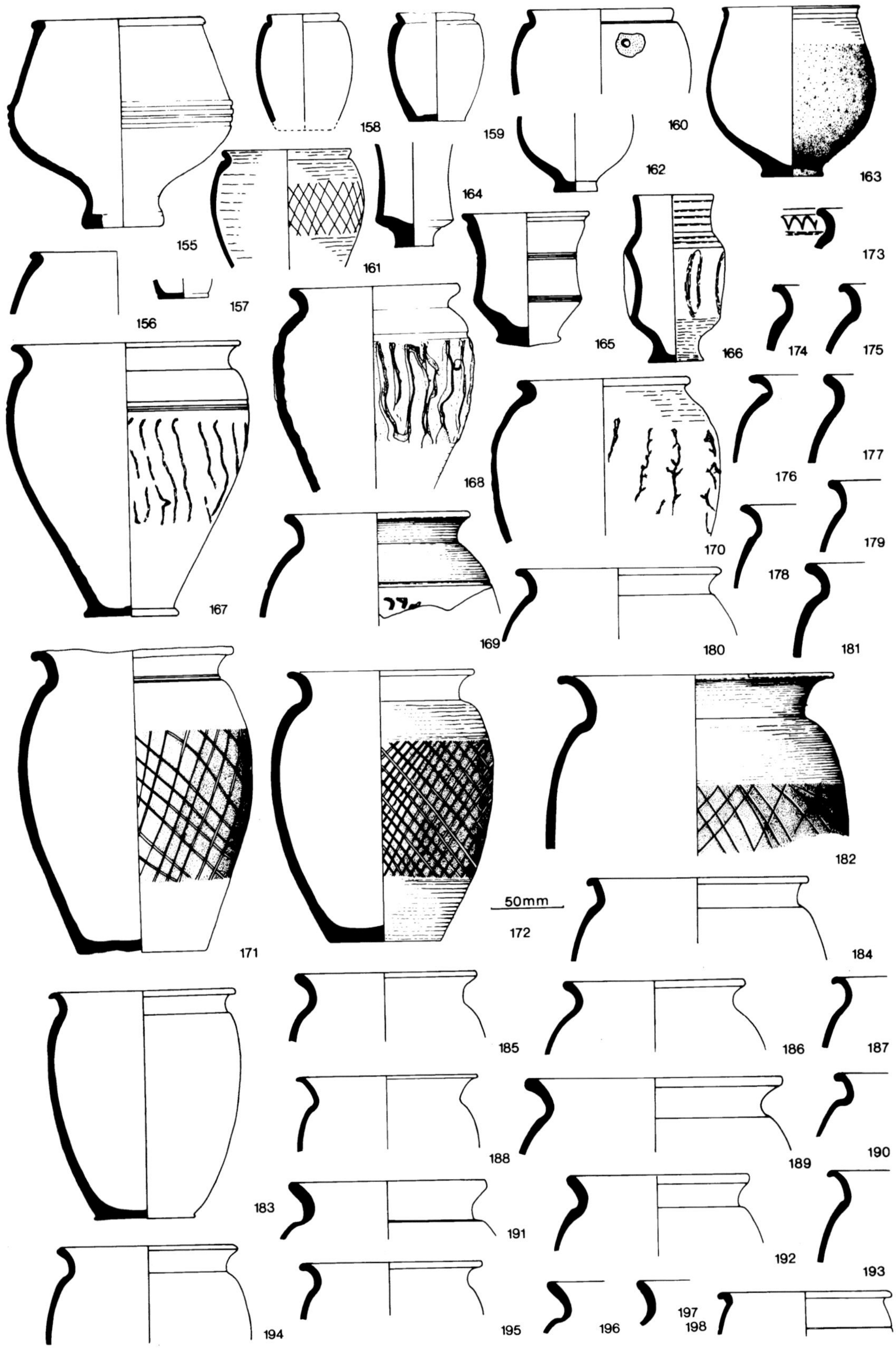

Figure 47. Rossington Bridge pottery: beakers, Nos 155–166, rusticated jars, Nos 167–170, and cooking pots/jars, Nos 171–198.

208. Jar rim, 150mm in diameter in light grey (2.5Y 7/2) fabric with traces of darker (N5) surface.
RB/2/- (L.4).

209. Jar rim in a gritty light grey (N7) fabric with traces of darker (N6) surface.
RB/4/S (stokehole to kiln 4).

210. Jar rim in a hard grey (N5) fabric, much sooted on surface. The vessel is clearly wheel thrown.
RB/8–9WMB/L.6.

211. Jar rim in a hard grey (N6) fabric, with very dark grey (N3) surface and lattice decoration; clearly wheel thrown.
RB/8WMB/L.6.

212. Jar rim in a hard grey (N6) fabric with slight traces of grey burnish on outer surface and inside rim; probably wheel thrown.
RB/2/S.1 (stokehole to kiln 2).

213. Jar rim, ?BB1, in a gritty light grey (N6) fabric, with light grey (2.5Y 7/2) outer zone and traces of a dark grey (N4) burnished surface.
RB/2/- (L.4).

214. Jar rim, BB1, in a dark grey (N4) fabric, with oxidised light red (2.5YR 6/6) surface and traces of lattice decoration.
RB/9WMB/L.5a.

215. Jar rim, BB1, in an oxidised light red (2.5YR 6/6) fabric with grey (N5) core; burnished over rim and with wavy line on neck.
RB/9.1/L.6.

Type E(b) Lid-seated jars

Todd (1968) has noted the widespread occurrence of grey ware lid-seated jars, distinct from the coarser harder fabric of Derbyshire Ware (Gillam (1970) type 152), on many sites in the East Midlands. It is apparent that kilns in south Yorkshire, particularly those at Blaxton (Buckland and Dolby 1980, nos 88–120), were major suppliers of this form from the mid-2nd century onwards, and occasional examples reached Hadrian's Wall (Dryden and Withell 1978, no 29, from Banks East Turret, west of Birdoswald). The form was also made in York, the butt-shaped jars of Gillam (1968, nos 48–68), where Swan (1994), whilst acknowledging the south Yorkshire parallels, has suggested a connection with Gallia Narbonensis for the type. Several of the Rossington vessels are in the same fabric as the Blaxton and Cantley vessels, but others are in an oxidised red fabric with much ironstone temper, and are more similar to the so-called pre-Derbyshire Ware products of the Derby Racecourse kilns (Brassington 1971, fig 11, 244–253), where production probably began in the Hadrianic period.

216. Complete lid-seated jar in a hard grey fabric with slightly sooted exterior, base string-cut and unfinished.
RB/8.1/L.6. The form also occurs among the wastage from the kilns.

217. Jar with shallowly lid-seated rim in a hard, oxidised reddish yellow (5YR 7/8) fabric, with traces of reddish brown (5YR 5/3) surface and some red ironstone temper.
RB/16.1/L.4.

218. Lid-seated jar in a hard, vitrified grey (N5) fabric with red (2.5YR 5/8) outer zone and grey (N5) surfaces.
RB/11WMB/L.5.

219. Rim of a lid-seated jar in a hard grey (N5–6) fabric.
RB/15.1/L.4.

220. Rim of a lid-seated jar, in an oxidised light reddish brown (5YR 6/4) fabric, with large quartz and ironstone temper; sooted over rim.
RB/9.1/L.5.
Despite the close resemblance to Derbyshire Ware (Gillam 1938), this is a Rossington product; see the further examples from kilns 3 and 4 below.

221. Lid-seated jar in a hard, oxidised light red (2.5YR 5/8) fabric, with grey (N6) surface and much red ironstone temper.
RB/3/S (stokehole to kiln 3).

222. Lid-seated jar rim in a hard, gritty dark grey (10YR 4/1) fabric with abundant red ironstone temper, as **220–1** above.
RB/4/S.2 (stokehole to kiln 4).
cf Derby Racecourse (Brassington 1980) fig 17, 497.

223. Bell-mouthed jar with gently rilled surface in a light red (2.5YR 7/8) oxidised fabric with evident quartz and ironstone temper, up to 3mm across, similar to **220** above.
RB/3/S (stokehole to kiln 3).
Rilled surfaces also occur occasionally on some of the Derby Racecourse products (eg Brassington 1971, fig 11, 348; 1980, fig 17, 467, 470–1), but in south Yorkshire are more typical of the flanged lid-seated jars from both Blaxton (Buckland and Dolby 1980, nos 121–129) and Cantley (Annable 1960, fig 9, 69–75).

Type F. Large jars

The vessels in this class (F) do not form a coherent group, and preservation is often insufficient to ascertain whether handles were intended. The few BB1 examples, however, (**224**) lack the countersunk handles typical of Dorset production of the type, and the remainder clearly belong to the grey ware wheel turned tradition evident at other Cantley, Blaxton and Branton kilns, continuing with little change through into at least the early 4th century.

224. Rim of large jar, BB1, with rather obtuse lattice. Light grey (N7) fabric with sooted (N6) surface. RB/9.1/L.5. A further example from the same layer has a lustrous black (N2.5) burnished surface and weak red (2.5YR 4/2) outer layer over a grey (N6) core.

225. Large jar with burnished wavy line on shoulder in a fine light grey (10YR 7/1) fabric with light grey (N7) core and dark grey (N4) slightly burnished outer surface and rim, with metallic lustre to outer surface.
RB/15WMB/L.5a.

226. Handle plugged through wall of vessel as **228** in a hard gritty grey (N6) fabric.
RB/3/S (stokehole to kiln 3).

227. Large jar, in a smooth, light grey (N6) fabric with light reddish brown (5YR 6/3) core and dark grey (N4) surface.
RB/12WMB/L.4.

228. Large jar with lugged handles in a hard light grey (N6) fabric, with lustrous (N5) surface sheen.
RB/25.1/L.5.

Type G(a). Flagons

Flagons and flasks form a small proportion of the products at Rossington, and the examples in finer fabrics have been dealt with previously under the heading parisian ware.

229. Neck of small flagon with dark grey (N4) surfaces, and pinkish grey (7.5YR 7/2) core.
RB/2/S (stokehole to kiln 2).

230. Body of small flagon in a hard, light grey (N3–5) fabric with metallic sheen and lighter (N6) core. RB/9L/L.6 (peat).

231. Body of a globular flagon in a fine, red-brown fabric, with a white slip on the outer surface.
RB/10.1/L.3.

232. Flagon neck, in a gritty oxidised pink (7.5YR 7/4) fabric with abraded white (10YR 7/2) slip.
RB/4/S.2 (stokehole to kiln 4).

233. Two-handled flagon in an oxidised pink (5YR 7/4) fabric with grey (N6) core. One handle attached, and traces of where the other had been applied.
RB/8.1/L.5.
Although an atypical fabric, the similarity to **244** *et seq* from kiln 2 below, suggests that these were Rossington products. cf Doncaster (Buckland and Magilton 1986), fig 37, 131) Hadrianic – Antonine.

234. Sherd from the pinched spout of a flagon, in a hard grey (N6) fabric with darker (N4) surface.
RB/9.1/L.5. (one example).

235. Handle, either of a small flagon or a beaker as **155** above. Smooth grey (N6) fabric, partly oxidised to light reddish brown (2.5YR 6/4).
RB/5/S (stokehole to kiln 5). A further example, unstratified, is in the same fabric as many of the parisian vessels.

236. Handle, probably from a two-handled flagon in a hard, partly vitrified grey (N5) fabric, with slight traces of lustrous surface.
RB/4/S (L.3) (stokehole to kiln 4). A similar, smaller example comes from the same group.

Type G(b). Narrow-necked jars

237. Narrow-necked jar with dark grey to black (N2–3) surfaces, black burnished on rim and below neck with grey (N6) core and white (N8) outer zone; metallic lustre on outer surface. The vessel was clearly without handles.
RB/8.1/L.5.

238. Rim of narrow-necked jar in an oxidised pink (5YR 7/4) fabric, with light grey (N7) core and crudely frilled decoration.
RB/9–10WMB/-.

239. Narrow-necked jar in a light grey (2.5Y 7/2) fabric, with grey (N6) surface.
RB/2/S (stokehole to kiln 2).

240. Narrow-necked jar with grey (N6) surfaces and a burnished metallic lustre on outer surface to inside of rim, and light grey (N5–6) sandwich core.
RB/10.1/L.5.

241. Two-handled narrow-necked jar/flagon, diameter indeterminate, with dark grey surfaces with metallic lustre and grey core. Frilled decoration at base of neck and attachment marks for handles, which are unplugged.
RB/7.1/L.5a.

242. Ribbed handle, probably from a narrow-necked jar in a hard dark grey (N5) fabric, with lustrous surface.
RB/8.1/L.5.

243. Narrow-necked jar in a gritty light olive-grey (5Y 6/1) fabric.
RB/2/S (L.4) (stokehole to kiln 2).

244. Narrow-necked jar, 110mm in diameter, in a light grey (N6) fabric, with darker (N4) outer layer and surface.
RB/2/S (stokehole to kiln 2).

245. Narrow-necked jar, 100mm in diameter, in a gritty light grey (N7) fabric, with abraded surfaces but traces of light brownish grey (10YR 6/2) burnished surface survive.
RB/2/S.1 (stokehole to kiln 2).

246. Narrow-necked jar in a light grey (2.5Y 7/2) fabric, with traces of grey (N5) surface.
RB/2/S (stokehole to kiln 2).

247. Narrow-necked jar in a gritty, grey (N5) fabric, with light grey (2.5Y 7/2) surface.
RB/2/S (stokehole to kiln 2).

248. Narrow-necked jar in a gritty, light red (2.5YR 6/6) fabric, with dark grey (N4) surface.
RB/4/S (stokehole to kiln 4).

249. Narrow-necked jar in a hard, light grey (N6) fabric, with dark grey (N4) lustrous surface.
RB/10WMB/L.5a.

250. Narrow necked jar in a gritty, grey (N5) fabric with darker (N6) core.
RB/- unstratified.

251. Ribbed handle from narrow-necked jar or flagon in a hard grey (N6) fabric, with metallic (N5) lustre on outer surface; handle burnished and plugged.
RB/11.1/L.5 The vessel is unique amongst the Rossington products and the single applied strip to one side of the handle indicates the possibility of a face jar / flagon; traces of three other applied strips occur below the handle.

252. The base of a small ribbed handle, probably from narrow-necked jar. Oxidised light red (2.5YR 6/8) fabric with grey (N5) core and traces of slip.
RB/4/S (stokehole to kiln 4).

253. Narrow-necked jar with dark grey (N4) surfaces, burnished on rim, with three burnished lines and intersecting wavy lines on neck; light brown (7.5YR 6/4) and grey (N6) sandwich core.
RB/8.1/L.3. A further example, distorted in firing, from RB/7.1/L.5a, has a groove on the top of the rim and is in a hard grey (N5) fabric.

254. Narrow-necked jar with a bead rim, in an oxidised reddish yellow (5YR 7/6) fabric, with grey (N6) core and traces of burnish and white (N8) slip on outer surface and inside rim. A joining sherd is reduced to grey (N6).
RB/4/S (stokehole to kiln 4).

Type H(a). Colanders

Both rounded and flat-based colanders or strainers appear to have been made on the Rossington Bridge site, the flat-based form with a flat reeded rim continuing into the 4th century at Branton (Buckland 1976).

255. Flat-bottomed colander or strainer in a grey (N5) fabric, with darker (N4) surface, burnished on rim and with wire marks on outside of base. The 2mm holes have been pushed through from the outside. Apparently hand made.
RB/WMB/- unstratified.

256. Rim, possibly from a strainer, in an oxidised light red (2.5YR 6/8) fabric, with patches of grey (N5) surface; very abraded.
RB/3/S (stokehole to kiln 3).

257. Rounded base of a colander or strainer in a hard grey (N6)

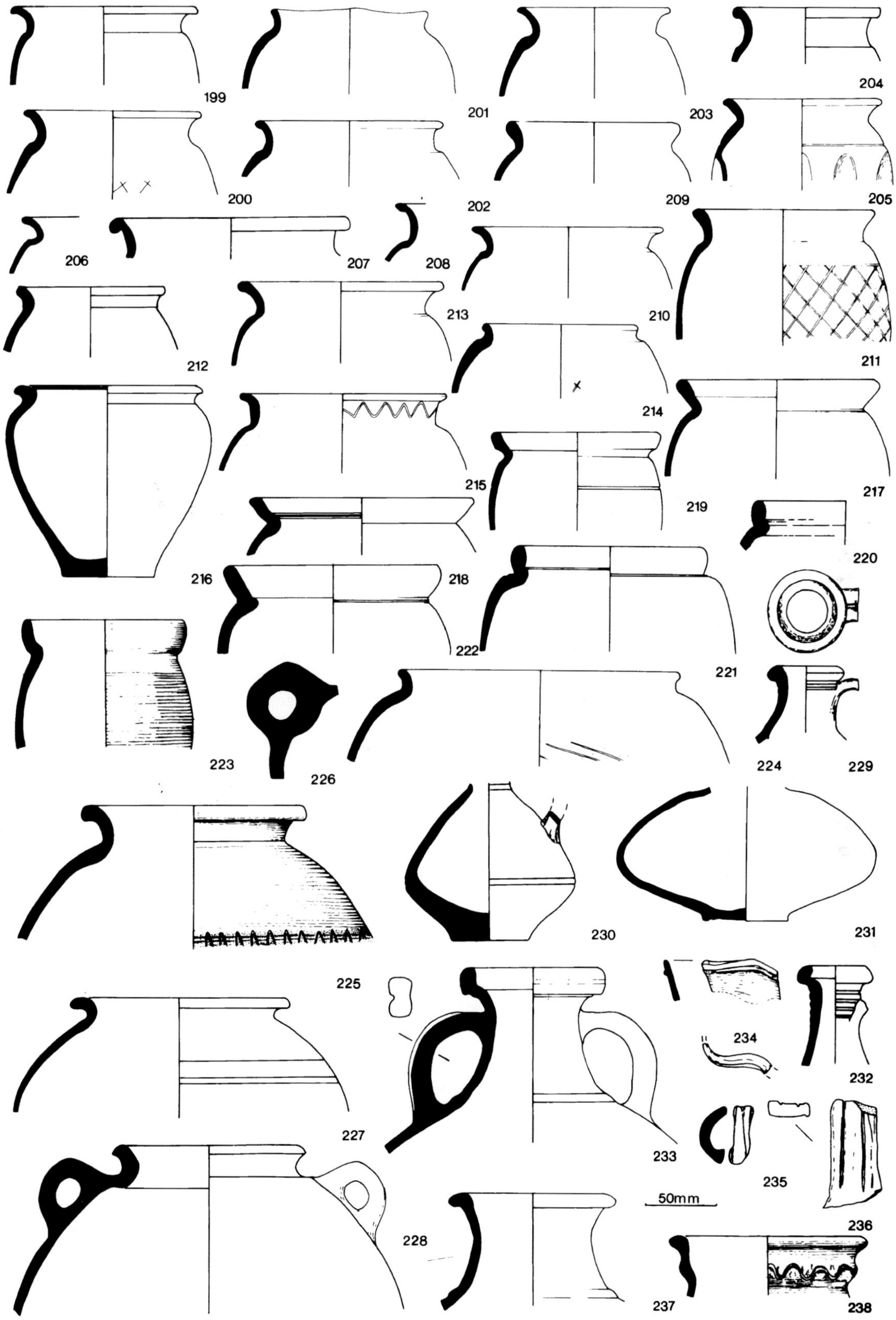

Figure 48. Rossington Bridge pottery: jars/cooking pots, Nos 199–215, lid-seated jars, Nos 216–223, large jars, Nos 224–228, flagons, Nos 229–236, and narrow-necked jars, Nos 237–238.

fabric, with lighter outer zone and dark grey (N4) burnished surface.
RB/8.1/L.5a.

258. Reeded rim of colander or strainer in a dark grey (N3) fabric, burnished on rim and outer surface.
RB/- unstratified.
For full profile, see Branton (Buckland 1976) no 64, where the type is 4th century.

259. Base of strainer, probably as **258**. Smooth light grey (N7) fabric with darker (N4) burnished surface. Circular holes, 2mm in diameter pushed through from inside the base.
RB/14.1/L.3.

260. Base of colander or strainer in a grey (N5) fabric, with lighter (N6–7) surface. Circular holes, 3.5mm in diameter, pushed through from outside of base.
RB/- unstratified.

Type H(b). Shoulder bowls/wide-mouthed jars

Problems of differentiating jar from bowl rims in the fragmented material from the waster tips led Samuels (1984) to include these groups together in his counts. They do, however, appear to provide a small proportion of the wastage, and all are wheel turned.

261. Wide-mouthed jar with dark grey to black surfaces and grey core. Burnished wavy line and horizontal decoration on outer surface.
RB/12.1/L.5/6.

262. Wide-mouthed jar in a smooth grey (N6) fabric with very dark grey (N3) surface, burnished over rim and between wavy line decoration.
RB/2/S (stokehole to kiln 2).

263. Wide-mouthed jar, 200mm in diameter, in a light grey (2.5Y 7/2) fabric, with dark grey (N4) surface.
RB/3/S (stokehole to kiln 3).

264. Wide-mouthed jar, 160mm in diameter, in a light grey (2.5Y 7/2) fabric, with darker (N5) surface. Trace of burnish on top of rim.
RB/4/S.1 (stokehole to kiln 4).

265. Wide-mouthed jar, diameter indeterminate, in a hard grey (N6) fabric, with light brownish grey (2.5Y 6/2) surface.
RB/2/S (stokehole to kiln 2).

266. Wide-mouthed jar, diameter indeterminate, in a hard grey (N6) fabric.
RB/2/S (stokehole to kiln 2).

267. Wide-mouthed jar, 160mm in diameter, with grey (N5) outer surface, gritty light grey (N7) core and inside surface.
RB/2/S (stokehole to kiln 2).

268. Wide-mouthed jar, in a hard, light grey (N6) fabric, with lighter (N7) core; a zone of wavy-line decoration between burnished zones and traces of pinkish white (7.5YR 8/2) on surface.
RB/15WMB/L3.

269. Wide-mouthed jar with grey (N5) surfaces with light grey (N7) core, metallic lustre and wavy-line decoration on outer surface.
RB/25.1/L.3.

270. Wide-mouthed jar in a light grey (10YR 6/1) fabric, with black (N2) burnished surface, burnished over onto inside of rim. Wheel thrown.
RB/10WMB/L.5.

271. Wide-mouthed jar, 170mm in diameter, in a hard, light grey (N6) fabric, with darker (N4) pimply surface. A further example from the same context is undecorated, in a roughly burnished light grey fabric with irregular black burnished outer surface; the base is poorly finished and distorted.
RB/15WMB/L.3.

272. Wide-mouthed jar, 220mm in diameter, in a gritty light grey (2.5Y 7/2) fabric, with dark grey (N4) surface.
RB/2/S (stokehole to kiln 2).

Types H(c) – (d). Medium-sized and large bowls

These types form a gradational series and cannot be subdivided easily in the Rossington assemblages. The truncated conical form is characteristic of the South Yorkshire potteries, first appearing at Rossington. The basic form is a truncated cone, usually with the base unfinished and showing the marks of string cut removal from the wheel. The bifid form of rim appears to be restricted to 2nd century kilns in the region, occurring also at Cantley (Annable 1960, fig 10, 128–132; Cregeen 1957, fig 4, 149–150), but absent from Blaxton (Buckland and Dolby 1980); Rigby and Stead (1976, fig 83, 87) note similar less pronounced forms from both Winterton and Norton Disney in Lincolnshire. The majority of vessels bear only a pair of shallow grooves on the body below the rim, although a few examples have incised wavy lines.

273. Rim of medium sized bowl, 180mm in diameter, in a grey (N6) fabric; traces of burnish survive on top of rim.
RB/3/S (stokehole to kiln 3).

274. Rim of medium sized bowl / wide mouthed jar in a hard, pimply grey (N4) fabric, with metallic (N5) lustre.
RB/10WMB/L.5.

275. Rim of medium sized bowl in a gritty light grey (N7) fabric, with traces of darker surface.
RB/4/S.2 (stokehole to kiln 4).

276. Rim of medium sized bowl in a hard, gritty grey (N5) fabric.
RB/4/S.2 (stokehole to kiln 4).

277. Complete medium sized bowl in a black (N2) fabric, with grey (N5) core, burnished on top of rim. A waster, cracked in firing. String cut and partly finished base.
RB/- unstratified.

278. Bowl rim, in a gritty light grey (N7) to yellowish red (5YR 5/8) fabric, with grey (N5) surface.
RB/2/S (stokehole to kiln 2).

279. Medium sized bowl / wide-mouthed jar, 200mm in diameter, in a gritty reddish yellow (5YR 6/8) fabric with grey (N5) core and traces of dark grey (N4) burnished surfaces.
RB/2/S (stokehole to kiln 2).

280. Bowl rim, 240mm in diameter, in a hard grey (N6) fabric.
RB/4/S.2 (stokehole to kiln 2). (One example).

281. Medium sized bowl rim, 220mm in diameter, in a very pale brown (10YR 7/4) fabric.
RB/2/S (stokehole to kiln 2).

282. Medium sized bowl rim, 180mm in diameter, in a light grey (N7) fabric, burnished on top of rim.
RB/4/- (kiln 4).

283. Bowl rim, 240mm in diameter, in a gritty pink (7.5YR 7/4) to light grey (10YR 6/1) fabric.
RB/4/S (stokehole to kiln 4).

284. Sherd from medium sized bowl with combed wavy line decoration bounded by grooves, in a light grey (2.5Y 7/2) fabric with greyish brown (2.5Y 5/2) abraded surface.
RB/2/S (stokehole to kiln 2).

285. Large bowl with grooved lip, 320mm in diameter, in a gritty grey (N5) fabric with darker grey (N4) surface. RB/5/K (interior of kiln 5).

286. Large bowl in a gritty pale brown (10YR 6/3) fabric, with traces of darker grey (N4) abraded surface. RB/2/S (stokehole to kiln 2).

287. Full profile of large bowl with black (N1) sooty outer surface, grey (N4) core and inner surface; string cut marks on base. RB/9WMB/L.5a.

288. Large bowl in a grey (N6) fabric, with darker (N1–5) surface. RB/- unstratified.

289. Large bowl/? large jar with grooved lip, 220mm in diameter, in a grey (10YR 6/1) fabric, with oxidised reddish yellow (5YR 7/6) surface and white (10YR 8/2) slip, as the mortaria. RB/4/S (stokehole to kiln 4). (One example, but cf **292** below).

290. Bowl with grooved lip, 210mm in diameter, in a gritty dark grey (N4) fabric with grey (5Y 5/1) surface; some burnish on top of rim. RB/4/S (stokehole to kiln 4).

291. Medium sized bowl rim in a grey (N5) fabric, with dark grey surface. RB/9.1/L.5.

292. Large bowl/? jar with grooved lip, in a gritty grey (2.5Y 7/2) fabric, with dark grey (N4) surface. RB/4/S (stokehole to kiln 4). (One example).

293. Bowl rim, 260mm in diameter, with a grooved lip, in a gritty dark grey (N4) fabric, burnished on top of rim. RB/- unstratified.

294. Bowl rim, 250mm in diameter, with lightly grooved lip, in a hard grey (N6) fabric, with traces of burnish on top of rim. RB/2/S (stokehole to kiln 2).

295. Bowl rim, diameter indeterminate, in a gritty, light grey (10YR 7/2) fabric, with darker (10YR 5/1) surface. RB/2/S (stokehole to kiln 2).

296. Bowl rim in a gritty light grey (2.5Y 7/2) fabric, with grey (N7) core. RB/2/S(stokehole to kiln 2).

297. Large bowl rim in a gritty, light brownish grey (2.5Y 6/2) fabric. RB/2/S (?L.3) (stokehole to kiln 2).

298. Large bowl rim, in a gritty grey (N6) fabric. RB/2/S (L.3) (stokehole to kiln 2).

299. Large bowl rim, in a gritty grey (N5) fabric with light greyish brown (2.5Y 6/2) surface. RB/2/S (stokehole to kiln 2).

300. Large bowl, 300mm in diameter. Gritty, grey (N4) fabric. RB/4/S (stokehole to kiln 4).

301. Large bowl, 260mm in diameter. Gritty grey (N4) fabric, with reddish brown (5YR 5/4) core and darker (N5) surface. RB/3/S (stokehole to kiln 3).

302. Medium sized bowl, diameter indeterminate, in a gritty light grey (10YR 7/2) fabric. RB/4/S.2 (stokehole to kiln 4).

303. Large bowl, 340mm in diameter, in a hard, gritty grey (N5) fabric, burnished on top of rim. The rim form is variable. RB/4/S.2 (stokehole to kiln 4).

304. Large bowl, 340mm in diameter, in a gritty grey (N6) fabric with light grey (2.5Y 7/2) surface and traces of burnish on top of rim. RB/3/S (stokehole to kiln 3).

305. Large bowl, 240mm in diameter, in a hard, gritty grey (N6) fabric with darker (N5) surface, roughly burnished on top of rim; slightly distorted in firing. RB/- unstratified.

306. Rim of a large bowl, 295mm in diameter. RB/- unstratified.

307. Rim of a large bowl, 280mm in diameter, in a grey (N6), with greyish brown (2.5Y 5–6/2) surface. RB/3/S (stokehole to kiln 3).

308. Sherd from body of large bowl with two rows of incised wavy line between grooves, in a hard, lightly vitrified grey (N5) fabric, with light brownish grey (10YR 6/2) core. RB/4/S (stokehole to kiln 4).

309. Sherd from large bowl with combed wavy line in a hard grey (N5) fabric, with darker (N4) surface. RB/2/- (kiln 2).

310. Rim of a large bowl, 340mm in diameter, in a gritty light grey (N7) fabric. RB/4/S (stokehole to kiln 4).

311. Large bowl, slightly distorted in firing, in a hard, grey (N5) fabric. RB/4/K (interior of kiln 4).

312. Large bowl, 320mm in diameter, in a gritty, light grey (N7) fabric with dark grey (N3) core. RB/1/S (stokehole to kiln 1).

313. Large bowl rim, 260mm in diameter, in a gritty light grey (2.5Y 7/2) fabric with darker (N6) core. RB/2/S (L.4) (stokehole to kiln 2).

314. Large bowl in a gritty light grey (N7) fabric with light brownish grey (2.5Y 7/2) surface, roughly burnished over rim. RB/4/S (stokehole to kiln 4).

315. Large bowl rim, 260mm in diameter, in a reddish brown (5YR 5/4) fabric with grey (N6) core and dark grey (N4) surface. RB/2/S (stokehole to kiln 2).

316. Large bowl rim, 280mm in diameter, in a gritty light grey (N7) fabric. RB/2/S (stokehole to kiln 2).

317. Large bowl rim, 320mm in diameter, in a gritty light red (2.5YR 6/8) fabric with traces of grey (N5) surface. RB/4/S.2 (stokehole to kiln 4).

318. Large bowl rim, 360mm in diameter, in a gritty, oxidised light red (2.5YR 6/8) fabric, with traces of grey (N5) surface, burnished on top of rim. RB/4/S.2 (stokehole to kiln 4).

319. Large bowl rim, in a gritty light grey (N7) fabric. RB/4/S (stokehole to kiln 4).

320. Bowl rim, 340mm in diameter, in a gritty light grey (2.5Y 7/2 – N7) fabric with traces of burnish on top of rim. RB/4/S (stokehole to kiln 4).

321. Bowl rim, diameter indeterminate, in a pinkish grey (7.5YR 7/2) fabric with dark grey (N4) surface. RB/4/S (stokehole to kiln 4).

322. Bowl rim, 240mm in diameter, in a gritty, light grey (N7) fabric with darker (N5) core. RB/4/S (stokehole to kiln 4).

Type J. Cheese Press

323. Cheese press in a hard light brownish grey (2.5Y 6/2) fabric. RB/- unstratified.

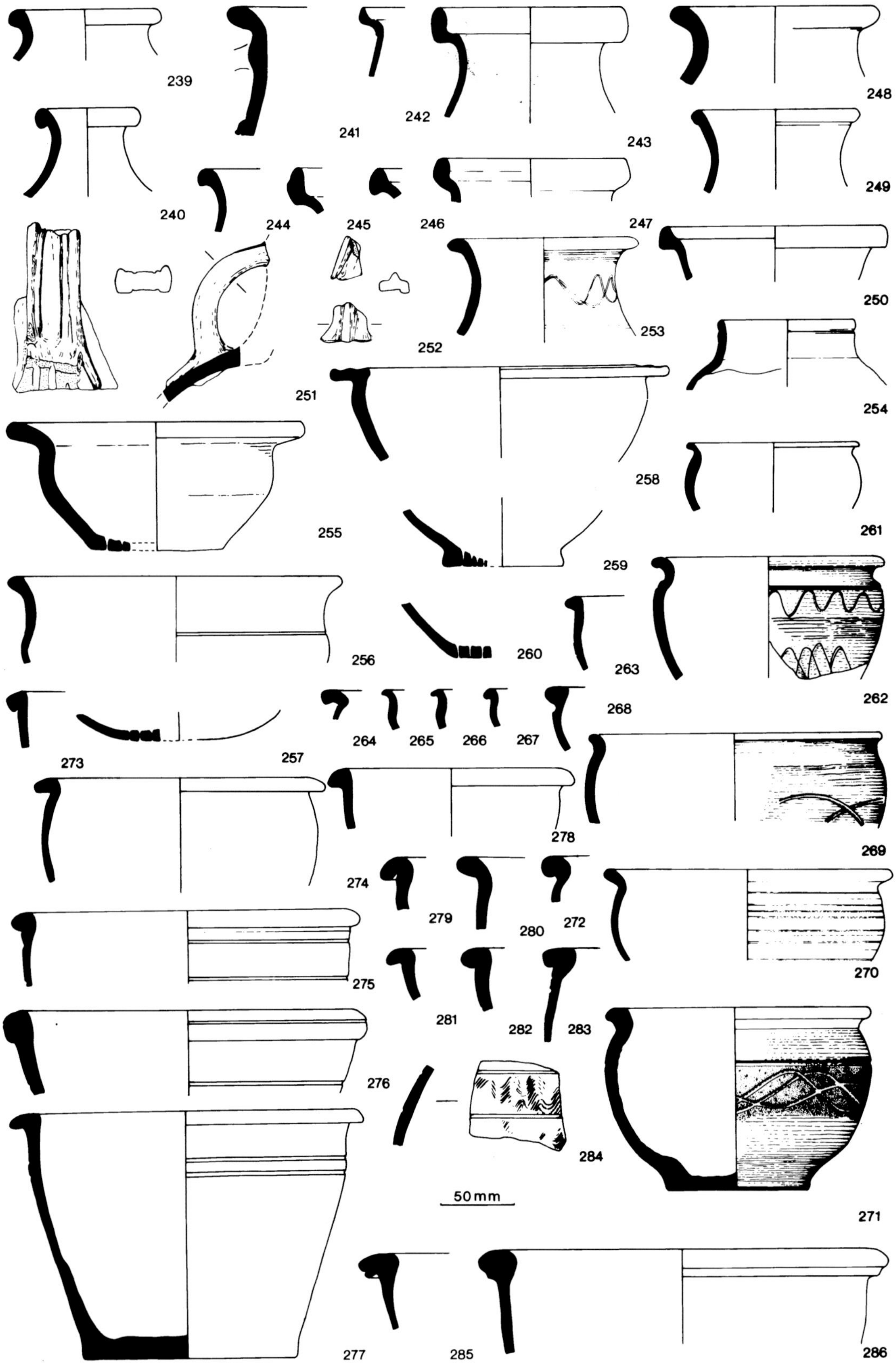

Figure 49. Rossington Bridge pottery: narrow-necked jars, Nos 239–254, colanders, Nos 255–260, shoulder bowls/wide-mouthed jars, Nos 261–271, and medium sized bowls, Nos 272–286.

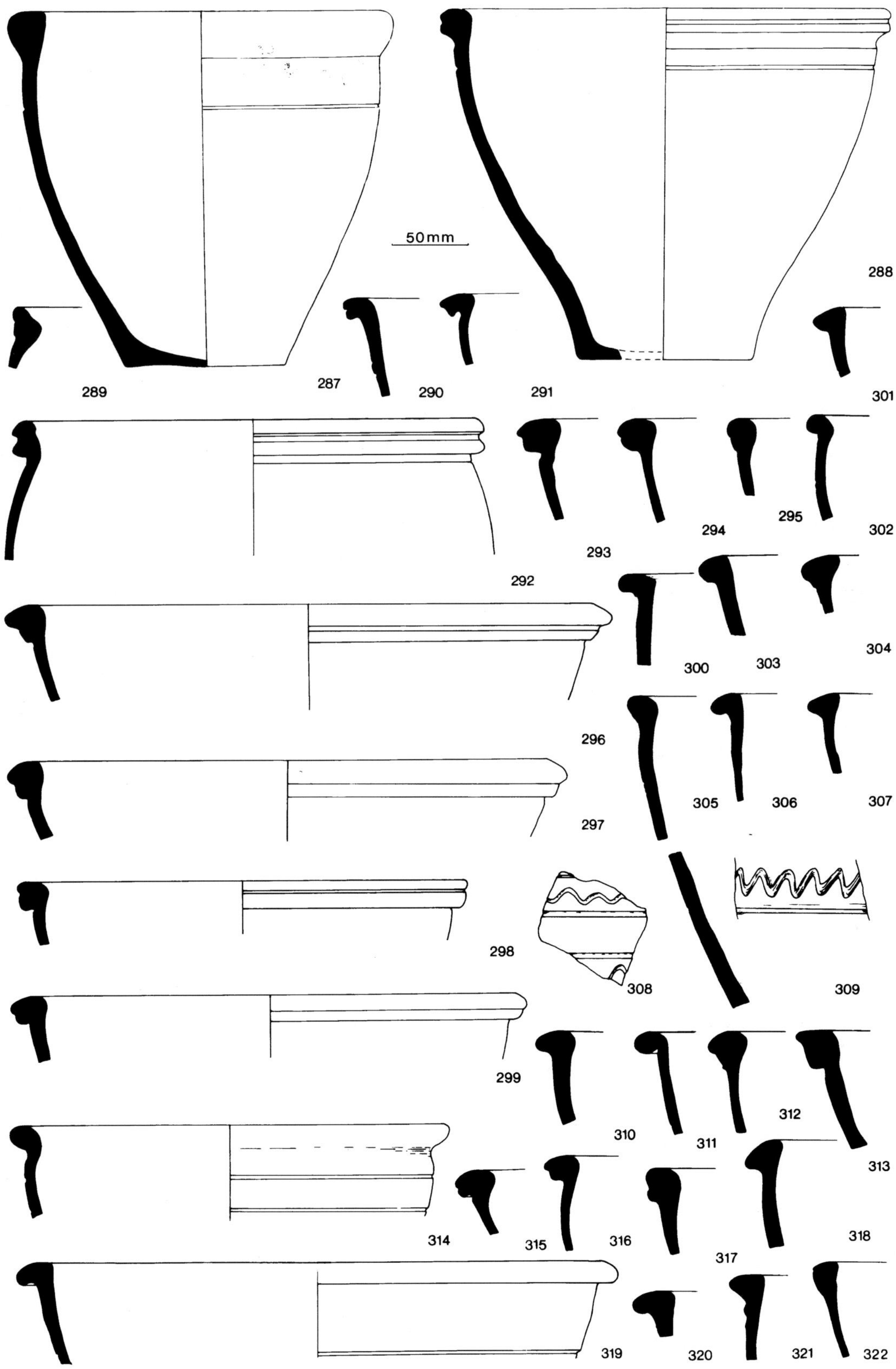

Figure 50. Rossington Bridge pottery: large bowls, Nos 287–322.

Type K. Samian imitations

324. Hemispherical bowl, hand made, probably imitating a glass pillar-moulded bowl, rather than a samian form. BBl, dark grey (N4) burnished surface with dark brown (7.5YR 4/4) core. Applied clay strips.
RB/8WMB/L.5a.
For the original form, see Price and Cottam (1998) fig 7, 1st to early 2nd century.

325. Imitation samian form 38 in a grey (N4) fabric, burnished to a darker grey (N3–4) surface.
RB/- Unstratified, but apparently a Rossington product.

326. Imitation samian form 38, in a hard grey (N6) fabric with reddish yellow (5YR 7/6) surfaces; a distorted waster.
RB/25.1/L.3.

327. Imitation samian form 38 / segmental flanged bowl in a pinkish-grey (7.5YR 7/2) to light brown (7.5YR 6/4) fabric with red (2.5YR 4/6) painted decoration on flange and irregular burnish.
RB/18.1/L.5a.

328. ? Imitation samian form 44 in a light reddish brown (5YR 6/3) fabric with burnishing on outer surface. Badly fire-cracked, a similar fabric to **113** above.
RB/10.1/L.5, a Rossington product.
cf Dragonby (Gregory 1996) no 903, early 2nd – early 3rd century.

329. Imitation samian form 44 in a gritty very pale orange (10YR 8/2) with traces of grey (N4) surface.
RB/2/S.1 (stokehole to kiln 2). (2 examples). Rossington products.
cf Derby Racecourse kilns (Brassington 1980) fig 14, 383–4, with white painted decoration above the flange. Gillam (1970) Type 200 from the Antonine Wall fort at Balmuildy (also figured in Swan 1999, no. 27) is similar but smaller and in an oxidised fabric thought to have been poduced locally.

Type L. Lids

330. Two sherds from a lid in BBl, with pinkish grey (7.5YR 6/2) burnished surfaces and grey (N5) core. Pierced through the top.
RB/11.1/L.5.

331. Lid with very dark grey (N3) surface, and grey (N6) core.
RB/12.1/L.5.
cf York (Monaghan 1997) no 4088, Antonine.

332. Lid in a dark grey (N4) fabric, with light grey (N7) core.
RB/25.1/L.4.

333. Lid with dark grey (N4) surfaces and grey (N6) core, with wire marks on top and rough, unfinished surface.
RB/11WMB/L.6.

Type M. Miscellaneous forms

334. Base, grey (N6) fabric with lighter (2.5Y 7/2) outer zone and slightly abraded surface with metallic grey (N4) burnish. ? Finger tip decoration at edge of base.
RB/8.1/L.4. (One example).
More likely to be a candlestick than a lid. cf Blaxton (Buckland and Dolby 1980) no 215.

335. Handle of ? patera in BBl. Black to grey (N3–6) lightly burnished surfaces with dark greyish-brown (7.5YR 4/2) core; wavy line burnished beneath.
RB/9.1/L.6 (peat) (one example).
cf examples in a mica-dusted fabric from London (Marsh 1978) fig 6.14, 32.1 *et seq.*

336. Perhaps a handle or even a child's toy, in a grey fabric.
RB/10WMB/L.5a.

337. Pedestal base, apparently pierced in the centre, in a grey (N6) fabric, with darker (N4) surface and much internal sooting.
RB/4/S.1 (stokehole to kiln 4).

338. Part of a triple vase in a grey (N5–7) fabric with a slightly pimply surface. Two pierced holes in the body of the vessel with the remains of two other attached vessels.
RB/16WMB/L.5a.

339. Small beaker/ triple vase in a grey (N6) fabric, with darker (N4) surface.
RB/- unstratified.

Non-local vessels

340. Corrugated jar in a hard grey (N5) fabric with a metallic sheen on outer surface, a generally harder and finer fabric than most of the Rossington products.
RB/9.1/L.5.
cf Dragonby kiln 3 (Rigby and Stead 1976) fig 64, 11. Flavian +?

341. Corrugated jar, wheel-made and burnished. Black (N2) outer surface, grey (N4) core and predominantly pale brown (10YR 6/3) interior, where a dark grey (10YR 6/3) surface has been eroded.
RB/D.1.2/-.
May (1922) regards an example, with handles, from Templeborough (pl 31, 189) in a white fabric as dating to 'soon after the middle of the first century'.

342. Mortarium, unstamped, in fabric 9, a fine light grey (N7) fabric, with pinkish grey (7.5YR 7/2) surface and small, angular flint grit extending over the rim.
RB/15.1/L.6.
Gillam (1970) type 238, NE. Gaul, AD 65–100+ (Hartley K.F. 1977, Group II).

343. Mortarium rim, 300mm in diameter, in Fabric 2, a fine white (10YR 8/1); no trituration grit survives.
RB/?3/- unstratified.
Mancetter/Hartshill, or possibly Lincoln, South Carlton, *c* AD 120–170.

344. Mortarium, with stamp of DOCCAS (die 5) (Fig 34, 4), in fabric 2. White (N9), with scattered subrounded multi-coloured trituration grit. Evidence of use in the worn interior.
RB/- unstratified.
Mancetter/Hartshill.

345. Mortarium, with stamps of GR]ATINV[S (Fig 34, 3) on either side some distance from the spout, in fabric 2, white (N9), with small, angular red and black trituration grit.
RB/12WMB/L.5a.
Mancetter/Hartshill.

346. Mortarium, in fabric 2, as **345**, with multicoloured sub-rounded trituration grit with much quartz. A small irregular hole, to 5mm, a firing fault, in the side goes completely through the side of the vessel.
RB/15.1/L.6.
Mancetter/Hartshill, *c* AD 140–180.

347. Mortarium, with stamp of ICOTASGVS (Fig 34, 2), in fabric 2, a fine white (N9) fabric with very pale brown (10YR 8/3) surface and multicoloured subangular to angular grit, largely of quartz.
RB/8.1/L.5a.
A Mancetter/Hartshill product, *c* AD. 140–180.

348. Mortarium, 260mm in diameter, with a stamp of S]ARRI(VS) (Die 3) (Fig.34, 1), in fabric 2.
RB/- unstratified.
Mancetter/Hartshill.

349. Flange of a mortarium, 310mm in diameter, in fabric 2, white (N9).
RB/11.1/L.3.
Mancetter/Hartshill, *c* AD 160–230.

350. Mortarium, with reeded rim, 190mm in diameter, in fabric 2, white (10YR 8/2), with small angular red trituration grit.
RB/9WMB/L.5a, joining sherd in 11.1/L.5.
Mancetter/Hartshill, *c* AD 210–260.

351. Mortarium, 290mm in diameter, in fabric 2, white (10YR 8/2), with traces of fine, black trituration grit.
RB/12.1/L.4.
Mancetter/Hartshill, *c* AD 210–300.

352. Mortarium rim with two slight grooves on the outer surface of the flange, 300mm in diameter, in fabric 2, as **351**, with scattered angular red grit.
RB/12WMB/L.5.
Mancetter/Hartshill, *c* AD 240–340.

353. Mortarium rim with two grooves on outer surface of flange, 230mm in diameter, in fabric 2, as **351**, with red and black trituration grit.
RB/11.1/L.3.
Mancetter/Hartshill, *c* AD 220–270.

354. Mortarium rim with three grooves on the outer surface of the flange, 290mm in diameter, in fabric 2, white (5YR 8/1), with traces of angular grit.
RB/7.1/L.4.
Mancetter/Hartshill, *c* AD 230–300.

355. Reeded rim of a mortarium, 310mm in diameter., pinkish white (5YR 8/2) to pink (5YR 7/4) fabric with angular black grit.
RB/13–14/ (peat, presumably the 'upper peat'), L3.
Mancetter/Hartshill, or Lower Nene Valley, *c* AD 250–350.

356. Mortarium rim with three slight grooves on outer surface of flane, 250mm in diameter, in fabric 2, as **350**.
RB/10/- unstratified.
Mancetter/Hartshill, *c* AD 230–280.

357. Mortarium, in fabric 2, fine white (N9) with small angular red grit.
RB/16–17/- unstratified.
Mancetter/Hartshill, *c* 230–300.

358. Mortarium, 200mm in diameter, in fabric 2, fine pinkish white (7.5YR 8/2), with angular red to black trituration grit; burnt.
RB/25.1/- unstratified.
Mancetter/Hartshill, *c* AD 240–340.

359. Mortarium, 300mm in diameter, in fabric 5, burnt, in a fine pink (5YR 7/3) fabric with light brownish grey (10YR 6/2) burnt surface and trace of angular black trituration grit.
RB/9.1/L.4 and 9WMB/L.3.
Nene Valley, AD 230–300.

360. Mortarium, with double finger impression spout, in fabric 6, a slightly gritty, very pale brown (10YR 7/4) fabric with brown (10YR 5/3) surface and small angular black grit. The outer surface has a combed acute wavy line.
RB/9WMB/L.3 and RB/13–14/ (peat, presumably the 'upper peat'), L3.
Probably a Crambeck product, cf Corder (1928) type 6, although the form and decoration are not directly paralleled in the published series, 4th century.

361. Rim of a small beaker in a cream fabric.
RB/- unstratified.

362. Rim of a rough-cast beaker in a white (10YR 8/1) fabric with reddish yellow (5YR 7/6) colour-coat and fine rough casting.
RB/8.1/L.5a.
A South Carlton product, cf Webster (1944).

363. Rim of a small, rough-cast beaker in a white (5YR 8/1) fabric with red (10R 5/6) colour-coat and fine rough casting.
RB/8WMB/L.5a.

364. Many sherds from a folded 'scale' beaker in a pinkish white (7.5YR 8/2) fabric with light grey (N7) core and dark grey (N4) colour-coat, orange internally.
RB/16WMB/L.5a.
Howe *et al* (180) suggest that this type first appeared in the 'second quarter of the third century'. If this is certain, then this vessel provides a *terminus post quem* of AD 225+ for the 'occupation layer'; this finds some support in the presence of a coin of Septimius Severus high in the same deposit.

365. Sherd of rouletted Castor Box, 150mm in diameter
RB/12WMB/L.5. (a small sherd also occurs in the stokehole to kiln 2).
The type appears to begin in the 3rd century (Howe *et al*, 1980, 24).

366. Base of a pedestal beaker, with rouletted decoration in a white (10YR 8/1) fabric with dark reddish brown (5YR 3/2) colour coat.
RB/- unstratified.

367. Pedestal base, in a fine, oxidised light reddish brown (5YR 6/3) fabric with grey (N5) core, burnished surface and red (2.5YR 5/8) slip run down the inside.
RB/13.1/L.3. Possibly a Rossington Product.

368. Rim, 110mm in diameter, of a carinated bowl, in a smooth micaceous pinkish white (5YR 8/2) fabric with grey (N5) core; brown (7.5YR 5/4) surface and light reddish brown (2.5YR 6/4) painted decoration.
RB/25.1/L.5.
Jars and bowls in this fabric with painted decoration occur widely in late 1st century contexts: cf Old Winteringham (Rigby and Stead 1976) fig 78, 73–4, Lincoln (Darling 1981) fig 33.2, and Doncaster (Buckland and Magilton 1986) no 79.

369. Carinated bowl in a light grey (N7) fabric with grey (N6) core and several grit inclusions; surface very dark grey (N3) to reddish brown (2.5YR 4/4). Slight trace of lattice between grooves on side of vessel.
RB/6.1/L.5.
The type appears in the Dorset BB1 industry at Worgret (Hearne and Smith 1991, fig 14, 60, type 36), where a 1st century date and a derivation from samian form 30 is suggested.

370. Imitation butt beaker in a hard, light red (2.5YR 6/6) fabric with grey (N6) core and very dark grey (N3) to reddish grey (5YR 5/2) surface, burnished at neck and base with two bands of incised vertical lines between cordons.
RB/16.1/L.5. Mid to late 1st century.

371. Rim of a rusticated jar in a light grey (N6) fabric with a darker (N5) metallic lustre on the surface.
RB/15.1/L.4 (one example).
The fabric is suggestive of a Rossington product, but the vigorous rustication, angular rim and lack of a groove defining the upper edge of decoration imply an earlier ?Hadrianic date.

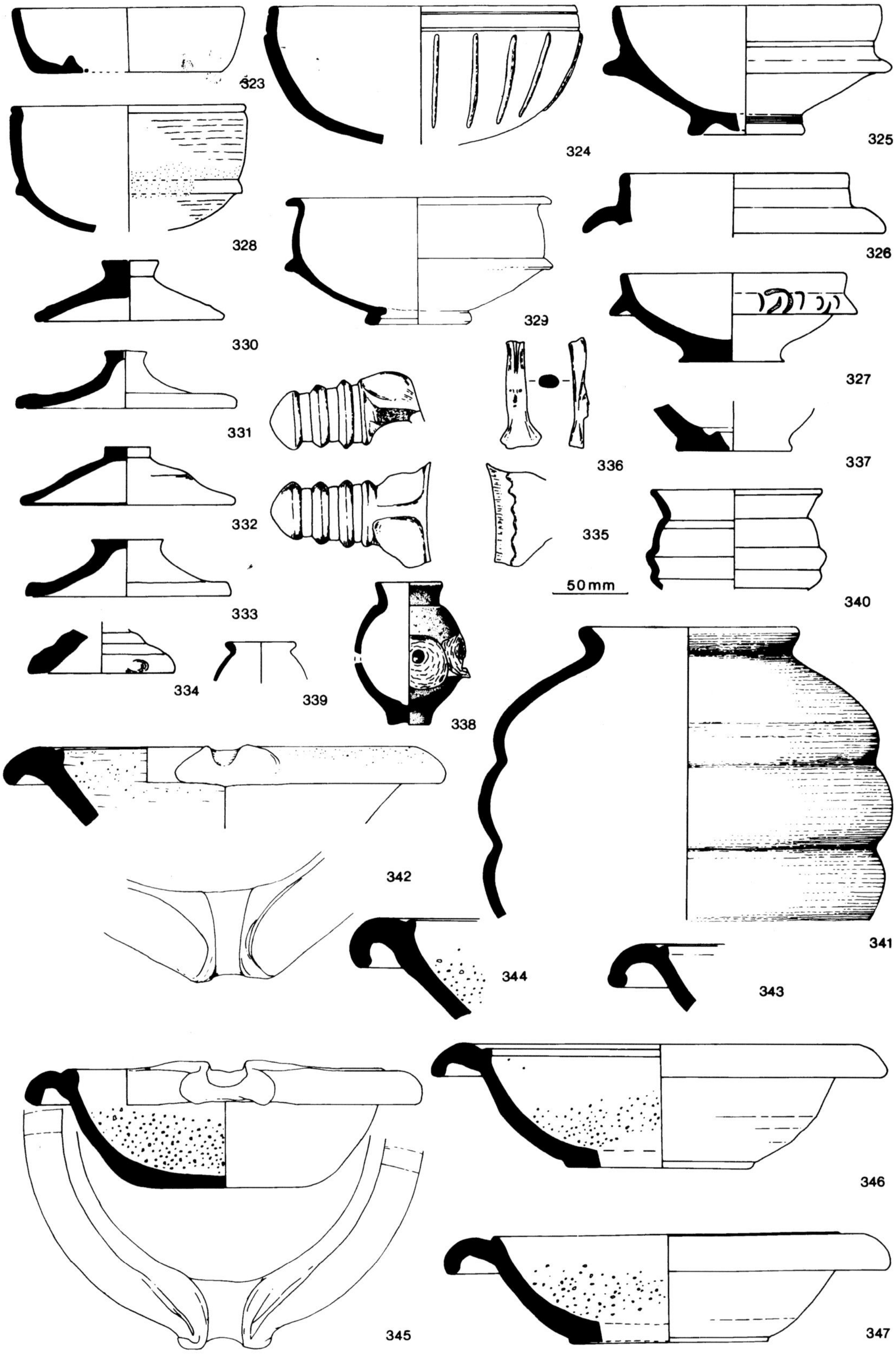

Figure 51. Rossington Bridge pottery: cheese press, No 323, imitation glass and samian vessels (Nos 324–329, lids, Nos 330–333, base, No 334, handles, Nos 335–336, triple vases, Nos 338–339, honey jars, Nos 340–341 and non-local mortaria, Nos 342–347.

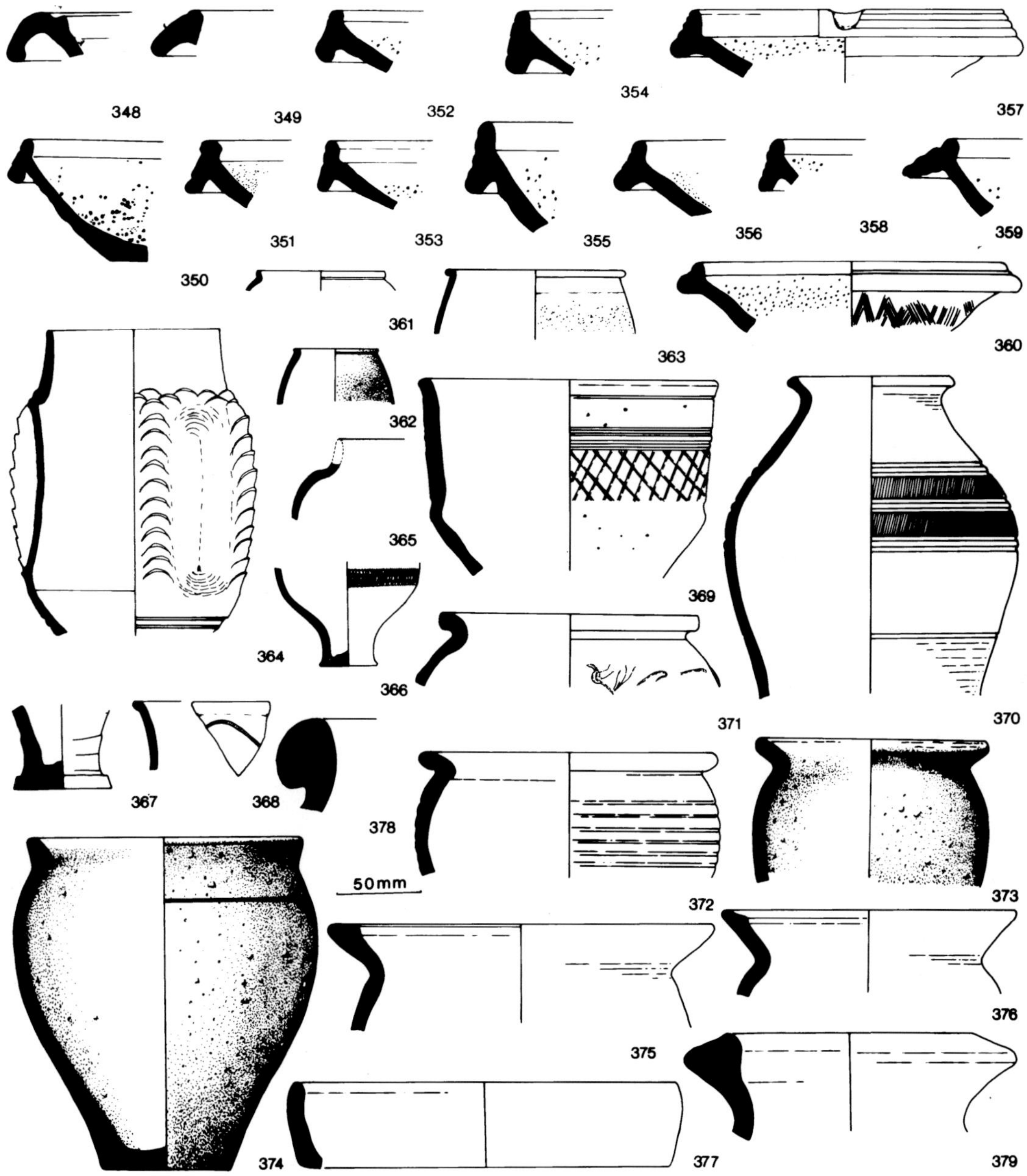

Figure 52. Rossington Bridge: non-local pottery, Nos 348–379.

372. Hand-made jar, with corrugated outer surface, in a very coarse black (N2) fabric with slightly pimply surface, containing some large subrounded quartz temper to 3mm; dark grey to black (N2–3) core and inside surface, surface pinkish grey (5YR 6/2).
RB/10–15WMB/-.
The type appears in the vexillation fortress at Longthorpe (cf Frere and St. Joseph 1974, fig 54, 109), pre- Flavian.

373. Jar rim. Pinkish grey (7.5YR 6/2) to very dark grey (N3) outer surface with grey (N6) core; heavily calcite-gritted, smoothed on neck and rim. A hard fabric with a soapy feel, probably wheel-finished.
RB/25.1/L.3.

374. Complete jar in a heavily grogged light grey (2.5Y 7/2) fabric with much dark grey angular grog up to 2mm, and a very dark grey (N3) patchy surface. A roughly made vessel but wheel-thrown. It would appear that the base has been added after the body has been cut off from the wheel. There are a number of blisters in the body of the pot which could make this a second or a local product but it is unlikely to be a 2nd century Rossington vessel.
RB/13WMB/L.6 (peat). The rim of a wide mouthed jar in a similar fabric occurs in RB/25.1/L.4, presumably derived from earlier deposits.
cf Dragonby (May 1996) no170, Claudio-Neronian; probably associated with the vexillation fortress occupation.

375. Rim of Dales ware jar in a soft, very dark grey (N2) to light brown (7.5YR 6/4) fabric, containing some crushed shell temper, but much leached out leaving a pitted surface. RB/11WMB/L.5a.

376. Dales Ware rim as **375** above. RB/?6/K.
For a full discussion of the type, see Loughlin (1977), where an additional vessel from Rossington Bridge (fig 1, 11) is figured. Loughlin (*op cit*, 89) notes several Dales ware rims from RB/1/S, but these vessels have since lost their documentation. In the most recent discussion of the type, by Monaghan (1997, 897–8) considering the York material, a starting date no earlier than AD 190 is proposed. The Rossington data are insufficiently well recorded to suggest otherwise, and the one piece from L.5a is associated with a coin of Septimius Severus. Additional vessels occur in the demonstrably 3rd century overlying deposits (Table 4).

377. Plain lipped dish in a grey (10YR5/1) fabric with a dark grey (N3–4) pitted surface, where calcite grit has been dissolved out by the acid soil conditions; surfaces burnished. Similar to Dales Ware, **375–6** above. RB/16WMB/L.5a.

378. Rim of a large storage jar, diameter indeterminate, in a dark grey (N4) fabric with grey (N5) to light brownish grey (2.5Y 6/2) surface, burnished on top of rim. RB/- unstratified.

379. Amphora rim, Dressel form 20, much burnt and abraded, in a light red (10R6/8) fabric with light grey (2.5Y 7/2) core. RB/2/S (stokehole to kiln 2). An unstamped handle belonging to the same form also occurs unstratified. Although the fabric is burnt, the vessel clearly belongs to the more frequent Baetican type. 2nd century.

380. Carinated bowl in a red-brown fabric with grey core and several large grit inclusions. RB/6.1/L.5. One example, not a local product.

The Animal Bones
Gillian Crawley

Introduction

The excavation of the Roman pottery kilns site at Rossington Bridge, near Doncaster took place, over four seasons, between 1958–1961. After the initial discovery by the cutting of the water main trench (WM), the site was hand excavated and this generated assemblages of bone which was stored at the Beechfield Museum, Doncaster, before being relocated to the present Museum building in 1964.

The recovered animal assemblage was relatively small, resulting 211 identifiable pieces, A further 43 fragments were also examined but these proved to be undiagnostic. The assemblage's small size is probably a direct reflection of the limited recovery techniques employed during excavation. When compiling the original list of specimens stratigraphical information was recorded where present, but on detailed examination this information showed-up sporadically and therefore the bone assemblage has, primarily for statistical reasons, been treated as a whole. All generated lists and tables have been included in the excavation archive housed at Doncaster Museum and Art Gallery.

Preservation

Generally the bone assemblage is not in a good state of preservation. The collection has suffered greatly over the intervening years since excavation because they were extracted from damp or waterlogged conditions, and then transferred to a dry museum store, without being given the time or the corrective environmental conditions to dry out slowly. Consequently, much physical stress can be witnessed throughout the bone assemblage, for example, longitudinal splitting has occurred on many of the longbone shafts and scaling, especially of the articular joints. Unfortunately this has resulted in the destruction of much of the surface evidence, such as knife marks, gnawing and shatter fracture patterns, as well as some pathology.

Methodology

All 'identifiable' fragments were sorted by species and then by anatomical type, this facilitates frequencies between species and skeletal survival, which in turn can be used to provide estimates of minimum numbers of individuals (MNI). As an aid to identification, fragments were compared with skeletal reference material curated by the Natural History Section at Doncaster Museum and the human material by comparison with a modern articulated teaching skeleton as used by Corporate Services, DMBC. Where possible, estimates of age were made by recording dental eruption, tooth wear patterns and epiphysial fusion. On the whole, this was not wholly satisfactory due to the paucity of identifiable parts and the physical damage the bone had undergone since excavation.

An attempt was made to identify all fragments but unfortunately not everything was able to be assigned to cation. This second group is predominantly made up of prove to come from cattle long bones.

Due to a) the sample size of this assemblage and b) the scarcity of diagnostic bones, a decision was made to not review the gender of individual animals.

Discussion: the animal bone

The combined limitations of a modestly sized bone assemblage, an assemblage which is heavily biased by the non-retrieval of small bone, plus its generally compromised conservation status means that any interpretation of the faunal collection is of a tentative nature. However small, in statistical terms, the assemblage may appear, it does provide enough evidence to show clearly that the 2nd–4th century inhabitants at Rossington Bridge were managing their domestic animals to provide them with meat, marrow, wool and traction. Within the cattle, horse and sheep faunal groups, there are cuts, borings and shatter fractures, all marks characteristic of filleting

Table 9. Anatomical distribution of bone fragments.

	Homo	*Lepus*	*Cervus*	*Sus*	bird	*Bos*	*Equus*	Ovi-caprid	total
skull	3					5		4	
horncore						5			
maxilla/premaxilla				1		1			
mandible						4	2	5	
loose teeth			1			22	23	9	
atlas	1								
vertebra						2		2	
sacrum	4								
ribs						2		2	
scapula				2		1	2	3	
pelvis			1			2	2	3	
humerus	2	1	1			2		1	
radius						6	1	4	
ulna					1	5		2	
femur	1					2		1	
tibia			1			10	1	1	
undet. long bone					1	3		2	
astragalus						7		2	
calcaneum						3			
metacarpals						4		5	
metatarsus						8	2	3	
other carpal/tarsal	1						2		
phalanges					3	1			
hoofcore				3					
unident fragments									
Total	12	2	3	5	2	100	37	49	211
group %	5.68	0.94	1.42	2.37	0.94	47.39	17.53	23.22	

Table 10. Minimum number of individuals.

Homo	*Lepus*	*Cervus*	*Sus*	bird	*Bos*	*Equus*	Ovi-caprid
1	1	1	1	1	5	2	4

Table 11. Evidence for post mortem butchery.

(based on a total of 253 bones examined)

type	frequency	%		
cut marks	8	3.16%	8.69%	16.60%
marrow shatter/boring	14	5.53%		
burning	20	7.9%		

and marrow extraction and indicative of human consumption. Five horncores survive in the excavation record and all are similarly sized and appear to be from the smaller shorthorn cattle prevalent in the late Iron-Age – early Roman periods.

Preliminary examination of the relative age of death within the faunal remains by dental record or epiphysial fusion does indicate that within the cattle and sheep assemblages some animals were being culled for meat before they were reaching maturity (the pig assemblage is too small to draw any valid conclusion). Whilst others were being allowed to live their adult lives because they were valued beasts for milk, wool, breeding stock and traction. Unlike the cattle and sheep bones, the horse assemblage does not included any specimens that were immature at death, although the group does include common post-mortem butchery marks. This probably indicates that the horse population had a 'working life' as traction or transportation beasts before their slaughter and consumption. The complete acetabulum (B69) and right metatarsus 3, 2 and 4 (B82, RBPS 8.1/9.1) reveal these animal as small Celtic-type ponies. What makes this horse assemblage notable is its percentage ratio of of horse bones indicates that they must have been of economic importance to the Rossington Bridge community. It is interesting to speculate as to the human strategic use of these animals as pack horses for transport some credence is provided by the two iron hipposandals from the site.

As stated, the interpretation of the faunal assemblage has been severely hampered by the salvage techniques as employed at Rossington. Many small bones and fragments were not retrieved or later salvaged by wet sieving, this certainly would explain the lack of fish and fowl bones in the assemblage, which one would have expected to see given the site's close proximity to the river Torne. The Torne and its floodplain would have providing the Rossington community with rich hunting opportunities. From the identified assemblage, it can be surmised that people were supplementing their deitary with hunted animals, as this is evidenced by the presence of hare (*Lepus europaeus*) and red deer (*Cervus elaphus*) bones with cut marks upon them.

The Human Bone

12 pieces of human bone have been identified from the faunal assemblage, including three cranial fragments, one atlas, four sacrum fragments, a left femur, as well as right and left humeri. In all likelihood, this probably represents one individual, but the remains do pose several difficult questions. Were the bones the remains of a Roman burial or from a disturbed earlier, probably Iron-Age context? If Roman why were they buried within the confines a settlement, against usual practice? And most perplexing of all why is the left humerus severely mutilated?

skull The skull survives in 3 pieces, examination of the visible sutures indicates that this person was adult.
sacrum Now in four badly degraded fragments

left femur Incomplete, both the proximal and distal articular joints are missing. Both ends of the mid shaft fragment look as if the marrow has been extracted, and there are three cut marks on the anterior surface just below the fractured proximal end. As only the mid shaft is present an estimate of the individual's height using Trotter and Gleser's regression equations has not been pursued, but from the bone's appearance it would be reasonable to suggest that it belonged to mature, robust male of medium height (*c* 5'4"–5'8").

right humerus Again both articular joints are missing and the break across the distal joint, immediately through the *coronoid fossa* looks suspicious and not natural. The break at the proximal end looks as it has been chipped away, exposing the marrow before its extraction.

left humerus Again another mid shaft fragment with missing proximal and distal articular joints, but this bone is different because it has been shaped by shave marks. The deltoid ridge and the ridges which flatten out the shaft toward the distal epiphysis have been shaved away in order to make the bone's usual prismoid section more cylindrical. The anterior surface has been severely cut back to form a flat wedged end. On the caudal surface, at least six shavings have been made to take off excess bone. When turned sidewards it becomes apparent that a notch has been cut into the wedge-shaped working 'end' making the whole object look like a tool (Fig. 53). To remove the splays of bone that have been taken off the bone must have been 'green', therefore workable in this manner, because to have done so at a later (unspecified) date would have resulted in shatter splintering. Any wear patterns either in the notch or on the bone defining tool function are obliterated by a coat of lacquer given to the bone post excavation but prior to any recent examination (*c*1989). Transverse cut marks, very similar to filleting cuts are visible along the bone shaft and give the impression that the meat had been removed from the bone before it was shaved into its current shape.

Discussion

Mutilated burials are not uncommon in Roman contexts. Although most consist of beheadings, a number show severed limbs (Harman *et al* 1981). An example from Adwick-le-Street, north of Doncaster, appeared to show the chopping off of hands and feet (Dolby 1969), although later examination of the poorly preserved bone was less conclusive (Buckland and Magilton 1986, 214–217; Nellist 1986). There is no indication that the fragments recovered at Rossington Bridge came from a disturbed single burial of either Iron Age or earlier Roman date or several individuals, and more detailed study is necessary before a case of cannibalism, adventitious use of human remains, or perhaps preparation of the body for deposition in some sort of ossuary can be suggested.

The Plant Remains

Despite the extensive nature of the preservation of waterlogged plant remains at Rossington Bridge Pumping Station, only one example survives in the Museum's collections (RBPS 16.1/L5 (DONMG: 1996.71), a nut from the common hazel (*Corylus avellana*). The reason this shell survives and others did not, is that it was deemed special because it had been gnawed. Examination by Colin Howes, Doncaster Museum and Art Gallery identifies this gnawing as that of a red squirrel (*Sciurus vulgaris*).

Rossington Bridge Farm

There are sufficient close parallels in stamps and types to indicate that the two kilns excavated south of the river belong to the same phase of local production as the main site. The forms, however, are sufficiently distinct to suggest different potters, and the rilled lid-seated jars (**25–29**) are better paralleled at Cantley kiln 2 (Annable 1960) than across the river Torne at Rossington Bridge Pumping Station. BB1 is absent from the group, and the site may belong to the later stages of production at Rossington Bridge.

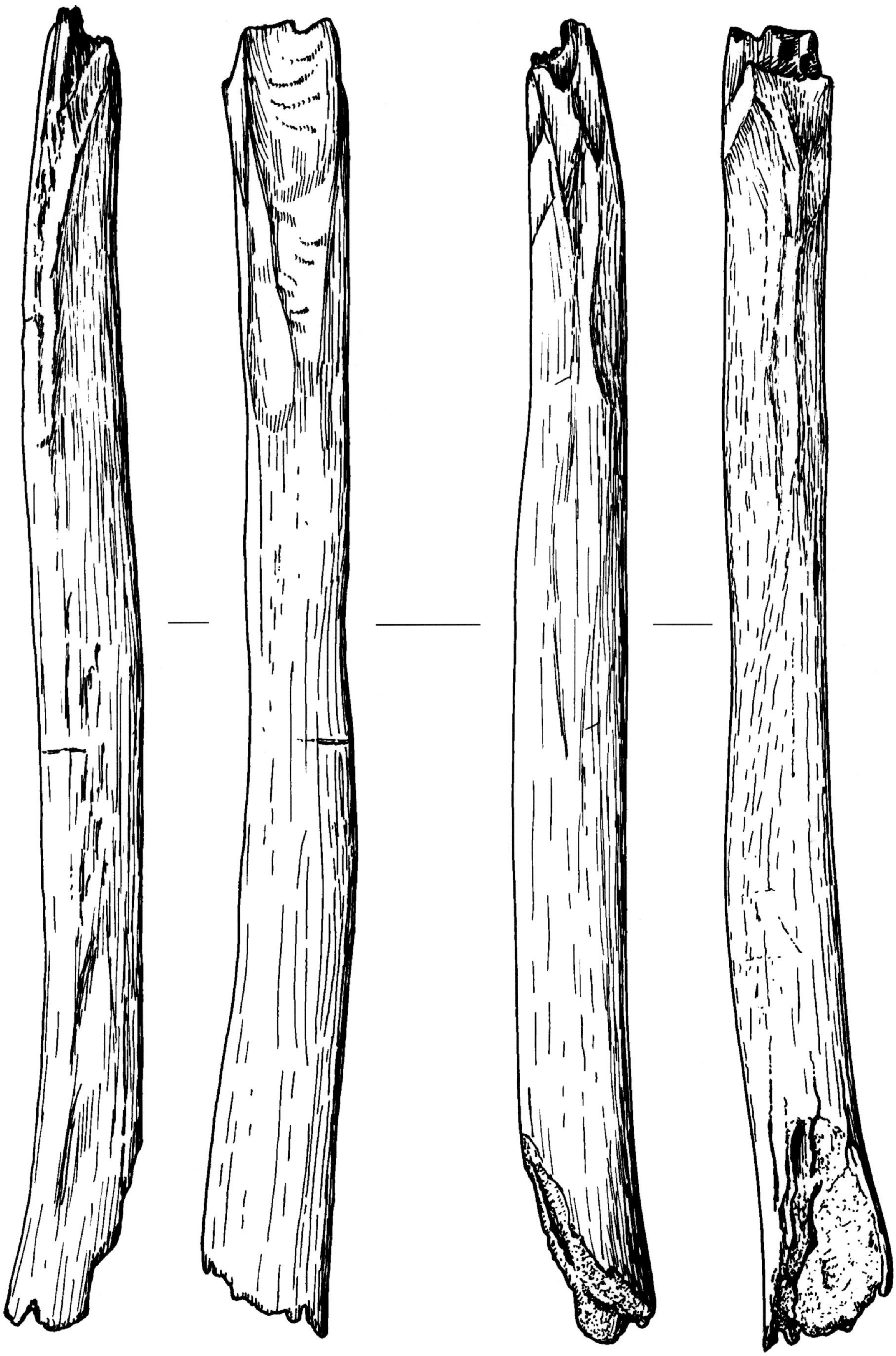

Figure 53. Modified human humerus from RBPS L.4. Drawing: M. Lucas.

The Pottery

The group also includes Trade-mark mortarium stamp 54 (Fig 33, 11).

1. Bead-rimmed dish, 130mm in diameter. Gritty, grey (N6) fabric, with patchy dark grey (N4) surface, with some trace of burnish.
RBF/2/F (from the flue of kiln 2).

2. Lipped dish, 250mm in diameter, in a hard, gritty grey (N5) fabric with very dark grey (N3) surface, burnished over rim and patchily on outer surface.
RBF/2/S (stokehole to kiln 2).

3. Lipped dish, 120mm in diameter, in a light grey (N7) fabric, with patchy greyish brown (2.5Y 5/2) burnished surface.
RBF/2/S (stokehole to kiln 2).

4. Lipped bowl/dish, 160mm in diameter, in a gritty light grey (2.5Y 7/2) fabric.
RBF/2/F (from the flue to kiln 2).

5. Lipped bowl, 140mm in diameter, in a gritty light grey (2.5Y 7/2) with patchy light brownish grey (2.5Y 6/2) burnished surface and traces of lattice as **7** below.
RBF/2/S (stokehole to kiln 2).

6. Lipped dish, 170mm in diameter; fabric as **5**.
RBF/2/S (stokehole to kiln 2).

7. Lipped bowl in a hard, gritty very dark grey (N3) fabric, roughly burnished on top of the rim.
RBF/1/S (stokehole to kiln 1).

8. Lipped bowl in a hard light grey (2.5Y 7/2) fabric with thin, light brownish grey (2.5Y 6/2) ?slipped surface, burnished over rim and below zone of wavy line decoration.
RBF/2/K (interior of kiln 2).

9. Lipped dish, 170mm in diameter, in a light brownish grey (2.5Y 6/2) fabric, with burnished dark grey (N4) surface. Inclusions in the fabric have resulted in a somewhat irregular form to the body but the vessel would appear to be wheel thrown.
RBF/2/S (stokehole to kiln 2).

10. Lipped bowl, 140mm in diameter, in a hard, gritty light grey (2.5Y 7/2) fabric with grey (N5) to light grey (N6) surface, burnished on top of rim and with decoration as **7**.
RBF/1/S (stokehole to kiln 1).

11. Flanged bowl, diameter indeterminate, in a light brownish grey (2.5Y 7/2) fabric with traces of dark grey (N4) surface, finely rilled on top of the flange. Possibly a colander?
RBF/2/S (stokehole to kiln 2).

12. Lid-seated bead-rimmed jar/beaker, in a hard, gritty grey (N5) fabric with traces of light grey (2.5Y 7/2) burnished slip inside rim.
RBF/2/S (stokehole to kiln 2).

13. Everted rim of a small beaker, 70mm in diameter, in a reddish yellow (5YR 6/2) fabric with grey (N6) core and dark grey (N4) burnished surface.
RBF/2/S (stokehole to kiln 2).

14. Sherd from a vessel of uncertain form, with triangular stabbed decoration, in a similar fabric to **13**.
RBF/2/K (interior of kiln 2). See **151** above, also from this kiln group, and the more complete profile of **127**. The use of this form and technique provides a positive link between the kiln groups.

15. Sherd, probably from a jar, with 'roller-stamp' decoration of uncertain form below a slight groove. Oxidised reddish yellow (7.5YR 8/6) fabric with traces of darker (7.5YR 7/6) surface.
RBF/1/F (flue of kiln 1).
For discussion, see pp 60–1 above.

16. Sherd from the shoulder of a jar, probably as **21** below, with ?'roller stamp' decoration below groove, in a light grey (2.5Y 7/2) fabric with greyish brown (2.5Y 5/2) burnished surface.
RBF/1/F (flue to kiln 1) (See also Fig 44).

17. Sherd from a jar with subdued rustication, in a hard gritty dark grey (N4) fabric.
RBF/1/K (interior of kiln 1).

18. Sherd from a jar with linear rustication, in a hard grey (N5) fabric.
RBF/1/S (stokehole to kiln 1).

19. Jar rim, diameter indeterminate, in a light grey (N7) fabric, with darker (N7) surface, burnished on neck and to inside of rim.
RBF/2/S (stokehole to kiln 2).

20. Jar rim, 120mm in diameter, in a pale brown (10YR 6/3) fabric with patchy, burnished light brownish grey (10YR 6/2) surface.
RBF/2/K (interior of kiln 2).

21. Jar rim, 100mm in diameter, in a gritty light grey (2.5Y 7/2) fabric with traces of burnished very dark grey (N3) to greyish brown (2.5Y 5/2) surface.
RBF/2/S (stokehole to kiln 2).

22. Jar rim, 100mm in diameter, in a gritty light grey (2.5Y 6/2) fabric with burnished light brownish grey (2.5Y 6/2) surface.
RBF/2/S (stokehole to kiln 2).

23. Jar rim, 110mm in diameter, in a hard grey (N5) fabric with pale brown (10YR 6/3) surface and patchily slipped grey (N5) surface; a cracked waster.
RBF/2/K (interior of kiln 2).

24. Jar base, in a hard grey (N5) fabric, with deeply burnished lattice and smoothed base.
RBF/2/K (interior of kiln 2).

25. Lid-seated rim of a jar, 140mm in diameter, in a gritty, light brownish grey (2.5Y 6/2) fabric with patchy dark grey (N4) surface.
RBF/2/S (stokehole to kiln 2).

26. Lid-seated jar rim, 160mm in diameter, in a gritty light grey (2.5Y 7/2) to greyish brown (2.5Y 6/2) fabric with grey (N4) surface; finely rilled on the inside of the rim and on the body.
RBF/2/S (stokehole to kiln 2).

27. Sherd from the shoulder of a vessel as **26** above, with cordon and faintly rilled surface, in a light grey (2.5Y 7/2) fabric with traces of grey (N5) surface.
RBF/2/S (stokehole to kiln 2).

28. Lid-seated jar, in a gritty light grey (2.5Y 7/2) fabric with greyish brown (2.5Y 5/2) patchy surface.
RBF/2/S (stokehole to kiln 2).

29. Lid-seated rim of a jar, 150mm in diameter, in a hard grey (N5) fabric, rilled inside the rim and on the outside.
RBF/1/S (stokehole to kiln 1).
cf Cantley kiln 2 (Annable 1960), fig 9, 69.

30. Rim of a large jar, 120mm in diameter, in a gritty, light grey (10YR 6/1) fabric, with traces of grey (10YR 5/1) surface.
RBF/2/F (flue to kiln 2).

31. Plugged handle from a large jar, in a gritty, light brownish grey (2.5Y 6/2) fabric with dark grey (N4) surface.
RBF/1/S (stokehole to kiln 1).

32. Basal sherd from a round-based colander, with circular holes, 2.5mm in diameter, pushed through from the outside,

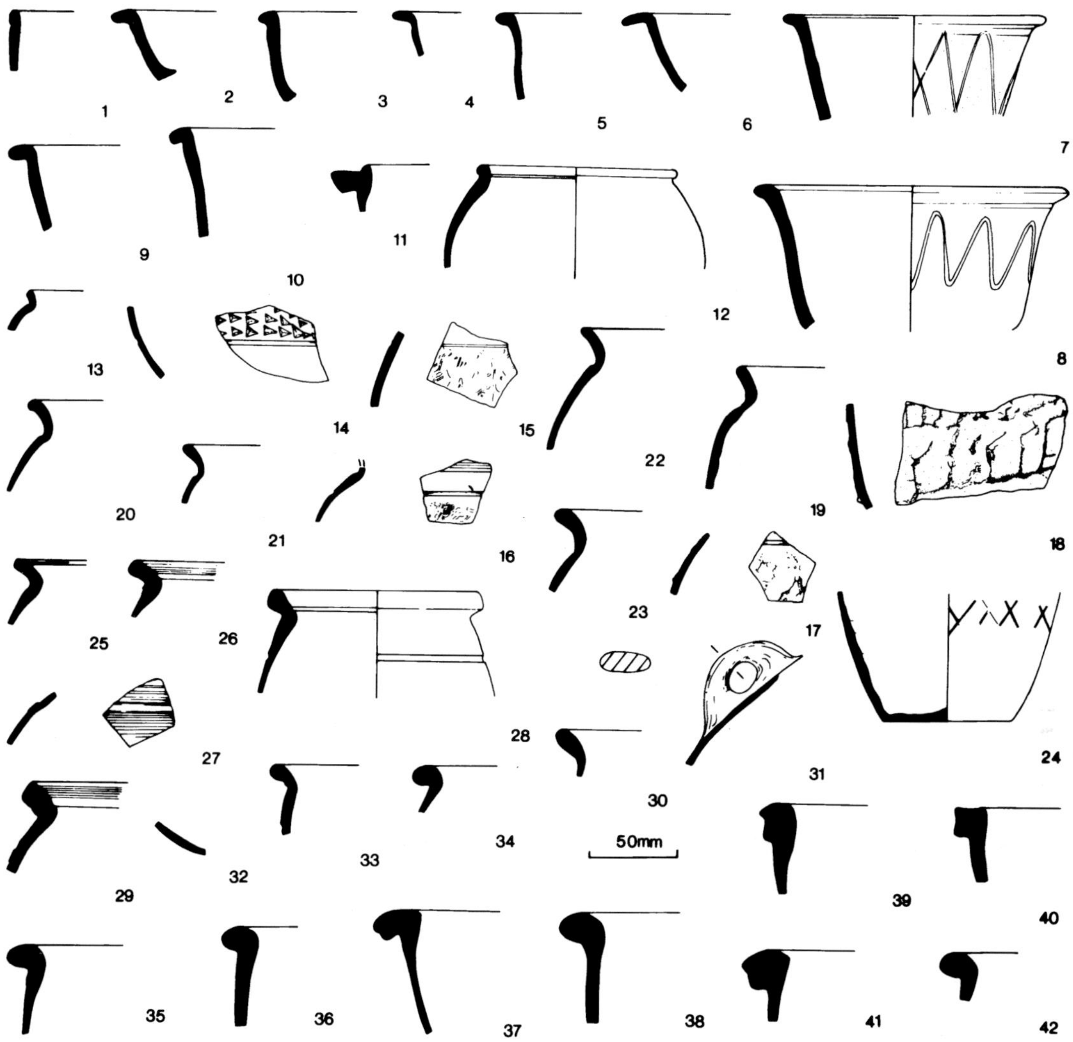

Figure 54. Rossington Bridge pottery: material from the Rossington Bridge Farm kilns, 1961.

in a gritty grey (N5) fabric. RBF/2/S (stokehole to kiln 2).

33. Wide mouthed jar, 180mm in diameter, in a hard greyish brown (2.5Y 5/2) fabric with dark grey (5Y 4/1) surface, burnished outside and to inside of rim.
RBF/2/S (stokehole to kiln 2).

34. Wide mouthed jar / medium sized bowl, 200mm in diameter, in a grey (N5) fabric.
RBF/2/S (stokehole to kiln 2).

35. Medium sized bowl, 270mm in diameter, in a light grey (2.5Y 7/2) to dark grey (N4) fabric, burnished on top of rim; a second sherd, apparently from the same vessel, is in an oxidised light red (2.5YR 6/6) fabric with light yellowish brown (10YR 6/4) surface. The profile appears rather variable.
RBF/2/F (flue to kiln 2).

36. Bowl rim, 280mm in diameter, in a gritty, grey (N6) fabric, with traces of darker (N4) surface.
RBF/2/S (stokehole to kiln 2).

37. Large bowl rim, 290mm in diameter, in a light grey (2.5Y 7/1) fabric with grey (N6) core and very dark grey (N3) surface, burnished on top of rim.
RBF/2/S.4 (stokehole to kiln 2).

38. Large bowl, 400mm in diameter, in a light grey (2.5Y 7/2) fabric with patchy dark grey (N4) surface, burnished on top of rim.
RBF/1/F (flue to kiln 1).

39. Large bowl with grooved lip, 310mm in diameter, in a gritty, light grey (5Y 7/2) fabric.
RBF/2/S (stokehole to kiln 2).

40. Large bowl, 240mm in diameter, in a gritty light grey (N6) fabric.
RBF/2/S (stokehole to kiln 2).

41. Large bowl, 340mm in diameter, in a gritty light grey (2.5Y 7/2) fabric with dark grey (N4) core and traces of grey (N5) burnished surface on top of rim.
RBF/2/S.4 (stokehole to kiln 2).

42. Large bowl, 310mm in diameter, in a gritty grey (N5) to light grey (2.5Y 7/2) fabric.
RBF/2/S (stokehole to kiln 2).

43. 'Roller-stamped' sherd, probably from a jar, in a gritty grey (2.5Y 7/2) fabric with traces of grey (N6) surface. RBF/1/K. (below kiln floor) (Fig 44; scale 1:1).

Discussion

The decision to locate a major production centre for a wide range of pottery types at Rossington Bridge during the Antonine period is usually seen simply as a reaction to the northward advance of the frontier to the Forth-Clyde line and the need to cut transport costs to the principal markets for the wares with the army (eg Buckland 1986, 45; Williams 1980, 257). Seen in terms of suitable raw materials, however, there are many sources much closer to the markets, even as at Bar Hill (Keppie 1985), Bearsden (K. Hartley, in prep) and Croy Hill (Robertson *et al* 1975) immediately adjacent to the Antonine Wall itself, and the question remains – why Rossington Bridge? It is evident that mortarium potters from the Hartshill-Mancetter kilns, principally Sarrius, but also possibly Iunius (Hartley, in Buckland *et al* 1980) were involved, and it is tempting to see constraints upon movement being imposed by the limits of the civitas territory of the Corieltauvi. As Mann (1985) has pointed out, the civil administration, in this case presumably based in Leicester, the civitas capital, was responsible for the collection of at least part of state taxation. In addition, this unit would also need to raise taxes for maintenance of roads and other civic utilities (cf Millett 1990, 123–126). If, for the purposes of discussion, the Rossington kilns are seen primarily as a secondary workshop of the Midland mortarium potter Sarrius, it can be hypothesised that his activities were limited by the bounds of his own tribal unit; to move further would have led to tax liability also to the Brigantian civitas. In a recent discussion, Booth (1996) has placed the south-western boundary of the Corieltauvi beyond Watling Street, with the Coleshill temple lying on the margins. This places Mancetter-Hartshill within the civitas, but, to substantiate the model, it remains to examine the evidence for the boundary between the Corieltauvi and Brigantes.

If the location of forts during the Roman conquest of Britain reflects the occupation of existing tribal units, then the existence of Claudio-Neronian forts along the line of Ryknield Street, at Strutts Park in Derby (Dool 1985), Chesterfield (Ellis 1989), and Templeborough, on the Don, west of Rotherham (May 1922; Simpson 1973) defines a western limit for the Corieltauvi against the gritstone uplands of the Derbyshire Peak. Eastwards, the river Don provides a logical boundary, as it did between Mercia and Elmet and later Northumbria in the post-Roman period, a line reinforced by the linear earthwork, known as the Roman Rig immediately north of the Don (Buckland *et al* 1989). Millett (1990, fig 16), however, apparently following Rivet (1958), takes a line close to the Trent, which would exclude south Yorkshire and the greater part of Nottinghamshire north of the Trent, and Ellis (1989) also follows this line. This would place the vexillation fortresses at Newton-on-Trent and Osmanthorpe (Bishop and Freeman 1993) close to the frontier, but cut across what would appear to be a coherent system of fields in Sherwood (Riley 1980), which are demonstrably oblique to later Roman features and must have pre-Roman origins (Buckland 1986; Chadwick 1997; *contra* Branigan 1989). Todd (1991) favours a boundary between the Don and Idle, whilst recognising the fluid nature of such divisions; this would again bisect the brickwork field pattern. Whitwell (1982) prefers the Don, but goes so far (*idem*, 59) as to suggest that Doncaster became a civitas capital administering a large area of the Humber Basin; there is no evidence to support this hypothesis. Field systems north and south of the Don, east of the Magnesian Limestone outcrop, do appear different, the large brickwork patterns being less evident to the north, but this may be as much a reflection of the underlying geology, the widening outcrop of the heavier clay-silt lands of the Late Devensian Lake Humber deposits of the Vale of York, as a cultural change. The essentially aceramic nature of the pre-Roman Iron age of north Nottinghamshire and south Yorkshire, more in common with west Yorkshire and the Vale than Lincolnshire and sites further south, further compounds the problem of defining any boundary; as Peacock (1968) has shown, the orbits of potters need have little to do with putative tribal affinities.

The extensive excavations on the site of Danum, beneath modern Doncaster, leaves no doubt that the fort is an early Flavian foundation (Buckland 1986; Buckland and Magilton, in prep b), but both Buckland (*idem*) and Webster (1981) have suggested that an earlier fort lay to the east of the town. A further fort on the Don at either Crowle (Buckland 2000) or at the confluence of the Don and Trent at Adlingfleet (cf Fenwick *et al* 1998) would fill the gap between it and Old Winteringham on the Humber (Stead 1976a). What is critical in defining the boundary is the date of the vexillation fortress on the south side of the river Torne at Rossington. Discovered by St. Joseph (1969), most authors (eg Bishop 1999; Bishop and Freeman 1993; Buckland 1986; Hanson and Campbell 1986; Hartley 1986; Hartley and Fitts 1988; Webster 1981) have preferred a Claudio-Neronian origin for the site, although van de Noort and Fenwick (1997, 224), quoting Frere and St. Joseph (1983) have recently suggested a Flavian date. The pottery and other finds, largely from the river crossing at Rossington Bridge (small finds **21** and **33**, loom weight, pottery **340**, **342**, and **369–374**), and the metal detector finds from the environs of the fortress (Appendix A below) confirm the pre-Flavian date. A foundation date of *c* AD 54, in line with Chesterfield (Anderson in Ellis 1989) and Templeborough (Simpson 1973), and associated with Didius

Gallus' activities in strengthening the frontier with the Brigantes (Webster 1981, 94–95), appears probable. The stability of this line until AD 69–70 (Hanson and Campbell 1986) would support the hypothesis that the Don formed the northern limits of the *Civitas Corieltauvorum*, and that Sarrius had set up another factory within his own canton. The recent realisation that similar products to Rossington Bridge were being produced on the line of the Antonine Wall near Bearsden (K. Hartley, in prep) complicates this model.

The nature of the industry: slaves, freedmen or independent potters?

The presence on a single kiln site of potters whose origins can be traced to a diversity of tribal units, Durotriges and Corieltauvi, and perhaps Aquitanians, requires an explanation which goes beyond the simplistic concept of migrating or wandering potters. The view that potters were free individuals. able to move and set up workshops at any suitable place within the Empire, appears to be a fundamental tenet of most British researchers. It is a view which appeals much to those used to a modern free market economy, but which, as Richmond (1950) once perceptively remarked in another context, would be 'found at best strangely unfamiliar and at worse grossly distasteful' in the Ancient World. Pollard (1988), for example, in his extensive review of Roman pottery production in Kent, a source of much BB2, makes no mention of slaves or freedmen. Swan (1992), in doubting the free movement of potters of diverse North African origins to York, prefers to see local production by skilled legionaries of African origin, whilst Greene (1977) favoured production by slaves of eastern origin at Holt and other military production sites. Swan (1999) proposes a range of possibilities for the presence of locally produced African forms, from slaves to auxiliaries returning with garrisons to the Wall from AntoninusPius' Mauritanian wars in *c* AD 150. Fülle, in a discussion of Italian Arretine manufacture (1997, 145), has urged caution in the use of modern terms in the description of large scale Roman pottery production. Graeco-Roman society was slave-owning at all levels, from the emperor's Greek tutor to the stokers in the *praefurnia*, and the purchase of suitably skilled potters is as probable as the purchase of the pots themselves. The relative status of potters in society was likely to have been low, whether free or slave (cf Peacock 1982), and there are few literary references. Only from Egypt is there sufficient surviving documentary evidence for the varying nature of contracts for pottery production (Cockle 1981; Fülle 1997). Potters leased existing potteries with all materials provided in exchange for both cash and product payments; elsewhere they had to provide their own materials, and a range of other arrangements is probable.

The stamping of fine wares, particularly Arretine and samian wares, provides a number of clues. The stamps upon the former are often sufficiently explicit to define the status of the individual, with the *tria nomina* of the Roman citizen owner juxtaposed with the name, often Greek (Greene 1986, 160), of the slave or freedman potter. In Gaul, Germany, England, and the Danube provinces, Brian Hartley (1977) has recorded a surprising degree of mobility of names and dies between production sites, and stamps consist of single names; only one stamp, an additional one on moulds by the 'firm' of Germanus used at Banassac reading SER(VUS), might indicate servile status. In contrast with Arretine, therefore, the samian manufactories appear to consist of relatively free individuals working co-operatively at particular sites (cf Polak 1998). Some caution, however, may be necessary in this conclusion. The Christian lady Melania in the early 5th century held estates in Italy, Sicily, Spain, North Africa and Britain, and is alleged to have owned 24,000 slaves (Finley 1980, 123); skilled artisans could be moved as freely as their products, and the orchestration of movement may have lain more with who owned the land than with the individual.

Which model applies to the Rossington kilns is impossible to divine, but the purchase of skilled slaves by an entrepreneur, putatively Sarrius utilising freedmen, Secundua and Setibogius, to run a secondary production centre seems a pattern worthy of consideration. There is some suggestion that a similar situation may have pertained slightly earlier in the 2nd century at Derby Racecourse, where other Mancetter/Hartshill mortarium potters were involved in producing a wide range of products, perhaps including Black Burnished Ware (Buckland, in Brassington 1980, 39–40) at a site again close to the suggested tribal boundary of the Corieltauvi.

Conclusion

The rescue work carried out at Rossington in the late 1950s and the subsequent research excavations directed by John Lidster revealed a site of considerable significance in Roman pottery studies, and it is unfortunate that events conspired against its early publication. Few major production centres lie adjacent to waterlogged deposits, and it is particularly unfortunate that both the artifactual and environmental potential of these sediments were not exploited. The site has dried out significantly over the past 40 years, although the assessment carried out by the Humber Wetlands Unit in 1997 shows that there is still some potential for recovery of materials from the abandoned meander of the River Torne (Dinnin, in van de Noort 1997, 444–447). Although a scheduled monument, the process of destruction by desiccation cannot be controlled. Changes in land use are also affecting the site. Although one of the few remaining areas of unploughed heath in the region and the only British locality for a species of ladybird, *Exochomus nigromaculatus* Goeze. (Skidmore 1985), the site has no

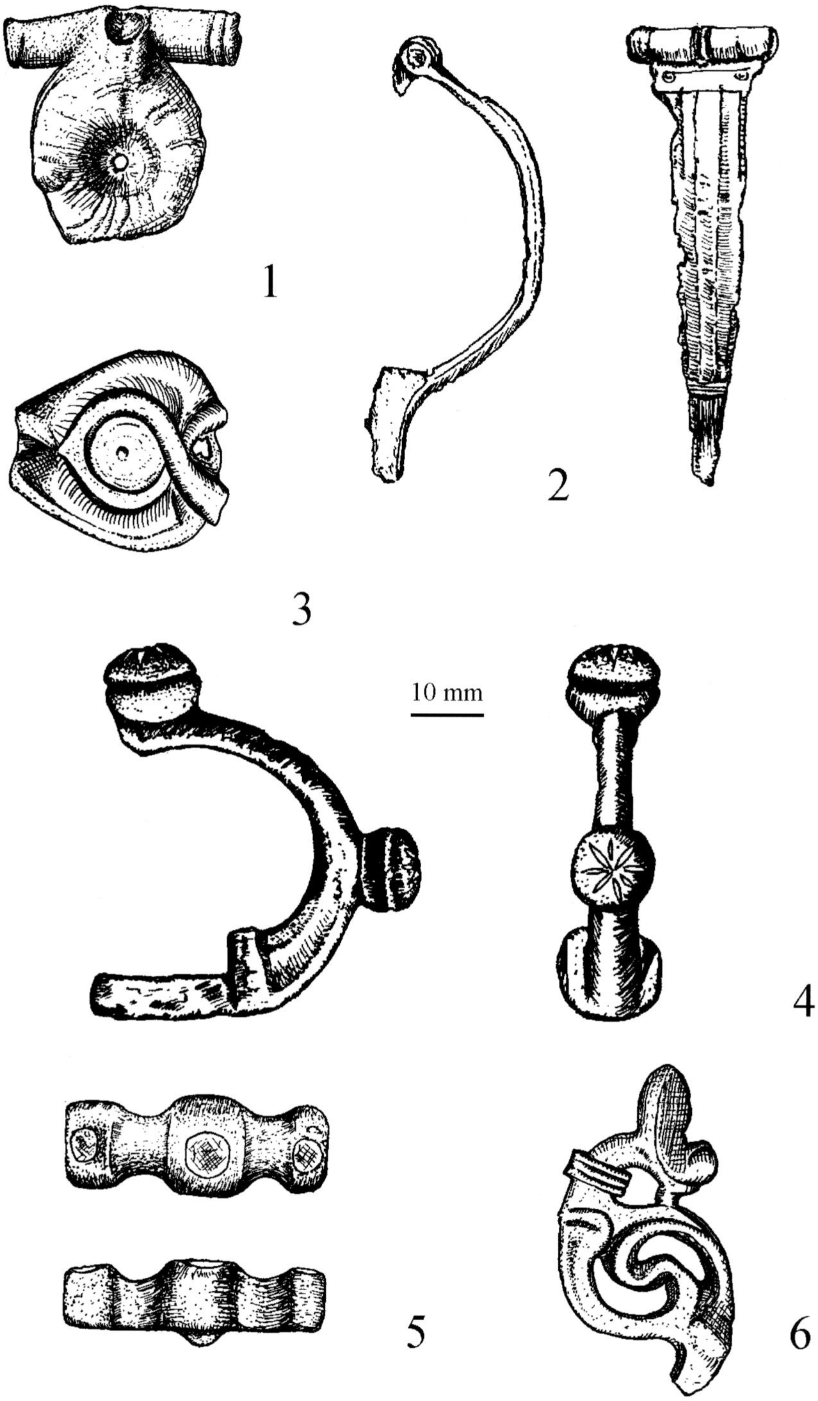

Figure 55. Metal-detector finds from south of the River Torne. Drawing: M. Lucas.

protection as a Site of Special Scientific Interest (SSSI), and part of it has recently been ploughed by an unsympathetic landowner. In addition, previously grazed by horses, these have now been excluded from the site, and it is rapidly being overgrown with birch and oak scrub, thereby causing additional damage to sub-surface structures. Lying on the southern edge of suburban Doncaster, the area is also under increasing pressure for housing development, and the former gardens of houses fronting onto Warning Tongue Lane to the north have now been infilled with houses, fortunately after archaeological evaluation (Atkinson and Merrony 1994). Unless action is taken soon, the unique record of the Rossington Bridge site will be lost.

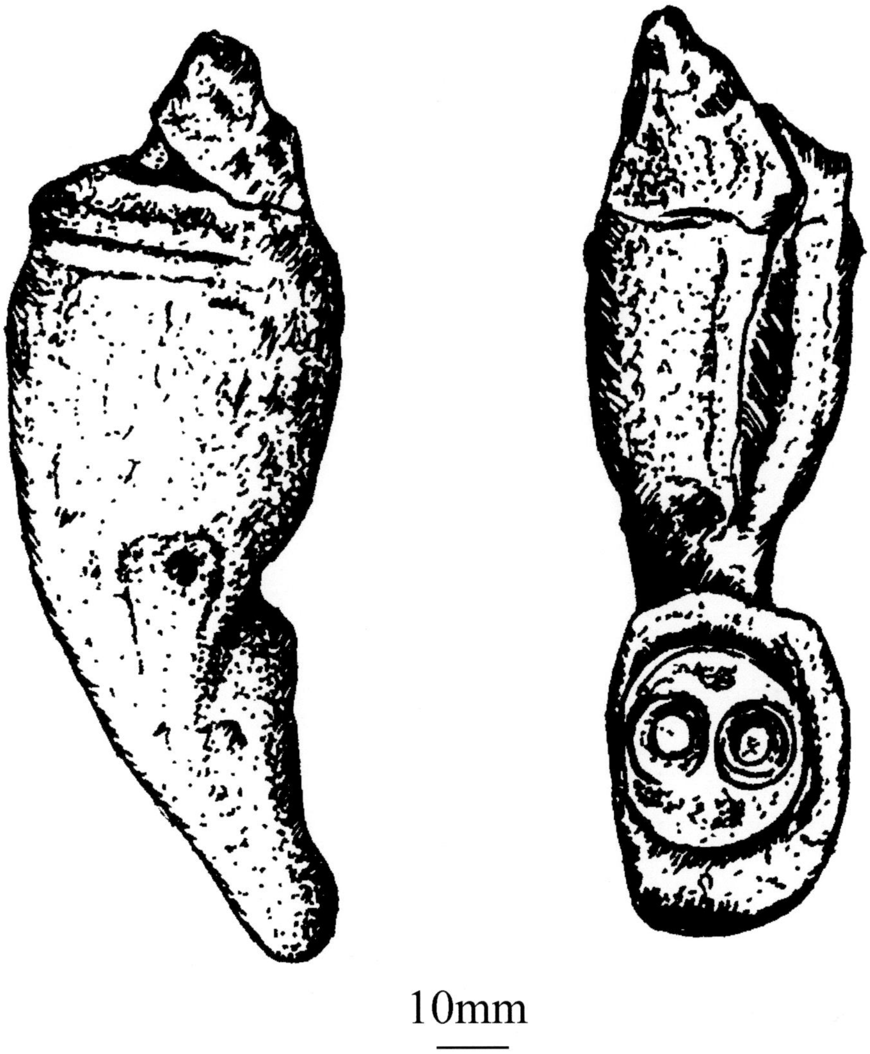

Figure 56. Enamelled linch pin metal detector find from south of Rossington Bridge. Drawing: M. Lucas.

Acknowledgements

The Museum records unfortunately do not include the names of the volunteers who assisted in the excavations of 1956–61; unknown, they are gratefully acknowledged. Only Chris Devlin of the Museum staff is noted as taking part. The magnetometer survey conducted in the early 1960's was directed by M.J. Dolby, then Deputy Keeper of Antiquities at Doncaster Museum, with help from PCB, J. Hinchliffe, E. Judkins and R.D. Steward, amongst others. Processing of the finds was largely the work of Joan Buckland, Ian McDonald, and Neil Loughlin, and John Samuels carried out the basic counts on material. Conservation of finds was carried out by Arthur Boulton and Janet Edmond. Dave Green kindly provided details of metal detector finds made in the region and allowed details to be incorporated in the report by Tony O'Connor. Drawings were prepared by Phil Buckland, M.J. Dolby, Mick Durrant, Mark Lomas, and Jo Minter, as well as the authors. The text has benefitted much from discussion with, and comments from Geoff Dannell, the late Ray Farrar, the late John Gillam, John Magilton, Eva Panagiotakopulu, Rob Perrin, Ian Stead and Vivien Swan over several years. Successive directors, curators and keepers of Doncaster Museum Service are acknowledged for assistance and continued access to collections. The finds and site archive are held by Doncaster Museum Service, part of the Education and Culture Department of Doncaster Metropolitan Borough Council.

Table 12. Metal detector finds of coins from Rossington Bridge.

	Date	Denomination
Q. Fabius Maximus	125–120 BC	*denarius* RRC 478
M. Aemilius Scarus & P. Platius Hypsaeus	58 BC	*denarius* RRC 912
Emperor		
Augustus	7–6 BC	*denarius* RIC 207
Claudius	AD 41–54	*dupondius* Rev. CERES AVGVSTA
Nero	64–68	*denarius* RIC 51
Nero	60–64	plated *denarius*
Nero	54–68	*as* Rev. Victory holding shield
Vespasian	72–73	*as* RIC 528
Vespasian	77–79	*as* RIC 595
Vespasian	69–79	*as* RIC 494
Vespasian	69–79	*as* Rev. female figure advancing rt.
Vespasian	71	*dupondius* RIC 473
Titus	77–78	*dupondius* RIC775(b)
Domitian	81–82	*sestertius* RIC 233a/240a
Trajan	114–117	*sestertius* RIC 671
Hadrian	134–138	*sestertius* Rev. FELICITAS AVG SC
Sabina	137	*as* RIC 1024
Antoninus Pius	140–144	*as* RIC 691a
Antoninus Pius	138–161	*as* illeg.
Antoninus Pius	158–159	*as* RIC 1026
Antoninus Pius	138–161	*sestertius* Rev. ? AVGVSTA SC
Faustina I	141	*denarius* RIC 141
Faustina I	141	*as* Rev. AETERNITAS SC
Faustina II	161–179	*sestertius* RIC 1686
Lucilla	179	*as* RIC 791
Lucilla	179	*sestertius* RIC 1779
Commodus	177–178	*sestertius* RIC 1588
Commodus	184–186	*sestertius* Rev. VICT BRIT
Commodus	175–192	*sestertius* Rev. LIBERTAS
Septimius Severus	196–197	*denarius* RIC 81a
Septimius Severus	202–210	*denarius* RIC 265
Julia Domna	196–211	*denarius* RIC 580
Geta	203	*denarius* RIC 105
Elagabalus	219	*denarius* RIC 19
Severus Alexander	222–235	*denarius* RIC 282
Maximinus	235–238	*antoninianus* RIC 13
Postumus	259–268	radiate Rev. female figure holding branch and cornucopiae
Posthumus	259–268	radiate illeg.
Gallienus	260–268	radiate Rev. PROV[ID]
Gallienus	260–268	radiate Rev. APOLLINI CONS AVG
Gallienus	260–268	radiate as RIC 332f
Victorinus	268–270	radiate Rev. PIETAS AVG type
Victorinus	268–270	radiate Rev. SPES PUBLICA
Claudius II	268–270	radiate RIC 102
Carausius	287–293	radiate RIC 98
Carausius	287–293	radiate Rev. PAX AVG type
Allectus	293–296	radiate RIC 33
Maximianus	298–299	*follis* RIC 91b Rome
Maximianus	300	*follis* RIC 500 Trier
Maximianus	303–305	*follis* RIC 33–34 London
Maximianus	307	*follis* (reduced) RIC 83–84
Constantius I	300–301	*follis* RIC 426ff Trier
Constantine I	321–322	*follis* RIC 223
Constantine I	320–330	*follis* Rev. Victory adv. lt. holdingwreath
Constantine I	324–330	3ae LRBC 38 Trier
Crispus	320	3ae Rev. BEATA TRANQUILLITAS
Crispus	320–321	3ae RIC 161 Siscia
Constantine II	323–324	3ae RIC 292 London
Constantine II	324–326	3ae LRBC 8 London
	330–341	3ae Urbs Roma type
Constantine II	324–330	3ae Rev. PROVIDENTIAE CAESS type
Constantine II	323–324	3ae RIC 217 Lyon
Constantine II	323	3ae RIC 218 Lyon
Constantine II	323–324	3ae RIC 441 Trier
Constantine II	330–335	4ae Rev. GLORIA EXERCITVS
Constans	341–346	4ae LRBC 137ff
Constantine II	346–350	3ae Rev. FEL TEMP REPARATIO (fallen horseman)
Magnentius	350–351	2ae LRBC 3 Amiens
Magnentius	350–351	2ae Rev. FELICITAS REIPVBLICAE
Gratian	367–375	3ae LRBC 511
Valens	367–375	*siliqua* RIC 27d

Appendix 1: Rossington Bridge: coins and copper-alloy objects reported to Doncaster Museum and Art Gallery
T. O'Connor

During the 1980s the area to the south of the River Torne, between the scheduled ancient monument of the fortress and the Rossington Bridge Pumping Station kilns, was extensively explored by a local metal detectorist, Mr David Green. The finds were identified, plotted and recorded at Doncaster Museum and Art Gallery. The material adds to our knowledge of the long usage of this site and goes some way towards confirming the early date of the occupation of the vexillation fortress. The coins and a selection of the copper-alloy metalwork finds are listed here; unfortunately drawings and detailed descriptions are not available for all the pieces.

Copper-alloy objects

1. Cast copper-alloy fitting with Celtic style decoration and a central rivet hole. Stead pers comm: has suggested that this is part of a La Tene III tankard handle (Fig 55, 3). cf. the more complete example from the Seven Sisters hoard, Glamorgan (Grimes 1939, fig 40, 9), where an associated horse trapping (no.12) would suggest an early Roman date of deposition.
2. Cast copper-alloy knobbed terret-ring, the knobs are decorated with 8 red enamel petals and grooves. (Fig 55, 4). The type is discussed by MacGregor (1976, 46–47), who suggests that the type originated in the pre-Roman Iron Age, but continued through the 2nd century AD. Stead (1991, fig 39) figures an example, decorated with bone inlay on the knobs, from an Iron Age burial at Garton Station, East Yorkshire.
3. Copper-alloy horse-harness toggle, decorated with 3 enamelled red roundels. (Fig 55, 5). The piece is clearly related to the examples figured by Stead (1965, fig 34) from pre-Roman Iron Age contexts at Eastburn, East Yorkshire and at Glastonbury, Somerset.
4. Copper-alloy distal end of a linch pin, decorated with red enamel (Fig 56). When complete, it would have been attached to a rectangular section iron shank. Compare the very similar pieces recently published by Cunliffe (1995, fig 16, 7) from Bury Hill, Hampshire, and by Stead 1991, (figs 37–38) from the Kirkburn cart burial, East Yorkshire. A date range of *c* 100–50 BC is suggested.
5. Rosette brooch, Collingwood and Richmond (1969) form W. The drawing (Fig 55, 1) indicates that the piece had an encased spring rather than a simple hinged pin. The perforation in the centre of the circular frame would have held an inlay. The type is discussed by May (1996, 247) in considering the few pieces from Dragonby, and he suggests that, despite a few examples in pre-Conquest contexts, the brooch type is essentially 1st century Roman. Stead and Rigby (1989, fig 99) record three examples in Grave 69 at the King Harry Lane Cemetery, St. Albans, which they date to AD 30–55.
6. Aucissa brooch, Collingwood and Richmond (1969), group C, although unstamped. (Fig 55, 2). May 1996, (fig 11.6, 66) provides a parallel from Dragonby, north Lincolnshire, and he comments that the type appears to have been introduced to Britain at the Roman Conquest and has largely ceased to be current by the end of the Claudio-Neronian period.
7. Dragonesque brooch. (Fig 55, 6). The type has been discussed by Feachem (1968), who figures an example from Cantley. The basic form is similar to an example from Old Winteringham Stead 1976a, (fig 99, 11), although the latter, like the Cantley piece, has enamel rather than curvilinear decoration. Stead (*op ci.*, 198) regards the form as late Neronian-Flavian.
8. Enamelled plate brooch in the form of a hare. Second century, cf. the examples from Dragonby (May 1996, fig 11.12, 127) and Old Winteringham (Stead 1976a, fig 100, 19).
9. Disc brooch with evidence of enamelling. Probably 2nd century.
10. Dolphin brooch. Hattatt (1987, 93) suggests that the form was being produced in the immediately pre-Conquest period, continuing to *c* AD 80.
11. Trumpet headed brooch, Collingwood and Richmond (1969) Form R.
12. Trumpet headed brooch fragment.
13. Trumpet headed brooch, mid section only. Late first to mid-second century (May 1996, 255).
14. Headstud brooch with lozenge band of enamelled decoration, Collingwood and Richmond (1969) Form Q.
15. Headstud brooch with traces of red enamel.
16. Headstud brooch, Collingwood and Richmond (1969) Form Q. May (1996, 255) dates the type to the late first to the end of the 2nd century.
17. Fantail brooch with lozenge enamelled decoration. 2nd century (May 1996, 257).
18. Fragment of patera handle.
19. Strap end decorated with red and blue enamel and hatched designs, probably a piece of military equipment.
20. Amphora-shaped strap end. Simpson (1976) associates the type with the late Roman army.

Discussion

It is unfortunate that no systematic field-walking of the area east of the Rossington Bridge fortress has been possible. The area of the fortress itself was examined shortly after its discovery but produced virtually no finds, and it was left to metal detectorists to make the extensive finds of copper alloy objects of which some are reported here. They indicate roadside settlement along the road south of the river crossing, as well as a scatter of pre-Flavian material sufficient to confirm the earlier foundation of the vexillation fortress. Three items, nos. 1, 3 and 4, however, horse and cart fittings, are suggestive of an earlier Iron Age presence, and these may relate to a now lost burial. A further item, an Anglo-Saxon garnet-inlayed gold fitment, found in the same field as the Rossington Bridge Farm kilns, hints at a later high status presence. This item was sold on the legal antiquities market and is now lost.

References

Adams, N. 1977: 'Leather shoes' in Rogerson 1977, 207–209.

Aitken, M.J. and Weaver, G.H. 1962: 'Magnetic dating: some archaeomagnetic measurements in Britain', *Archaeometry* **5**, 4–22.

Allason-Jones, L. and Miket, R. 1984: *The Catalogue of small finds from South Shields Roman Fort,* Soc Antiq Newcastle upon Tyne Mon Ser, **2**.

Anderson, A.C. and Anderson, A.S. (eds.) 1981: *Roman pottery research in Britain and North-West Europe*, Brit Archaeol Rep **S123**.

Annable, F.K. 1954: 'The Roman Pottery Kilns at Cantley Housing Estate, Doncaster. Kilns 1–8', *Yorkshire Archaeolog J*, **38**, 403–6.

Annable, F.K. 1960: *The Romano-British Pottery at Cantley Housing Estate Doncaster Kilns 1–8*, Doncaster Mus Pub. **24**.

Arthur, P. and Marsh, G. (eds.) 1978: *Early Fine Wares in Roman Britain*. Brit Archaeol Rep **57**.

Atkinson, S. and Merrony, C.J.N. 1994: 'An archaeological evaluation of land off Warning Tongue Lane, Bessacarr, Doncaster', *Archaeol S Yorkshire 1993–1994.* 23–27.

Bell, M. 1976: 'The excavation of an early Romano-British site and Pleistocene landforms at Newhaven, Sussex', *Sussex Archaeol Coll*, **114**, 256–287.

Bidwell, P.T. 1979: *The Legionary Bath-House and Basilica and Forum at Exeter*, Exeter Archaeol Rep **1**.

Bird, J. (ed.) 1998: *Form and Fabric. Studies in Rome's material past in honour of B.R. Hartley*, Oxbow Mon **80**.

Birley, E. 1930: 'Excavations on the line of Hadrian's Wall west of Newcastle upon Tyne', *Archaeologia Aeliana*, 4th Ser., **7**, 150–180.

Birley, E. and Gillam, J.P. 1948: 'Mortarium stamps from Corbridge, 1906–1938', *Archaeologia Aeliana*, 4th Ser., **26**, 172–201.

Bishop, M.C. 1999: 'The historical and archaeological context of the *Castra* at Castleford' in P. Abramson, D.S. Berg and M.R. Fossick, *Roman Castleford. Excavations 1974–85, II. The structural and environmental evidence*, 307–312, Yorkshire Archaeol **5**.

Bishop, M.C. and Freeman, F.W.M. 1993: 'Recent work at Osmanthorpe, Nottinghamshire', *Britannia*, **24**, 159–190.

Boon, G.C. 1974: *Silchester The Roman Town of Calleva*. (2nd. ed).

Boon, G.C. 1978: 'Glass', in James 1976, 84.

Boon, G.C. 1983: 'Potters, oculists and eye-troubles', *Britannia*, **14**, 1–12.

Booth, P. 1996: 'Warwickshire in the Roman period: A review of recent work', *Trans Birmingham Warwickshire Archaeol Soc*, **100**, 25–57.

Branigan, K. 1989: 'An early landscape revisited', in Kennedy 1989, 161–166.

Brassington, M. 1971: 'A Trajanic Kiln Complex near Little Chester, Derby, 1968', *Antiq J*, **60**, 8–47.

Brassington, M. 1980: 'Derby Racecourse kiln excavations 1972–3', *Antiq J*, **60**, 8–47.

Brodribb, A.C.C., Hands, A.R. and Walker, D.R. 1978: *Excavations at Shakenoak Farm, near Wilcote, Oxfordshire.* **V**: *Sites K and E.*

Buckland, P.C. 1976: 'A Romano-British Pottery Kiln Site at Branton, near Doncaster', *Yorkshire Archaeol J,* **48**, 69–82.

Buckland, P.C. 1986: *Roman South Yorkshire. A source book.*

Buckland, P.C. 2000: Review of van de Noort and Ellis 1998: *Environmental Archaeol*, **5**, 122–123.

Buckland, P.C. and Dolby, M.J. 1980: *A Roman Pottery Kiln Site at Blaxton Quarry, near Doncaster.*

Buckland, P.C. and Magilton, J.R. 1986: *The Archaeology of Doncaster. 1. The Roman Civil Settlement,* Brit Archaeol Rep **148**.

Buckland, P.C. and Magilton, J.R. and Hayfield, C.1989: *Archaeology of Doncaster 2. The medieval and later town*, Brit Archaeol Rep **202**.

Buckland, P.C. and Magilton, J.R. in prep. a: *Excavations on Roman Pottery Kiln Sites in Cantley Parish, south Yorkshire, kilns 30–44, 1956–1974.*

Buckland, P.C. and Magilton, J.R. in prep. b: *Archaeology of Doncaster 3. The Roman fort.*

Buckland, P.C., Magilton, J.R. and Dolby, M.J. 1980: 'The Roman pottery industries of South Yorkshire: a review', *Britannia,* **11**, 145–164.

Buckland, P.C. and Sadler, J. 1986: 'Late Flandrian Alluviation in the Humberhead Levels', *E Midland Geog*, **8**, 239–251.

Buckley, D.G. and Major, H. 1990: 'Quernstones', in Wrathmell and Nicholson 1990, 105–120.

Buckley, D.G. and Major, H. 1998: 'The quernstones', in Cool and Philo 1998, 241–246.

Cameron, H. and Lucas, J. 1969: 'Tripontium. First interim report on excavations by the Rugby Archaeological Society at Cave's Inn, near Rugby, Grid Reference SP 57, 535795', *Trans Birmingham Warwickshire Archaeol Soc*, **83**, 130–179.

Carrington, P. 1977: 'Severn Valley Ware and its place in the Roman pottery supply at Chester: a preliminary assessment', in Dore and Greene 1977, 147–162.

Chadwick, A. 1997: 'Towards a social archaeology of later prehistoric and Romano-British field systems in south Yorkshire, West Yorkshire and Nottinghamshire', *Assemblage*, **1**, 1–15 http://www.shef.ac.uk/~assem/2/2chad.html:.

Charlesworth, D. 1972: 'The Glass', in Frere 1972, 196–215.

Clarke, G. 1979: *Winchester Studies 3: Pre-Roman and Roman Winchester. Part 2: The Roman Cemetery at Lankills.*

Cockle, H. 1981: 'Pottery manufacture in Roman Egypt', *J Roman Stud*, **71**, 87–97.

Coles, J.M. 1987: 'Meare Village East. The excavations of A. Bulleid and H. St. George Gray', *Somerset Levels Papers*, **13**.

Collingwood, R.G. and Richmond, I.A. 1969: *The Archaeology of Roman Britain.*

Collis, J. 1984: *Oppida. Earliest Towns North of the Alps .*

Cool, H.E.M. 1998: 'The needles, weights, table utensills, seal boxes, furniture, fittings, fastenings and miscellaneous objects', in Cool and Philo 1998, 91–116.

Cool, H.E.M. and Philo, C. (eds.) 1998: *Roman Castleford. Excavations 1974–85, I. The small finds*, 241–246, Yorkshire Archaeol **4**.

Corder, P. 1928: *The Roman Pottery at Crambeck, Castle Howard,* Roman Malton Dist Rep **1**.

Corder, P. 1950: *A Romano-British Pottery Kiln on Lincoln Racecourse.*

Corder, P. 1954: *The Roman town and villa at Great Casterton Rutland. Second interim report for the years 1951–1953.*

Corder, P. 1956: 'Parisian Ware', *Yorkshire Archaeol J*, **39**, 48–52.

Corder, P. 1959: 'The Structure of Romano-British Pottery Kilns', *Archaeol J*, **114**, 10–27.

Corder, P. and Birley, M. 1937: 'A pair of fourth century pottery kilns near Crambeck: with a note on the distribution of Crambeck ware', *Antiq J*, **17**, 392–413.

Corney, M. 1984: 'Objects of Iron', in Fulford 1984, 112–115.

Cregeen, S.M. 1957: 'The Romano-British Excavations at Cantley

Estate, Doncaster. The Pottery from Kilns 9–25', *Yorkshire Archaeol J*, **39**, 364–388.

Crummy, N. 1983: *Colchester Archaeological Reports 2: The Roman small finds from Excavations in Colchester 1971–9.*

Cunliffe, B. 1975: *Excavations at Portchester Castle 1 Roman*, Rep Res Comm Soc Antiq London, **32**.

Cunliffe, B. 1995: 'The Celtic chariot: a footnote', in Raftery *et al.* 1995, 31–40.

Curle, J. 1911: *A Roman Frontier Post and its People: The Fort at Newstead in the Parish of Melrose.*

D. = Figure types in Dechelette, J. 1904: *Les Vases céramiques ornés de la Gaule romaine.*

Dannell, G.B. and Wild, J.P. 1987: *Longthorpe II. The military works-depot: an episode in landscape history*, Britannia Mon Ser **8**.

Darling, M.J. 1981: 'Early red-slipped ware from Lincoln', in Anderson and Anderson 1981, 397–416.

Detsicas, A.P. (ed.) 1973: *Current Research in Romano-British Coarse Pottery*, Counc Brit Archaeol Res Rep **10**.

Detsicas, A.P. 1974: 'Exhibitions at ballots, no.2. Finds from the pottery kilns: at Eccles, Kent', *Antiq J*, **54**, 305–306.

Dolby, M.J. 1969: 'Roman remains from Adwick-le-Street, W.R.', *Yorkshire Archaeol J*, **42**, 252–253.

Dool, J. 1985a: 'Derby Racecourse: Excavations on the Roman Industrial Settlement', *Derbyshire Archaeol J*, **105**, 155–221.

Dool, J. 1985b: 'Excavations at Strutt's Park, Derby, 1974', *Derbyshire Archaeol J*, **105**, 15–32.

Dore, J. and Greene, K. (eds.) 1977: *Roman Pottery Studies in Britain and Beyond*, 147–162, Brit Archaeol Rep **S30**.

Down, A. 1989: *Chichester Excavations **VI**.*

Draper, J. 1985: 'Excavations by Mr H.P. Cooper on the Roman Site at Hill Farm, Gestingthorpe, Essex', *E Anglian Archaeol* **25**.

Dryden, J.S. and Withell, A.R. 1978: 'The pottery from Turret 52a, Banks East', *Trans Cumberland Westmoreland Antiq Archaeol Soc*, 2nd ser. **78**, 37–45.

Duhamel, P. 1973: *Les fours céramiques en Gaule romaine.* Thesis, Ecole practique des Hautes Etudes, IVe section.

Ellis, P. 1989: 'Roman Chesterfield: excavations by T. Courtney 1974-78', *Derbyshire Archaeol J*, **109**, 51–130.

Elsdon, S. 1982: *Parisian Ware: a study of the stamped wares of the Roman period in Lincolnshire, Humberside and South Yorkshire*, Vorda Res Ser **4**.

Farrar, R.A.H. 1973: 'The Techniques and Sources of Romano-British Black-burnished Ware', in Detsicas 1973, 67–103.

Farrar, R.A.H. 1975: 'Interim Report on Excavations at the Romano-British Potteries at Redcliff near Wareham', *Proc Dorset Nat Hist Archaeol Soc*, **97**, 49–51.

Farrar, R.A.H. 1977: 'A Romano-British black-burnished ware industry at Ower in the Isle of Purbeck, Dorset', in Dore and Greene 1977, 199–228.

Farrar, R.A.H. 1981: 'The first Darfield hoard and the dating of Black-Burnished ware', in Anderson and Anderson 1981, 417–440.

Feachem, R.W. 1968: 'Dragonesque fibulae', *Antiq J*, **48**, 100–102.

Fenwick, H., Chapman, H., Head, R. and Lillie, M. 1998: 'The archaeological survey of the lower Trent valley and Winterton Beck', in van de Noort and Ellis 1998, 143–197.

Finley, M.I. 1980: *Ancient slavery and modern ideology.*

Frere, S.S. 1972: *Verulamium Excavations **I***, Rep Res Comm Soc Antiq London **27**.

Frere, S.S. 1984: *Verulamium Excavations **III***, Oxford University Comm Archaeol.

Frere, S.S. and St. Joseph, J.K. 1974: 'The Roman fortress at Longthorpe', *Britannia*, **5**, 1–130.

Frere, S.S. and St. Joseph, J.K. 1983: *Roman Britain from the air.*

Frere, S.S. and Wilkes, J.J. 1989: *Strageath. Excavations within the Roman fort 1973–86*, Britannia Mon Ser **9**.

Fulford, M.G. 1975: *New Forest Roman Pottery,* Brit Archaeol Rep **17**.

Fulford, M. 1984: *Silchester Defences 1974–80*, Britannia Mon Ser **5**.

Fülle, G. 1997: 'The internal organisation of the Arretine *Terra sigillata* industry: problems of evidence and interpretation', *J Roman Stud*, **87**, 111–156.

Gaunt, G.D. 1981: 'Quaternary History of the Southern Part of the Vale of York', in Neale and Flenley 1981, 82–97.

Gaunt, G.D. 1994: Geology of the Country around Goole, Doncaster and the Isle of Axholme, *Mem Brit Geol Surv,* Sheets 79 and 88 (England and Wales).

Gillam, J.P. 1939: 'Romano-British Derbyshire Ware', *Antiq J*, **19**, 429–437.

Gillam, J.P. 1960–61: 'The Coarse Pottery', in Steer 1961, 113–129.

Gillam, J.P. 1968: 'Coarse Pottery', in Wenham 1968, 56–86.

Gillam, J.P. 1970: *Types of Roman Coarse Pottery Vessels in Northern Britain,* (3rd ed.).

Gillam, J.P. 1973: 'Sources of Pottery on Northern Military Sites', in Detsicas 1973, 53–62.

Gillam, J.P. 1976: 'Coarse Fumed Ware in North Britain and Beyond', *Glasgow Archaeol J*, **4**, 57–80.

Gilmour, E.F. 1954: 'The Roman Pottery Kilns at Cantley Housing Estate, Doncaster Kilns 9–15', *Yorkshire Archaeol J,* **38**, 407–412.

Gilmour, E.F. 1955: 'The Roman Excavations at Cantley Housing Estate, Doncaster. 1. The Roman Well. 2. Kilns 16–21', *Yorkshire Archaeol J*, **38**, 536–545.

Gilmour, E.F. 1956: 'The Roman Excavations at Cantley Housing Estate, Doncaster. Kilns 26–29', *Yorkshire Archaeol J*, **39**, 16.

Green, C.M. 1976: 'The coarse pottery', in Bell 1976, 256–287.

Greene, K. 1977: 'Legionary pottery and the significance of Holt', in Dore and Greene 1977, 113–132.

Greene, K. 1986: *The archaeology of the Roman economy.*

Greep, S. 1998: 'The bone, antler and ivory artefacts', in Cool and Philo 1998, 267–285.

Gregory, A.K. 1996: 'Romano-British pottery', in May 1996, 513–586.

Grew, F. and Frere, S.S. 1989: 'The objects of metal and jet', in Frere and Wilkes 1989, 141–174.

Grimes, W.F. 1939: *Guide to the collection illustrating the prehistory of Wales.*

Guido, M. 1978: *The glass beads of the Prehistoric and Roman periods in Britain,* Rep Res Comm Soc Antiq London **35**.

Hanson, W.S. and Campbell, D.B. 1986: 'The Brigantes: from clientage to conquest', *Britannia*, **17**, 73–92.

Harman, M., Molleson, T.I. and Price, J.L. 1981: 'Burials, bodies and beheadings in Romano-British and Anglo-Saxon cemeteries', *Bull Brit Mus Nat Hist (Geology)*, **35(3)**, 145–188.

Harold, M.R. 1960: 'Magnetic dating: the spinning magnetometer', *Archaeometry*, **3**, 47–50.

Hartley, B.R. 1977: 'Some wandering potters', in Dore and Greene 1977, 251–262.

Hartley, B.R. 1988: 'Plus ça change...or reflections on the Roman forts of Yorkshire', in Price and Wilson 1988, 153–160.

Hartley, B.R. and Fitts, L. 1988: *The Brigantes.*

Hartley, B.R. and Wacher, J. (eds.) 1983: *Rome and her Northern Provinces.*

Hartley, K.F. 1960: 'Mortarium stamps', in Jarrett 1960, 158–160.
Hartley, K.F. 1962: 'The kilns at Hartshill', *Archaeometry*, **5**, 22–24.
Hartley, K.F. 1973: 'The kilns at Mancetter and Hartshill, Warwickshire', in. Detsicas 1973, 143–147.
Hartley, K. 1975: 'The Mortarium Stamps', in Robertson, 236–239.
Hartley, K. 1977: 'Two major potteries producing mortaria in the first century A.D.', in Dore and Greene 1977, 5–18.
Hattatt, R. 1982: *Ancient and Romano-British Brooches.*
Hattatt, R. 1985: *Iron Age and Roman Brooches; a second selection of brooches from the author's collection.*
Hattatt, R. 1987: *Brooches of Antiquity.*
Hawkes, C. and S. Hawkes (eds.) 1973: *Greeks, Celts and Romans. Studies in venture and resistance.*
Hawkes, C.F.C. and Hull, M.R. 1947: *Camulodunum. First Report on the Excavations at Colchester 1930–39*, Rep Res Comm Soc Antiq London **14**.
Head, R., Fenwick, H., Chapman, H., van de Noort, R. and Dinnin, M. 1997: 'The archaeological survey of the Rivers Idle, Torne and Old River Don', in van de Noort and Ellis 1997, 267–367.
Henig, M. 1978: *A Corpus of Roman Engraved Gemstones from British Sites*, Brit Archaeol Rep **8**.
Henig, M. 1998: 'Romano-British art and Gallo-Roman samian', in Bird 1998, 59–67.
Holbrook, N. and Bidwell, P.T. 1992: 'Roman pottery from Exeter 1980–1990', *J Roman Pottery Stud*, **5**, 35–80.
Howe, M.D., Perrin, J.R. and Mackreth, D.F. 1980: *Roman Pottery from the Nene Valley: a Guide.*
Hull, M.R. 1963: *The Roman potters' kilns of Colchester,* Rep Res Comm Soc Antiq London **21**.
James, H. 1976: Excavations at Church Street, Carmarthen, 1976, *Cambrian Archaeol Assoc Mon Coll I. Roman Sites.*
Jarrett, M.G. 1960: 'Roman coins and potters' stamps from Halton Chesters'. *Archaeologia Aeliana* 4th Ser., **38**, 153–160.
Jones, D.M. *Excavations at Billingsgate Buildings 'Triangle', Lower Thames Street 1974,* London Middlesex Archaeol Soc Spec Pap **4**.
Jones, G.B.D. and Grealey, S. (eds.) 1974: *Roman Manchester.*
Kennedy, D. (ed.) *Into the sun. Essays in air photography in archaeology in honour of Derrick Riley.*
Kenyon, K.M. 1948: *Excavations at the Jewry Wall Site, Leicester,* Rep Res Comm Soc Antiq London **15**.
Keppie, L. 1975a: 'Iron', in Robertson *et al.,* 96–114.
Keppie, L. 1975b: 'The Leatherwork', in Robertson *et al.,* 59–90.
Keppie, L.F.J. 1985: 'Excavations at the Roman fort of Bar Hill, 1978–82', *Glasgow Archaeol J*, **12**, 49–81.
Lloyd Morgan, G. 1986: 'Small Finds from Doncaster', in Buckland and Magilton 1986, 83–86.
Loughlin, N. 1977: 'Dales Ware: A Contribution to the Study of Roman Coarse Pottery', in Peacock 1977, 85–146.
Maaskant-Kleibrink, M. 1978: *Catalogue of the Engraved Gems in the Royal Coin Cabinet, The Hague. The Greek, Roman and Etruscan Collections.*
MacGregor, M. 1976: *Early Celtic Art in North Britain.*
MacIvor, I., Thomas, M.C. and Breeze, D.J. 1980: Excavations on the Antonine Wall fort of Rough Castle, Stirlingshire, 1957–61, *Proc Soc Antiq Scotland*, **110**. 256–257.
Magilton, J.R. 1977: *The Doncaster district: an archaeological survey.*
Mann, J.C. 1985: 'Two 'Topoi' in the *Agricola*', *Britannia*, **16**, 21–24.
Manning, W.H. 1983: 'The Cauldron Chains of Iron Age and Roman Britain', in Hartley and Wacher 1983, 132–154.
Manning, W.H. 1985: *Catalogue of the Romano-British Iron Tools, Fittings and Weapons in the British Museum.*
Manning, W.H. 1998: 'A hoard of late Roman ironwork from Sibson, Huntingdonshire', in Bird 1998, 281–295.
Marsh, G. 1978: 'Early second century fine wares in the London area', in Arthur and Marsh 1978, 119–223.
May 1996, *Dragonby. Report on excavations at an Iron Age and Romano-British settlement in North Lincolnshire.*
May, J. (ed.) 1996: A.K. Gregory and S.M. Elsdon, 'Pottery descriptions : catalogue and drawings', in May 1996, 446–512.
May, J. 1996: 'Metal artefacts other than coins', in May 1996, 231–317.
May, T. 1922: *The Roman forts of Templebrough near Rotherham.*
Megaw, V. and Merrifield, R. 1969: 'The Dowgate Plaque: a bronze mount of the Belgic Iron Age from the City of London', *Archaeol J*, **126**, 154–159..
Miket, R. 1983: *The Roman fort at South Shields. Excavation of the Defences 1977–1981.*
Millett, M. 1990: *The Romanization of Britain. An essay in archaeological interpretation.*
Monaghan, J. 1997: 'Roman pottery from York', *Archaeology of York* **16/8**.
Neale, J. and Flenley, J. (eds.) 1981: *The Quaternary in Britain.*
Nellist, M. 1986: 'Inhumations from Adwick-le-Street, Doncaster, 1968', in Buckland and Magilton 1986, 218–220.
Orton, C. 1989: 'An introduction to the quantification of pottery'. *J Roman Pottery Stud*, **2**, 94–97.
Oswald, F. 1952: *Excavation of a traverse of Margidunum.*
Ottaway, P. 1993: *Roman York.*
Peacock, D.P.S. 1968: 'A petrological study of certain iron age pottery from western England', *Proc Prehistoric Soc*, **34**, 414–427.
Peacock, D.P.S. (ed.) 1977: *Pottery and Early Commerce: characterisation and trade in Roman and later ceramics.*
Peacock, D.P.S. 1980: 'The Roman millstone trade: a petrological sketch', *World Archaeology*, **12**, 43–53.
Peacock, D.P.S. 1982: *Pottery in the Roman world. an ethno-archaeological approach.*
Perrin, R. 1980: 'Pottery of 'London Ware' type from the Nene Valley', *Durobrivae. A review of Nene Valley archaeology*, **viii**, 9–10.
Perrin, J.R. 1991: Roman Pottery from the Colonia: 2, *Archaeology of York* **16/4**.
Perrin, J.R. (ed.) 1999: Roman pottery from excavations at and near to the Roman small town of Durobrivae, Water Newton, Cambridgeshire, 1956–58', *J Roman Pottery Stud*, **8**, 1–142.
Philp, B., Parfitt, K., Wilson, J., Dutto, M. and Williams, M. 1993: *The Roman villa site at Keston, Kent, First report Excavations (1968–1978)*, Kent Archaeol Mon Ser **6**.
Piggott, C.M. and Seaby, W.A. 1937: 'Early Iron Age Site at Southcote, Reading', *Proc Prehistoric Soc*, **3**, 54.
Polak, M. 1998: 'Old wine in new bottles. Reflections on the organisation of the production of terra sigillata at La Graufesenque', in Bird 1998, 115–121.
Pollard, R.J. 1988: *The Roman pottery of Kent,* Kent Archaeol Soc Mon **5**.
Potter, T.W. 1979: *Romans in North-West England. Excavations at the Roman forts of Ravenglass, Watercrook and Bowness on Solway*, Cumberland Westmoreland Antiq Archaeol Soc Res Ser. **1**.
Price, J. 1988: 'Romano-British Glass Bangles from East Yorkshire', in Price and Wilson 1988, 339–366.
Price, J. and Cottam, S. 1998: *Romano-British glass vessels : a*

handbook, Council for British Archaeology Practical handbook in archaeology **14**.

Price, J. and Wilson, P.R. (eds.) 1988: *Recent research in Roman Yorkshire. Studies in honour of Mary Kitson Clark Mrs Derwas Chitty*, Brit Archaeol Rep **193**.

Raftery, B., Megaw, V. and Rigby, V. (eds.) 1995: *Sites and sights of the Iron Age. Essays on fieldwork and museum research presented to Ian Mathieson Stead.*

Rhodes, M. 1980: 'The Leatherwork', in Jones1980, 99–108.

Ricken, H. and Fischer, C. 1963: *Die Bilderschusseln der Romischen Topfer von Rheinzabern.*

Rigby, V. 1986: 'Vessels with decoration in relief', in Stead and Rigby 1986, 246–254.

Rigby, V. 1989: 'The Roman Imported Fine Wares', in Down 1989, 109–124.

Rigby, V. 1998: 'Where did CEN, REDITAS and SACE produce pots? A summary of the range and distribution of Romano-British stamped wares', in Bird 1998, 191–198.

Rigby, V. and Stead, I.M. 1976: 'Coarse Pottery', in Stead 1976, 134–190.

Riley, D.N. 1980: *Early Landscape from the Air. Studies of Crop Marks in South Yorkshire and North Lincolnshire.*

Riley, D.N., Buckland, P.C. and Wade, J. 1995: 'Excavations and aerial reconnaissance at Littleborough on Trent, Nottinghamshire', *Britannia* **25**, 253–284.

Rivet, A.L.F. 1958: *Town and country in Roman Britain.*

Robertson, A. 1975: *Birrens Blatobulgium.*

Robertson, A., Scott, M. and Keppie, L. 1975: *Bar Hill: A Roman Fort and its Finds*, Brit Archaeol Rep **16**.

Rodwell, W. 1976: 'Iron Pokers of La Tène II–III', *Archaeol J*, **133**, 43–49.

Rodwell, W. 1978: 'Stamp-decorated pottery of the early Roman period in Eastern England', in Arthur and Marsh 1978, 225–292.

Rogers, G.B. 1974: 'Potérie sigillée de la Gaule centrale', *Gallia Suppl.* **28**.

Rogerson, A. 1977: 'Excavations at Scole', *E Anglian Archaeol*, **5**, 97–224.

Rush, P. 2000: 'The coarse pottery', in Rush *et al.* 2000, 89–166.

Rush, P., Dickinson, B., Hartley, B. and Hartley, K.F. 2000: *Roman Castleford. Excavations 1974–85, III. The pottery*, Yorkshire Archaeol **6**.

St. Joseph, J.K. 1969: 'Air reconnaissance in Roman Britain, 1965–68', *J Roman Stud*, **59**, 104–128.

Samuels, J. 1984: *The Roman Pottery Industry in the East Midlands*, Unpubl. Ph.D. thesis, University of Nottingham.

Samuels, J. and Buckland, P.C. 1978: 'A Romano-British settlement at Sandtoft, South Humberside', *Yorkshire Archaeol J*, **50**, 65–75.

Skidmore, P. 1985: '*Exochamus nigromaculatus* Goeze: Col., Coccinellidae: in Britain', *Entomologist's Monthly Mag*, **121**, 239–240.

Santrot, M.H. and Santrot, J. 1979: *Céramique Communes Gallo-Romaines d'Aquitaine.*

Simpson, C.J. 1976: 'Belt-buckles and strap-ends of the later Roman Empire: a preliminary survey of new groups', *Britannia*, **7**, 192–223.

Simpson, G. 1973: 'Roman Manchester and Templebrough: the forts and dates reviewed', in Hawkes and Hawkes 1973, 69–93.

Smith, A.H.V. 1986: 'The Palynology of a Sample of Coal from a Mid-Second Pit Site DG, pit 9: in Frenchgate, Doncaster', in Buckland and Magilton, 197.

Smith, A.H.V. 1997: 'Provenance of coals from Roman sites in England and Wales', *Britannia*, **28**, 297–324.

S. and S. Stanfield, J.A. and Simpson, G. 1958: *Central Gaulish Potters.*

Stead, I.M. 1965: *The La Tène cultures of eastern Yorkshire.*

Stead, I.M. 1967: 'A La Tène III burial at Welwyn Garden City', *Archaeologia*, **101**, 1–62.

Stead, I.M. 1976a: 'The Finds', in Stead 1976b, 195–234.

Stead, I.M. 1976b: *Excavations at Winterton Roman Villa and other Roman Sites in North Lincolnshire.*

Stead, I.M. 1991: *Iron Age cemeteries in East Yorkshire,* English Heritage Archaeol Rep **22**.

Stead, I.M. and Ribgy, V. 1986: *Baldock. The excavation of a Roman and pre-Roman settlement, 1968–72*, Britannia Mon Ser **7**.

Stead, I.M. and Ribgy, V. 1989: *Verulamium. The King Harry Lane site,* English Heritage Archaeol Rep **12**.

Steer, K.A. 1961: 'Excavations at Mumrills Roman Fort, 1958–60', *Proc Soc Antiq Scotland*, **94**, 86–132.

Swan, V.G. 1981: 'Caistor-by-Norwich reconsidered and the dating of Romano-British pottery in East Anglia', in Anderson and Anderson 1981, 123–156.

Swan, V.G. 1984: *The Pottery Kilns of Roman Britain*, Royal Commission on Historical Monuments suppl. Ser. **5**.

Swan, V.G. 1992: 'Legio VI and its men: African legionaries in Britain', *J Roman Pottery Stud*, **5**, 1–33.

Swan, V.G. 1999: 'The Twentieth Legion and the history of the Antonine Wall reconsidered', *Proc Soc Antiq Scotland*, **129**, 399–480.

Symonds, R.P. 1990: 'The problems of roughcast beakers, and related colour-coated wares', *J Roman Pottery Stud,* **3**, 1–17.

Thompson, F.H. 1958: 'A Romano-British pottery kiln at North Hykeham, Lincolnshire: with an appendix on the typology, dating and distribution of 'Rustic' Ware in Great Britain', *Antiq J*, **38**, 15–51.

Thompson, F.H. 1960: 'The Rustic Ware (Type 8)', in Annable 1960, 49–50.

Todd, M. 1968: 'The commoner late Roman coarse wares of the East Midlands', *Antiq J*, **48**, 192–209.

Todd, M. 1991: *The Coritani.* (2nd. ed.).

Tomber, R. and Dore, J. 1998: *The national Roman fabric reference collection. A handbook.*

Tomlin, R.S.O. 1983: '*Non Coritani sed Corieltauvi*', *Antiq J*, **63**, 353–355.

van de Noort, R. and Fenwick, H. 1997: Introduction to the archaeological survey. In, van de Noort, R. and Ellis, S. eds.: 1997:, 219–226.

van de Noort, R. and Ellis, S. (eds.)1997: *Wetland heritage of the Humberhead Levels.*

van de Noort, R. and Ellis, S. (eds.) 1998: *Wetland heritage of the Ancholme and Lower Trent Valleys.*

Wacher, J.S. 1969: *Excavations at Brough-on-Humber 1958–61.* Rep Res Comm Soc Antiq London **25**.

Waugh, H. and Goodburn, R. 1972: 'The non-ferrous objects', in Frere 1972, 114–162.

Webster, G. 1944: 'A Roman Pottery at South Carlton, Lincs', *Antiq J*, **24**, 130–143.

Webster, G. 1981: *Rome against Caratacus. The Roman campaigns in Britain AD 48–58.*

Webster, G. 1999: 'Excavations by the Water Newton Excavation Committee', in Perrin 1999, 10–18.

Webster, P.V. 1974: 'The Coarse Pottery', in Jones and Grealey 1974, 89–118.

Webster, P.V. 1977: 'Severn Valley Ware on the Antonine frontier', in Dore and Greene 1977, 163–176.

Wedlake, W.J. 1958: *Excavations at Camerton, Somerset.*

Wenham, L.P. 1968: *The Romano-British cemetery at Trentholme Drive, York.*

West, S.E. 1989: 'West Stow, Suffolk: the prehistoric and Romano-British occupations', *E Anglian Archaeol Rep* **48**.

Wheeler, H.M. 1985: North-west sector excavations 1979–80. Roman Derby: Excavations 1968–83, *Derbyshire Archaeol J*, **105**, 130–132.

Wheeler, R.E.M. 1930: *London in Roman Times*, London Mus Cat **3**.

Wheeler, R.E.M. 1943: *Maiden Castle Dorset,* Rep Res Comm Soc Antiq London **12**.

Wheeler, R.E.M. and Wheeler, T.V. 1932: *Report on the Excavation of the Prehistoric, Roman and Post-Roman Site in Lydney Park, Gloucestershire*, Rep Res Comm Soc Antiq London **9**.

Wheeler, R.E.M. and Wheeler, T.V. 1936: *Verulamium. A Belgic and two Roman cities,* Rep Res Comm Soc Antiq London **11**.

Whitehouse, N.J. 1999: *The evolution of the Holocene wetland landscape of the Humberhead Levels from a fossil insect perspective.* Unpubl. Ph.D. dissertation, University of Sheffield.

Whitwell, J.B. 1982: *The Coritani. Some aspects of the Iron Age tribe and Roman Civitas*, Brit Archaeol Rep **99**.

Wild, J.P. 1987: 'Objects of clay', in Dannell and Wild 1987, 113-114.

Williams, D.F. 1977: 'The Romano-British black-burnished industry: an essay on characterization by heavy mineral analysis', in Peacock 1977, 163–220.

Williams, D.F. 1980: 'The Black-Burnished Ware', in MacIvor *et al.*, 256–257.

Williams, D.F. 1985: 'Black-burnished ware and amphorae', in Wheeler 1985, 130–132.

Wrathmell, S. and Nicholson, A. (eds.) 1998: *Dalton Parlours. Iron Age settlement and Roman villa*, 105–120, Yorkshire Archaeol **3**

Wright, M.E. 1988: 'Beehive quern manufacture in the south-east Pennines', *Scottish Archaeol Rev*, **5**, 65–77.

Young, C.J. 1977: *The Roman Pottery Industry of the Oxford Region*, Brit Archaeol Rep **43**.

Zadocks-Josephus Jitta, A.N. and Witteveen, A. 1977: 'Roman Bronze Lunulae from the Netherlands', *Oudheidkundige Mededelingen uit het Rijksmuseum van Oudheden te Leiden*, **58**, 167–195.

Plate 1. General view of site looking south (1957). The series of 2m (9ft) square boxes (1–22WMB) running down to the River Torne appear top centre. The Rossington Bridge Farm kilns lay on the field beyond the power pole.

Plate 2. Construction trench for the water main close to the river Torne (1956), showing the extensive peat deposits downslope of the kilns. (Ranging poles are marked in feet).

Plate 3. Rossington Bridge Pumping Station kilns 1–3, looking south. Kiln 1 is partly truncated by the water main trench to the west, although the fired clay blocking remains in the flue. The line of stakeholes between kilns 1 and 2 is unrecorded elsewhere and the poorly preserved remains of kiln 3 are in the foreground.

Plate 4.Rossington Bridge Pumping Station kiln 1, showing twin pedestals, plinth against south wall of the chamber and, sectioned, the clay blocking to the flue. The pebbly nature of the construction material is evident.(Scale in inches).

Plate 5. Rossington Bridge Pumping Station kiln 1 looking east, with blocking and plinth removed.(Scale in inches).

Plate 6. Rossington Bridge Pumping Station kiln 2 looking west, showing well preserved flue from stokehole.(Scales in inches and feet).

Plate 7. Rossington Bridge Pumping Station kiln 2 chamber, showing three plinths and the finished top to the kiln wall, essentially at the Roman ground surface. (Scale in inches).

Plate 8. Rossington Bridge Pumping Station kiln 3, a poorly preserved surface-built kiln with deep stokehole. The kiln fragment lies beneath the 12 inch (300mm) rule; the relationship with the ?stokehole is uncertain.

Plate 9. Rossington Bridge Pumping Station kiln 3; the preserved arc of the base of the kiln wall is evident. (Scale in inches).

Plate 10. Rossington Bridge Pumping Station kilns 4 and 5 and stokehole. (Scale in feet and inches).

Plate 11. Rossington Bridge Pumping Station kilns 4 and 5.The massively constructed flue of kiln 4, with rows of postholes/stakeholes in the top leads into a deep stokepit; kiln 5 lies adjacent at virtual surface level.

Plate 12. Rossington Bridge Pumping Station kiln 4, showing the thick primary chamber wall and pockets or stakeholes between it and the relining.

Plate 13. Rossington Bridge Pumping Station kiln 4, showing the scars of two parallel elongate pedestals on the floor of the chamber.

Plate 14. Rossington Bridge Pumping Station: evidence for clamp or bonfire firing. Remains of black burnished ware vessels lie inverted in a layer of soot and sand on a burnt surface. (Scale in inches).

Plate 15. Rossington Bridge Pumping Station kiln 6, the potter's oven of the site records, viewed from the flue. The use of stone in both flue and chamber is evident. (Scale in feet).

Plate 16. Rossington Bridge Pumping Station kiln 6. The finished upper surface of the chamber wall survives below the ruler.

Plate 17. Rossington Bridge Pumping Station, 1957. The base of a wickerwork fence preserved in waterlogged deposits close to the river Torne. (Scale in inches).

Plate 18. Rossington Bridge Pumping Station, 1957. Wickerwork fence as above.

Plate 19. Rossington Bridge Pumping Station, 1957. Iron cauldron chain and piece of wooden moulding preserved in the peat; the latter does not survive. (Scale in inches).

Plate 20. Rossington Bridge Pumping Station, 1957. A single plank trackway laid across logs. The photograph is the only record of this structure. (Scale in feet).

Plate 21. Rossington Bridge Pumping Station, 1957. Groups of posts in bed of river Torne on the line of the Doncaster-Lincoln Roman road. The strings are at 3 ft (0.9m) intervals.

Plate 22. Rossington Bridge Pumping Station, 1957. ?Boundary ditch to kiln site (Scale in feet).

Plate 23. Rossington Bridge Farm, 1960. Kilns 1 and 2, partly cleared, looking south. (Scale in feet).

Plate 24. Rossington Bridge Farm, 1960. Kiln 1 looking south. (Scale in feet and inches).

Plate 25. Rossington Bridge Farm, 1960. Kiln 1 from the flue. The slight ledges for the insertion of the ends of firebars in the chamber are evident. (Scale in inches).

Plate 26. Rossington Bridge Farm, 1960. Kiln 2 looking north. The carefully finished top of the shallow chamber is evident. (scale in feet and inches).

Plate 27. Rossington Bridge Pumping Station. Complete wooden trug from layer 5a. Photo: G. Dowling.

Plate 28. Rossington Bridge Pumping Station. Wooden ?palette from layer 6 (peat). Photo: G. Dowling.

Plate 29. Rossington Bridge Pumping Station. Fragment of Millstone Grit quern with red ochre pigment on grinding surface. Photo: G.Dowling.

Plate 30. Rossington Bridge Pumping Station. Sandstone pebble with polished surface – ? burnisher. Photo: G. Dowling.

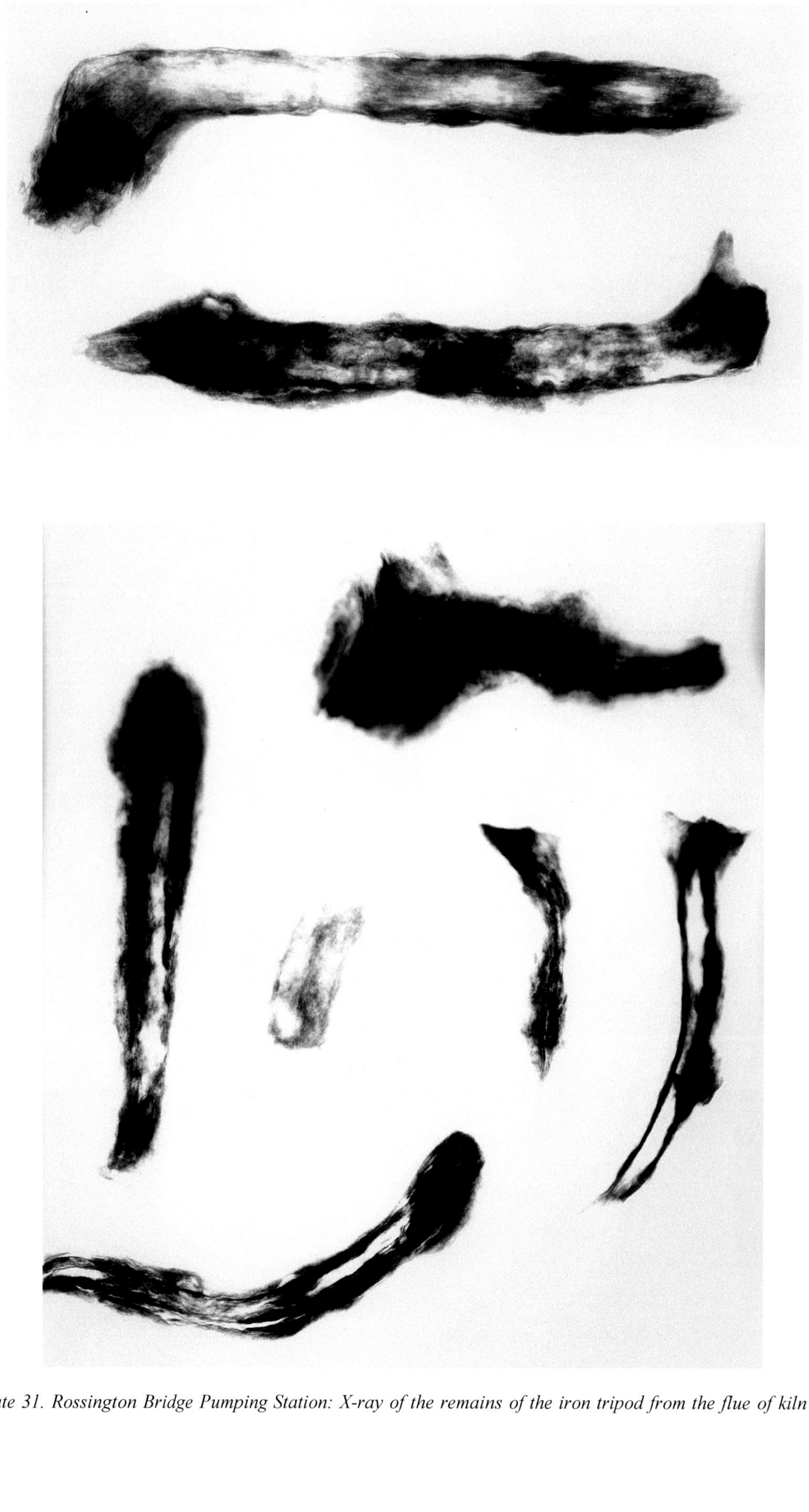

Plate 31. Rossington Bridge Pumping Station: X-ray of the remains of the iron tripod from the flue of kiln 4.